Human Rights for Communicators

Cees J. Hamelink

Universiteit van Amsterdam

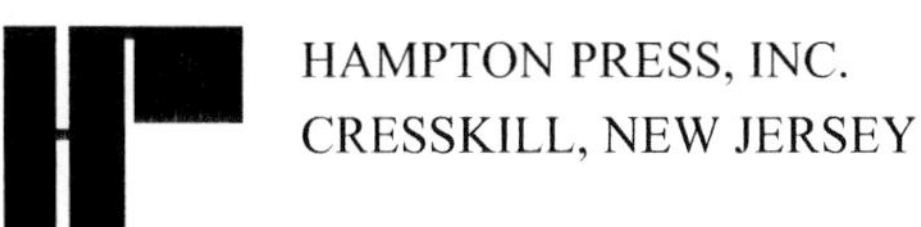

HAMPTON PRESS, INC.
CRESSKILL, NEW JERSEY

Printed in the United States of America

Library of Congress Cataloging-in-Publication Data

Hamlink, Cees J., 1940-
Human rights for communicators / Cees J. Hamelink.
p. cm.
Includes bibliographical references and indexes.
ISBN 1-57273-568-6 -- ISBN 1-57273-569-4
1. Human rights. 2. Communication--Political aspects. I. Title.
JC571.H3295 2004
323--dc22

2004054327

Hampton Press, Inc.
23 Broadway
Cresskill, NJ 07626

Contents

Preface

Some books are the result of a long-cherished wish to write them. For many years, my work on human rights has created the desire to produce a text that could be used by those professionals in the fields of communication studies, practice, and policy who have an interest in contributing to a more humane society.

As so often happens in our professional lives, too many tasks, challenges, and e-mails interfere with the initial planning schedule. However, eventually the time was found to complete the present book. This would not have been possible without the patience and support from publisher Barbara Bernstein. Our regular encounters at IAMCR and ICA conferences over the past years were a constant reminder of a project that had to be finished.

The completion of the manuscript over the past months was certainly assisted by the fact that the project of the international recognition of the right to communicate is back on the international public agenda. The right to communicate is one of the challenges for the United Nations World Summit on the Information Society, which is currently being prepared to be held in Geneva in December 2003 and in Tunis in 2005. Being actively involved in these preparations through such initiatives as the Communication Rights for the Information Society (CRIS) campaign made me—once again—realize that considerable progress has been made in the articulation of human rights for communicators and that this should be recorded.

At the same time, however, it needs to be realized that most of these human rights provisions are universally violated or under threat of being violated. International mechanisms for the implementation and defense of existing human rights are urgently needed. Moreover, it is important to observe that within the present framework of human rights the interactive dimension of communication—communication as public and private dialogue—is not adequately protected. This is a serious omission, particularly in view of the fact that so many social groups engaged in violent conflicts around the world desperately need to learn the art of the dialogue. The right to communicate represents a view of communication as a process of both speaking and listening. In the spirit of the right to communicate, I would also like to invite the readers to engage in dialogue with me if they have comments, suggestions for improvement, or discover omissions.

Various earlier versions of the text were critically read and commented on by my colleague D. Flud van Giffen. For this I am very grateful. As always, I found a lot of support in the presence of someone who prefers not to be named.

Cees J. Hamelink
Amsterdam/Marin July 2003

1

A Common Standard of Achievement

HUMAN RIGHTS

The Oxford Dictionary informs us that a *right* is the entitlement to have or do something. Following this we could define *human rights* as the entitlements human beings have to something. In a series of documents the international community has agreed that this *something* means that human beings should be treated in accordance with some fundamental moral standards. These standards are based on the principle of human dignity. From this moral consensus on the dignity of all human beings flow such standards as equality, liberty, and security.

Immediately after World War II, the international community, as it established the United Nations (in 1945), pointed at human rights as essential building blocks for the effort to realize a peaceful world. When in 1945 the Charter of the United Nations was adopted in San Francisco, several member states urged that a Bill of Rights should be included in the document. This did not happen, but it was agreed to establish a Commission on Human Rights, which was to prepare an International Bill of Human Rights for the General Assembly.

The UN Charter made explicit reference to human rights in its Preamble and Articles 1, 13, 55 56, 62, and 68. It stated herewith that human rights are seen as integral to the mandate and mission of the United Nations. Its visionary drafters expressed their fundamental conviction that the respect for human rights would be basic to international peace and development.

Following the UN Charter, human rights standards have been formulated in the so-called International Bill of Rights, which consists of the Universal Declaration of Human Rights (adopted on December 10, 1948, by the UN General Assembly) and the two key human rights treaties, the International Covenant on Economic, Social and Cultural Rights [ICESCR] (adopted in 1966 and in force since January 3, 1976) and the International Covenant on Civil and Political Rights [ICCPR] (adopted in 1966 and in force since March 23, 1976). Different dimensions of human rights have also been codified in a series of international treaties, in regional instruments (such as the European Convention for the Protection of Human Rights and Fundamental Freedoms [1950], the American Convention of Human Rights [1969], the African Charter on Human and Peoples' Rights [1981], and in the Islamic Declaration of Human Rights, which was prepared by the Islamic Council 1980 and presented to UNESCO in 1981. (Appendix I gives a comprehensive overview of the major human rights instruments.) In 2003, 148 countries have ratified the ICCPR and 146 countries have ratified the ICSECR.

The documents (often called *instruments*) in which human rights are formulated have different legal meanings. In international relations, rules and practices among states over time can be accepted as international custom and, as such, become a source of international law. Increasingly, however, such customary law is replaced by conventions or treaties that have become the essential instruments of international cooperation. Treaties impose binding obligations on the parties who ratify them. Often treaties are preceded by international declarations, which may have a strong moral impact (such as is the case with the Universal Declaration of Human Rights), but do not have a legally binding character. In addition to treaties and declarations, the international community can also recommend certain types of action through resolutions of its decision-making bodies such as the General Assembly of the United Nations.[1]

The essential instrument in the field of human rights remains the 1948 Universal Declaration of Human Rights (UDHR). The Declaration continues to be a source of inspiration for thought and action in the field of human rights. The UDHR, although not a binding treaty, carries important legal weight. Among legal scholars there is a considerable consensus that, in accordance with Article 38 of the Statute of the International Court of Justice, the UDHR constitutes binding law as international custom. The Declaration is certainly an essential part of international customary law and is recognized by civilized nations as a binding standard of achievement. The text proclaims a fairly com

[1]For more details, see Akehurst (1991), Buergental (1985), Hannikainen (1988), Sieghart (1986), and McWhinney (1984).

prehensive set of rights (and puts civil and political rights on the same level as social, economic, and cultural rights) and also proposes the implementation of these claims in a social, and international order.

THE UNIVERSAL DECLARATION OF HUMAN RIGHTS

The emergence of the UDHR has to be seen against the background of the repression, aggression, and violence experienced during World War II. The aspiration toward a new moral and legal world order was expressed by Franklin D. Roosevelt in January 1941 in his Message to the U.S. Congress. Basic to his vision of the New World Order were four freedoms: freedom of expression, freedom of faith, freedom from want, and freedom from fear.

Shortly after the establishment of the United Nations, a Commission on Human Rights began to draft an International Bill of Human Rights. The Commission used as resources drafts that were prepared by states and regional institutions like the Organization of American States and various nongovernmental organizations like the American Federation of Labour. Also constitutions from around the world were used by the secretariat headed by the Canadian law professor John Humphrey. The Chair of the Human Rights Commission, Mrs. Eleanor Roosevelt, had to find a compromise within her own U.S. delegation where two factions collided: the liberal school of the Roosevelt period and a more traditional and isolationist approach.

The text of the Declaration was drafted over 2 years. Between January 1947—when the Commission on Human Rights first met—and December 1948. The preliminary text was prepared by a committee of eight chaired by Mrs. Roosevelt. The committee found a consensus on the need to affirm fundamental human rights and freedoms and to include not only civil and political rights, but also social, economic, and cultural rights. Member States replied to the draft, and the committee revised the text and then submitted it to the General Assembly. The 58 member states in the General Assembly studied the text very closely and voted some 1,400 times on words and sentences. There was a good deal of debate. Some Islamic states, for example, objected against the right to change religion, and Western countries were critical of the inclusion of social and economic rights. On December 10, the Declaration was adopted with eight abstentions. This date remains the world's Human Rights Day. The fact that the UN General Assembly titled its human rights declaration universal, and not international, is a manifestation of the crucial importance it attached to the all-encompassing nature of the entitlements it provided to the world's people. All the claims the Declaration makes on the recognition and protection of rights and freedoms extend to all people.

The Preamble of the Universal Declaration

This first part of the Declaration begins with reference to the recognition of human dignity: "Whereas recognition of the inherent dignity and of the equal and inalienable rights of all members of the human family is the foundation of freedom, justice and peace in the world. . . ."

The notion *human dignity* is not without difficulties, and its grounding is seriously contested in religion and philosophy. A special problem is that human dignity tends to be defined in terms of the substantially superior nature of the human being in comparison with all other beings in the universe. To a large extent this justifies questionable human conduct regarding nonhuman forms of life such as animals. Human dignity remains a vague notion and yet it provides the ground for freedom, justice, and peace.

The Response to Human Rights Violations

> Whereas disregard and contempt for human rights have resulted in barbarous acts which have outraged the conscience of mankind, and the advent of a world in which human beings shall enjoy freedom of speech and belief and freedom from fear and want has been proclaimed as the highest aspiration of the common people. . . .

The barbarous acts of World War II are seen as resulting from a disregard for human rights. In this second paragraph, we find the four freedoms that President Franklin D. Roosevelt spoke about in his 1941 Message to the U.S. Congress.

The International Dimension

The Preamble points to the international dimension of human rights and the key mission of the United Nations with this phrase: "Whereas it is essential to promote the development of friendly relations between nations, . . . "

The Commitment

The Preamble confirms the commitment of the peoples of the United Nations to the defense of human rights and uses the following phrasing:

> Whereas the peoples of the United Nations have in the Charter reaffirmed their faith in fundamental human rights, in the dignity and

> worth of the human person and in the equal rights of men and women and have determined to promote social progress and better standards of life in larger freedom,
>
> Whereas Member States have pledged themselves to achieve, in co-operation with the United Nations, the promotion of universal respect for and observance of human rights and fundamental freedoms. . . .

It is important to note that the text states that the protection by law is essential for human rights: "Whereas it is essential, if man is not to be compelled to have recourse, as a last resort, to rebellion against tyranny and oppression, that human rights should be protected by the rule of law."

The Implementation

The Preamble continues with the observation that the implementation of human rights will, to a large extent, depend on the creation of a common worldwide understanding of what human rights are: "Whereas a common understanding of these rights and freedoms is of the greatest importance for the full realization of this pledge. . . ."

The Nature of the Declaration and Future Action

The General Assembly

> Proclaims this Universal Declaration of Human Rights as a common standard of achievement for all peoples and all nations, to the end that every individual and every organ of society, keeping this Declaration constantly in mind, shall strive by teaching and education to promote respect for these rights and freedoms and by progressive measures, national and international, to secure their universal and effective recognition and observance, both among the peoples of Member States themselves and among the peoples of territories under their jurisdiction.

Following the Preamble, there are 30 articles that identify a series of human rights of civil-political and socioeconomic and cultural nature. The concluding articles of the Declaration deserve some special attention. Article 28 is crucial to the whole system of human rights and is unfortunately often given little attention. It reads, "Everyone is entitled to a social and international order in which the rights and freedoms set forth in this Declaration can be fully realized." Article 29 says that everyone has duties to the community in which alone the free and full development of his personality is possible, and Article 30 warns that nothing in the declaration may be interpreted as implying for any state, group, or person any right to engage in any activity or to perform any act aimed at the destruction of any of the rights and freedom set forth in the Declaration.

THE HUMAN RIGHTS STANDARDS

A common distinction among the rights and freedoms that form the core of international human rights standards refers to three generations of human rights. According to this division, civil and political rights (sometimes referred to as the *classic human rights*) are seen as the first generation. Economic, social, and cultural rights make up the second generation, and a series of collective rights form the third generation. The latter include the right to development, the right to peace, and the right to a clean, natural environment. As Baehr (1999) rightly remarked "The term 'generations' is somewhat unfortunate. It suggests a succession of phenomena, whereby a new generation takes the place of the previous one. That is, however, not the case with the three 'generations' of human rights. On the contrary. The idea is rather that the three 'generations' exist and be respected simultaneously" (p. 7).

In the International Bill of Rights alone we find 76 different human rights. In the totality of major international and regional human rights instruments, this number is even greater. With the tendency among human rights lobbies to put more and more social problems in a human rights framework, the number of human rights is likely to further increase.

Because this proliferation of rights does not necessarily strengthen the cause of the actual implementation of human rights, various attempts have been made to establish a set of core human rights that are representative for the totality.

One effort concluded in the existence of 12 core rights (Jongman & Schmidt, 1994):

1. The right not to be discriminated against
2. The right to education
3. The right to political participation
4. The right to fair working conditions
5. The right to life
6. The right not to be tortured
7. The right not to be arbitrarily arrested
8. The right to food

9. The right to health care
10. The right to freedom of association
11. The right to political participation
12. The right to freedom of expression

These rights are the legal articulation of some underlying moral principles and their implied standards of human conduct. These basic principles and their related norms are:

Equality and the implied norm that discrimination—on any ground—is inadmissible.

Liberty and the implied norm that obstruction of the self-determination of the human person is inadmissible.

Security and the implied norm that intentional harm against human integrity is inadmissible.

THE MECHANISMS OF ENFORCEMENT

Crucial for the protection of human rights is the notion that there can be no rights without the option of redress in case of their violation. Rights and remedies are intrinsically related; where human rights instruments do not provide accessible and affordable means of redress, they erode the effective protection of the rights they proclaim. The old adagium of Roman law states, "ubi ius, ibi remedium"—where there is law, there is remedy. One can turn this around and propose that when no remedy is available, there is no law. People should be able to seek effective remedy when state or private parties violate their human rights.

Human rights not only require mechanisms of redress. They also imply that those who rule on behalf of others are accountable (i.e., they are obliged to justify their decisions on behalf of others). It is a basic requirement of human rights standards that provisions on public policy imply a mechanism for accountability. "The requirement that every citizen have a right to take part in the conduct of public affairs is satisfied if appointed officials are in some way responsible to elected representatives" (Partsch, 1981, p. 239).

The realization of human rights requires limitations on the power of the state as well as a defense against horizontal abuses of fundamental rights and freedoms. People should have access to effective redress when private actors interfere with their privacy, distribute misleading information, threaten their cultural autonomy, fail to protect their intellectual property, or hamper their access to telecommunication and data networks.

On the basis of these principles (effective remedy, accountability, and horizontal effect), the procedures for individuals and communities to seek redress have to contain at least the following three components. First, the recognition of the formal right to file complaints in case public or private actors do not comply with the adopted standards. Second, the recognition of the competence of an independent tribunal that receives complaints from both state and nonstate actors, individuals, and communities. Third, the recognition that the opinions of the tribunal are binding on those who accept its jurisdiction.

Present remedial procedures are mainly based on the Optional Protocol (OP) to the International Covenant on Civil and Political Rights (1966) and Resolution 1503 adopted by the Economic and Social Council of the UN (ECOSOC) in 1970. The Protocol authorizes the UN Human Rights Committee to receive and consider communications from individuals subject to its jurisdiction who claim to be victims of a violation by that State Party of any of the rights set forth in the Covenant. Individual complaints can only come from nationals of states that are party to the OP (presently 75 states). The OP provides for communications, analysis, and reporting, but not for sanctions. Resolution 1503 recognizes the possibility of individual complaints about human rights violations. It authorizes the UN Human Rights Commission to examine "communications, together with replies of governments, if any, which appear to reveal a consistent pattern of gross violations of human rights." The 1503 procedure is slow, confidential, and provides individuals with no redress.

Other institutional mechanisms for implementation are in addition to the UN Commission on Human Rights, and the Human Rights Committee to monitor the ICCPR, the Committee on the Elimination of Racial Discrimination, the Committee on Economic, Social and Cultural Rights, the Committee on the Elimination of Discrimination against Women, the Committee against Torture, and the Committee on the Rights of the Child.

However important these bodies' work is, their powers to enforce human rights standards are limited. The UN Commission on Human Rights is a permanent body of the ECOSOC. Its members are state representatives. Findings of the Commission have a certain significance, but are not binding. The Human Rights Committee consists of 18 experts supervising the implementation of the ICCPR. The work of the Committee covers only parties that ratified the covenant (presently 148 states) and provides international monitoring on the basis of reports provided by states. The Committee's monitoring does not imply any sanctions, but it can generate some negative publicity on a country's human rights performance. For the implementation of the Race convention, the Committee on the Elimination of Racial Discrimination has been established. The Committee can receive complaints from states, but only 14 states authorize the Committee to receive communications from individuals. The implementation body for the 1979 Convention on the Elimination of Discrimination Against Women is the Committee on the Elimination of Discrimination Against Women. Since 1999, an Optional Protocol to the Convention makes it possible for the Committee to process individual complaints. The Committee that examines the implementation of the Convention on the Rights of the Child does not have the authority to receive individual complaints. The Committee on Economic, Social and Cultural Rights has no right to receive complaints from individuals or groups. In its submission to the 1993 UN World Conference on Human Rights, the Committee argued for a formal complaints procedure in stating, "As long as the majority of the provisions of the Covenant (and most notably those relating to education, health care, food and nutrition, and housing) are not subject of any detailed jurisprudential scrutiny at the international level, it is most unlikely that they will be subject to such examination at the national level either" (United Nations, 1993a, para 24).

In 1997, the 53rd session of the UN Commission on Human Rights discussed a draft protocol for a complaints procedure and affirmed in a resolution the interest of its members for the draft. This was the first step in the long process toward an optional protocol.

International human rights law remains a weak and largely nonenforceable arrangement. It should not be ignored that this is a conscious political choice. Most nation-states have shown little interest in interference with their human rights record. The state-centric arrangement of world politics, in which states are unwilling to yield power over their citizens, is still dominant and stands squarely in the way of universal respect for human rights. In current world politics, states still maintain a considerable measure of sovereignty in the treatment of their citizens. Yet the UN World Conference on Human Rights of 1993 has reaffirmed that "the promotion and protection of all human rights is a legitimate concern of the international community." If indeed the most important issue for the significance and validity of the human rights regime is the implementation of the standards it proposes, the present worldwide lack of implementation of human rights standards poses the most serious challenge to the human rights regime. There is abundant evidence that human rights standards around the world are almost incessantly violated and by actors with different political and ideological viewpoints. Usually in wars of liberation, for example, one finds gross violations by the hands of both the oppressors and the liberators. Although it is obvious that the world would be a different and far more humane place for many people if human rights standards were respected, if one studies the annual reports from such bodies as Amnesty International, there appear to be no countries where human rights are not violated.

For moral philosophers, this is actually not a terribly surprising problem. It represents the classic gap between the moral knowledge human beings possess and their intention to act morally.

HUMAN RIGHTS IN THE WORLD

Taking the state of human rights in the world in the early 21st century, various reports published in 2002 give the following picture.[2]

The Right to Life

Violations: Death penalties were carried out in 28 countries. Thousands of unarmed civilians, including women and children, were killed in Burundi, Congo, and the Democratic Republic of Congo by government troops and opposition forces. In Brazil and Colombia, large numbers of street children were killed. A report from Honduras says that over 165 street children under the age of 18 were killed between January 1998 and September 2000. From India, human rights activists reported that some 14 women are murdered each day by their husbands' relatives. Domestic violence continued to be a critical issue for women worldwide. This type of violence caused more death among women—age 15 to 44—than cancer and malaria. Extrajudicial executions took place in 61 countries.

The Right Not to Be Tortured

Violations: Torture by security forces or police was reported in 125 countries. Torture of detainees was widely applied in Uzbekistan and Russia. Also in Turkey, torture remained a common phenomenon. The U.S. government submitted in 2000 a report on its compliance with the Convention against Torture and Other Cruel, Inhuman or Degrading treatment, in which concern, contention, and criticism were noted with regard to police abuse, excessive use of force in prisons, and physical and mental abuse of inmates. In May 2001, the UN Committee against Torture issued a statement that highlighted a range of U.S. practices that contravened the convention.

The Right Not to Be Arbitrarily Arrested

Violations: People were arbitrarily arrested and detained in 72 countries. In Rwanda, tens of thousands of detainees were held without charge or trial for

---

[2]Sources: Amnesty International Annual Reports; Human Rights Watch World Reports; IFEX Alerts; UNDP, Human Development Reports, World Bank Reports, Index on Censorship publications.

prolonged periods of time. Palestinians who publicly criticized policies of the Palestinian Authority were arbitrarily arrested and detained. In Mexico, peasants, indigenous people, and human rights activists were arbitrarily arrested and detained.

The Right to Food

Violations: More than 2 billion people did not get enough food and 800 million were chronically undernourished.

The Right to Health Care

Violations: 56% of the developing world lacked basic sanitation, and over 1 billion people worldwide lacked access to safe drinking water. Almost 1.5 billion people lacked access to health services.

The Right Not to Be Discriminated Against

Violations: Roma continued to be exposed to crude forms of discrimination in Croatia, Hungary, Romania, the Czech Republic, Bulgaria, Serbia, Macedonia, and Slovakia.

In September 2001, the U.S. government issued a report on its compliance with the Convention on the Elimination of All Forms of Racial Discrimination, in which it was concluded that racism, racial discrimination, and segregation persisted in the United States.

Women in the Middle East and North Africa continued to suffer severe forms of discrimination in all aspects of their lives. In Zimbabwe, the highest court ruled that women were perpetual minors without the right to inherit property. Across the world, women continued to face discriminatory hiring practices.

The Right to Due Process of Law

Violations: In several parts of Central Asia, politicians of incumbent governments were jailed on trumped-up charges. For example, in Kyrgyzstan, the government jailed prominent candidates for the opposition before the presidential elections.

Across the world, street children were arbitrarily detained and often locked up for excessively long periods of time. No legal presentation was provided to them, and unfair hearings took place in Brazil, Bulgaria, Guatemala, India, Jamaica, Kenya, Pakistan, and Russia. Human Rights Watch found, for example, that in Kenya street children were committed to many years of juvenile correctional institutions after summary proceedings without legal defense. In Paraguay, street children were detained because they were in a "state of danger."

The Right to Education

Violations: For more than 100 million children, there were no schools. Almost 1 billion adults were illiterate. Roma children often lacked access to schools in Croatia.

The Right to Fair Working Conditions

Violations: Some 1.4 billion working people in the Third World earned on average $695 per year. Throughout the world, women were trapped in forced labor and slavery-like conditions through the coercive practices of traffickers.

The Right to Freedom of Association

Violations: Internationally recognized labor rights were widely violated across industries in the United States. According to Human Rights Watch "Each year thousands of workers in the United States are spied on, harassed, pressured, threatened, suspended, fired, deported or otherwise victimized by employers in reprisal for their exercise of the right to freedom of association." Human Rights Watch found that millions of workers, including farm workers, household domestic workers, and low-level supervisors, were expressly excluded from protection under the law guaranteeing the right of workers to organize.

Freedom of association was nonexistent in Iraq, Syria, and Saudi Arabia. Oman, Saudi Arabia, and the United Arab Emirates prohibited any type of labor organization.

The Right to Political Participation

Violations: In Lebanon, the government suppressed peaceful political demonstrations by students against the role of Syria in the country. In Bahrain, individuals as well as associations with views critical of the government faced serious restrictions. In Myanmar, the military government reinforced its suppression of the National League for Democracy and arrested scores of its members. In Kuwait, dozens of political prisoners remained in prison following unfair trials.

The Right to Freedom of Expression

Violations: Journalists were killed (among them was Martin O'Hagan in Northern Ireland), editors were forced to quit (Pakistan), journalists received death threats (Bangladesh), TV station licenses were suspended (Kazakhstan), journalists were assaulted by police officers (Burundi), cameramen were arrested (Egypt), and radio programs were taken off the air (Thailand). In Angola, a campaign of harassment against journalists continued. In Zambia, the trial against six journalist—detained in 1999—continued. There were many incidents of detention and ill treatment of journalists in Liberia. Journalists were assaulted in Zimbabwe. In Ethiopia, eight reporters remained behind bars without due process. In Iran, some 30 independent newspapers and magazines were closed down. No critical and independent media could operate in Saudi Arabia, Libya, Iraq, and Syria. Journalists were harassed, arrested, and imprisoned in Egypt, Morocco, Tunisia, and Yemen.

Even this limited survey seems to indicate that it is difficult to enforce human rights standards across the world. During the presentation of Amnesty International's Report for 2002 (May 2003), A.I. Secretary General Irene Khan observed that human rights violations in 2002 had been greater than in any period since the cold war ended. Khan commented that the world's most powerful countries turned their backs on human rights violations all over the world. "These countries are now upholding human rights a la carte; you just pick and choose as you go" (IPS news report of May 28, 2003).

THE OBSTACLES

The existence of several obstacles to the implementation of human rights is responsible for this sad state of affairs.

The Limited Vision on Human Rights

Human rights are commonly perceived as civil and political rights. This short-sighted vision is a danger to the implementation of human rights. Processes of economic growth that immiserate ever larger groups of people are usually not perceived as a gross violation of human rights by most Western governments, donor institutions, or, as a matter of fact, many human rights organizations. If in the normal course of free market operations, World Trade Organization rules, or IMF conditions, millions of people are uprooted, impoverished, or unemployed, this is usually not seen as a human rights violation. Human rights advocates usually attack murder and torture, but not poverty. The exclusive perception of human rights as civil and political rights creates explosive contradictions between political conditionalities that press for good governance, democracy and respect for human rights, and economic conditions that impose such austere measures that the resulting inequalities can only be controlled by highly undemocratic policies. The policies of the IMF have—across the Third World—undermined the economic conditions for democracy, such as education, social equality, and reduction of poverty. The structural adjustment programs of the IMF in many countries weakened the capacity of governments to meet international human rights obligations. The neglect of basic social and economic rights undermines such civil and political rights as freedom of expression and freedom of association.

Another limited vision of human rights restricts them mainly to the public realm. Human rights are violated not only by state institutions, but also by civil institutions such as the family. In many countries, women's and children's rights are grossly violated within the family. Discrimination, cruelty, violence, and censorship often take place within family relations. The place where people should learn first about the respect for others is often the prime locus of violence against others.

Human rights are effectively threatened by people (e.g., by majorities that limit the rights of minorities). Whenever in the world innocent civilians are killed, tortured, or raped, this often happens with the silent consent, if not active participation, of other *innocent* civilians. Also the poor often violate the human rights of other destitute people.

The problem here is that human rights provisions tend to have little effectiveness in spheres outside the realm of the state. This goes back to the liberal origins of human rights protection. It was foreseen by the first human rights drafters (in the 18th century) that citizens needed protection against the state, but protection against fellow citizens was not considered an issue. However, often the perpetrators of human rights abuses are citizens (e.g., in the form of privately owned corporations).

Politics

It is a sobering thought that the post-World War II human rights system was created by a strange assortment of political leaders among which there were Latin American dictators, representatives of authoritarian regimes in Eastern Europe, and U.S. politicians who had little desire to be bound by supranational rules. Most likely the political initiators never seriously wanted a universal system of rights for their citizens that would erode their sovereign state powers. The fact that such rights acquired a prominent place on the world agenda is mainly due to the activities of nongovernmental organizations and civil movements. In the late 1940s, it could not be foreseen that civil society would play such a decisive role in the defense of human rights. However, even so governments have by and large been successful in securing that human rights remained moral standards not supported by robust enforcement and remedial measures.

It is harmful to the implementation of human rights that the more powerful Western nations have repeatedly been hypocritical in their enforcement of human rights standards. Usually human rights violations in so-called *client states* have been generously overlooked, whereas the readiness to intervene in countries of progressive leaning if they violated human rights has been much greater.

Often a double standard has been applied that served geopolitical and economic interests. Cases can be found in the different ways the international community has treated its enemies in Iraq or in former Yugoslavia. Moreover, there is an abundance of cases to demonstrate that many states are willing to trade the defense of human rights for their business interests. The motivation to defend human rights only rarely survives the attractions of commercial contracts. Western attitudes toward the Chinese People's Republic are a case in point. A particularly serious problem in this context is caused by the stakes the five permanent members of the UN Security Council have in the world's arms trade. Almost 90% of the world's weaponry is sold by these five countries. As Garcia-Sayan (1995) rightly observed, "Weapons on the world market are one of the major sources of corruption of both political and, especially, military institutions. If this issue is not clearly and directly tackled, it is impossible to speak seriously about economic, social, and cultural rights in the Third World" (p. 76).

A striking illustration came when in August 2002 the Bush administration decided to resume military ties with the Republic of Indonesia. These ties had been interrupted because of the grand-scale human rights violations by the Indonesian army in East Timor during 1999. The war on terrorism provided the convenient argument to restore military contacts. In this context, the State department took the initiative to intervene in a lawsuit filed against Exxon Mobil (in the United States) for alleged complicity in human rights abuses in Indonesia. The suit states that Indonesian security forces that protected the operations of Exxon Mobil had committed gross atrocities. The State department urged the presiding judge to dismiss the case. The key argument was that the suit would hinder the struggle against international terrorism because it would negatively affect the cooperation with the Indonesian authorities.

Despite overwhelming lip-service paid to the respect for human rights, it should be recognized that the desire to seriously implement human rights standards is not universally shared. In the major religious movements around the world today, there are certainly strong supporters for the implementation of the international human rights standards. There is a recognition in the different world religions (Christianity, Judaism, Islam, Hinduism, and Buddhism) that they share respect for human dignity and basic principles such as tolerance, integrity, and equality. Yet the religious support for human rights is not universally shared. It remains in many quarters a contested issue. As a matter of fact, in countries with strong religious presence there is often a great disparity between the theory and the practice of human rights. There is also a long history of gross human rights violations by religious movements. Moreover, today there are traditional religious movements (fundamentalists of various origins) and all kinds of new religious sects that perpetrate—as part of their sacred mission—human rights violations as they limit the freedom of conscience of their followers.

Actually, in the history of religions, an essential human rights principle such as "freedom of thought, conscience and expression" has always been a contested issue because it fundamentally challenges the institutional hierarchy in religions.

Even if religious movements recognize the universality of the human rights principles, their local interpretation may be influenced by religious idiosyncrasies (e.g., ideas on male–female relations) that are difficult to harmonize with these principles. These conflicting interpretations are often defended with references to the Western and imperialist nature of the human rights regime. This is corroborated by the fact that many countries are indeed experiencing a process of cultural colonization (sometimes referred to as *McDonaldization*) of which the introduction of human rights is perceived as an important part. This is reinforced by the fact that Western nations (and in particular the United States) have so often practiced in the pursuit of their foreign policy human rights imperialism. Against this, the supporters of human rights in religious movements will propose that conflicting interpretations of human rights principles can be resolved by rethinking the religious doctrines. However, this may not be so easy because there are real differences between religious and secular conceptions on the notion of "rights." The disparity between the secular conception that rights are derived from inherent human dignity is not so easily reconciled with the theocentric position that rights are the gift of God. In the latter view, rights are obtained on the basis of the fulfillment of obligations toward the Divine Will.

In line with this, it should also be recognized that in most world religions the dominant discourse is about duties and not about rights. In the religious world of the Islam, a complex question is also whether Islamic conformity with human rights principles should also imply that Shari'a should be in conformity with human rights standards. Shari'a comprises "the laws derived from the Qu'ran, the Sunnah, the Hadith and decisions of Muhammed, Ijma'—the consensus of opinion of the Ulama (Judges) and Ijtihad—the counsel of judges on a particular case" (Traer, 1991, p. 115).

If conformity of national jurisdiction with Shari'a is demanded, as certainly the fundamentalist theologians would prefer, there is an insurmountable problem. Although the Qu'ran may contain paragraphs that support religious liberty, this is not the case in Shari'a and has often not been the political practice in Muslim countries where the state has the responsibility to enforce the Shari'a.

Shari'a fundamentally rejects such basic human rights principles as nondiscrimination and equality: ". . . it is impossible for Shari'a to acknowledge any set of rights to which all human beings are entitled by virtue of their humanity, without distinction on grounds of religion or gender" (An-Na'im, 1995, p. 238).

Economics: Globalization

The effects of the processes of economic globalization on the defense of human rights are not homogeneous.[3] In different societies and in different strata of the same society, these effects are different. Globalization processes may both promote and threaten human rights. Global network technologies strengthen free speech, but also disseminate hate speech.

At the core of economic gobalization stands a societal model in which economic and contractual relations determine the nature of social relations. In the modern contract society, human rights are subsumed under economic rationales, and its key actors are driven primarily by self-centered interests. This clashes with human rights standards that are inspired by compassion with the interests of others.

It is a peculiar development that in current economic gobalization there is a strong drive toward deregulation and a minimal role for the state, whereas in the 19th and 20th centuries societies learned that deregulated free markets spell enormous social disaster. As Ghai (1999) argued ". . . few states, even the colonial, have found it possible or expedient to let markets unfold in the fullness of their logic, because the consequences of free markets threaten social peace and stability" (p. 245). Government had to intervene to keep the social costs of free markets under control. Modern markets, despite all the claims to freedom, are dependent on the coercive power of national states. This power benefits some people more than others.

If on the national level free markets pose serious threats to social stability, people's welfare, and natural resources, it is difficult to see why anyone would expect that the project of a global free market would not face instability, poverty, and resource depletion. A close reading of current statements and reflections on economic gobalization does not reveal any serious argument to support the thesis that global autonomous markets would cause any less disaster than would national autonomous markets.

As the role of the market becomes more dominant in modern societies, the outcome is in general more access to better educational and health services for few people and a deterioration of welfare for most people.

---

[3]UN Economic and Social Council, Sub-Commission on the promotion and protection of Human Rights, The realization of economic, social and cultural rights: Globalization and its impact of the full enjoyment of human rights; report by J. Olola-Onyango and Deepika Udugama; http://www.globalpolicy.org/socecon/un/wtonite.htm

The marketization of societies clashes fundamentally with the concept of human rights on the issue of equality. Whereas equality is a core standard in international human rights, the modern market does not foster equality.

HUMAN RIGHTS IN CONFLICT

The implementation of human rights is often problematic as a result of conflicts among human rights, conflicts between human rights and significant societal interests, or conflicts between human rights and cultural values.

Rights Versus Rights

A classical case for communicators is the situation in which the human right to the protection of privacy (Article 12 of the UDHR) conflicts with the human right to freedom of expression (Article 19 of the UDHR) or situations in which the free speech standard clashes with the prohibition to discriminate. This is complicated because there is no hierarchy of rights that can provide a definitive arbitration. A crucial characteristic of the human rights regime is the indivisibility of its constituent rights. In 1993, the UN World Conference on Human Rights (at Vienna) emphasized this by stating, "All human rights are universal, indivisible and interdependent and interrelated." In the conflict among human rights, one can only neglect one category of rights at the expense of other rights.

In reality, however, situations that represent irresolvable dilemma's occur infrequently. Choices made in Hell, such as in the movie "Sophie's Choice," in which a mother is forced by a German soldier to decide which one of her children will be deported, are fortunately scarce.

In most situations, dilemmas can be resolved when the pertinent elements of a confrontation are adequately analyzed. The analysis often shows that one of the claims is ill-founded; although rights can be considered of equal significance, the grounds on which their realization is claimed may be of a different order. It may well be that the claim to the protection of privacy is grounded on a limited private interest, whereas the claim to free speech is based on a broad public interest. If the parties involved fail to resolve this conflict through the social dialogue, courts of law will usually come to acceptable judgments.

Rights Versus Significant Interests

This conflict has become prominent after the events of September 11, 2001. In the aftermath of the attacks in the United States, human rights (such as the protection of privacy, free speech, due process of law) across the world have been severely limited on grounds of national security and the war against terrorism.

As Ronald Dworkin (2002) wrote in an essay for the *New York Review of Books* "What has al-Qaeda done to our Constitution, and to our national standards of fairness and decency? Since September 11, the government has enacted legislation, adopted policies, and threatened procedures that are not consistent with our established laws and values and would have been unthinkable before" (p. 44).

After September 11, the international agreement to cooperate against terrorism has shifted to the language of *war on terrorism*. For human rights, this is problematic because the emphasis in many states came to be on security and order, and many national experiences have demonstrated that this tends to go together with limits to the enjoyment of basic rights. With this change in approach, it is not always clear that efforts at controlling terrorism should remain within the boundaries of international human rights standards.

The core difficulty is this: Because no human right—however fundamental—can be absolute, there is always the possibility that significant national or personal interests demand qualification of basic rights. However, because this qualification may undermine human rights to unacceptable levels, each conflict between rights and interests needs to be judged in the light of the following four criteria. Proportionality: Is the restriction of a right proportional to the protection of the proposed aim? In other words, is there a pressing social need for the restriction. Subsidiarity: Is there no alternative measure to achieve the proposed aim? Effectiveness: Is there evidence that the proposed restriction will indeed achieve the proposed aim? Duration: is the restriction only of a temporary duration?

In many cases around the world, where state authorities propose to restrict citizens' basic civil and political rights, the proposals do not measure up to these criteria and should therefore be rejected.

Rights Versus Cultural Values

Under this heading, one finds conflicts between the right to physical integrity and the cultural practice of female genital mutilation, between the right to freedom of religion and culture-specific religious rulings (like *fatwas*), or between the right to be protected against discrimination and culture-based rejections of homosexuality. In such conflicts, it should always be questioned whose cultural values are at stake. What is presented as the cultural preferences of whole communities often only reflects the bias and interest of a cultural elite. Moreover, it should be realized that cultures are human constructs and, as such, are changeable and not sacrosanct. More often than not, the cultural argument is based on a selective interpretation of a culture's sources (e.g., its sacred scriptures), and a different reading of these sources may not conflict with human rights standards. Although many rights versus culture conflicts can probably be resolved in a serious dialogue among those concerned, it should not be ignored that there may indeed be situations in which the standards of international human rights law and those cherished by cultural communities clash in non-negotiable ways. There remains, for example, an inherent tension between the universality of human rights and transcendental religious values.

THE KEY FEATURES OF INTERNATIONAL HUMAN RIGHTS

The human species does not distinguish itself by a historical record that radiates benignity. Throughout most of its history, the human being occupies himself (and, to a more limited extent, herself) with an impressive variety of humiliating acts against fellow human beings.

Against this gross indecency of human history, the more enlightened individuals have throughout the ages committed themselves to the articulation and codification of basic moral standards that were intended to restrain human aggression, arbitrariness, and negligence.

Basic to the concept of human rights is the notion that the human being is entitled to respect for his or her inalienable dignity. This means that the human being is worthy of treatment in accordance with certain basic standards. The recognition of the dignity of the human person implies that human beings cannot treat each other arbitrarily in ways they see fit.

The standards of human conduct have evolved in a long history of different schools of religious and philosophical thought. The modern notion of human rights has many different parents. Among them are those European thinkers who developed the idea of natural rights that became so central to political thinking from the 18th-century Enlightenment period onward. Liberal theories on natural rights articulated such rights in universal terms as rights by birth belonging to all people because they are human beings. For example, one finds this in the thinking of John Locke (1632–1704), who proposed that individuals are born free and equal and are endowed with natural rights in virtue of their common humanity. Yet Locke excluded from these natural rights women and slaves, and from his right to religious tolerance he excluded Catholics and atheists. The modern idea that human rights are a reflection of universal moral principles was strongly influenced by the thinking of Immanuel Kant (1724–1804). Individuals can act autonomously and in accordance with reason. They can choose to act in accordance with universal moral principles. Such principles can be derived from reason. People can develop—when they distance themselves from their individual desires and interests—moral rules that would be freely adopted by all people under the same conditions. Such universal maxims imply moral obligations that are unconditional to all. The primary moral obligation is that I ought never to act except in such a way that I can also will that my maxim should become a universal law. The secondary moral obligation is to always act in such a way that no individual is treated as a means to an end. The underlying notion is that the dignity of all individuals should be respected. Kant suggested that for the implementation of such universal principles international political institutions are needed such as a league of nations.

The Enlightenment philosophers were primarily supporters of decent forms of public governance (Gay, 1973). Thinkers such as Montesquieu, Diderot, Beccaria, Voltaire, and Lessing strongly emphasized the need for social morality. Important moral principles for them were tolerance, pluralism, international peace, abolition of slavery (Montesquieu) and capital punishment, and the humanization of criminal law (Beccaria).

Yet such humanist conceptions also have many non-Western antecedents. The notion of human beings as rights bearers, which reflects a basic respect for human dignity, and a tradition of tolerance, freedom, and compassion, did not emerge from one single cultural source.

It is a strange and unwarranted underestimation of non-Western cultural traditions to assume that only the West could have come up with a defense of the inherent dignity of all human beings. Actually the West has been as much a place where ideas about rights to freedom, equality and democracy developed as it was the arena of slavery, racism, sexism, and fascism.

As UN Secretary General Kofi Annan stated in a speech in 1997, "The principles enshrined in the Universal Declaration of Human Rights are deeply rooted in the history of humankind. They can be found in the teachings of all the world's cultural and religious traditions."

Some illustrations of non-Western groundings of humanist values are to be found in Islam. It can be argued (Othman, 1999) that the Qur'anic notion of a common human ontology provides for a conception of rights of human beings because they are human. Also,

> Qur'anic conceptions of the rights and duties of men and women—in the family, to own and manage property, and to participate in public life and hold public office, for example, provide the basis for a far more enlightened and egalitarian view of gender relations than the regressive ideas that are currently offered, misleadingly in the name of Islam, by fundamentalist Islamists the world over. (p. 173)

"According to the Qur'an a Muslim person who suffers oppression and does not do anything about it is a sinner. . . . Implied in this is a profound affirmation of human freedom, dignity, and autonomy—and of the human as a rights-bearing being " (Othman, 1999, p. 189).

One could also refer to Confucian antecedents. The Confucian code of ethics recognized each individual's right to personal dignity and worth (quoted from Tai Hung-Chan in Donnelly, 1999, p. 66). There is in Confucianism a recognition of the importance of human dignity and human well-being. The Buddhist tradition also has a strong concern for human salvation—a set of moral rules somewhat comparable to the Decalogue of the Jewish Old Testament and the basic notion of compassion.

Most of the historic moral prescriptions had a limited scope in terms of the agents they addressed and/or the geographies they covered. The novelty of the international human rights system—as it was established after 1945—is the formulation of these standards into a catalogue of universal moral standards.

Moreover, one could argue that despite these antecedents most of the pre-1945 reflections on human dignity and human values are grounded in conceptions of human entitlements that are significantly different from what after 1945 is defined as human rights. The interesting observation is that the post-1945 emerging human rights are new for all parties in the international community. Human rights confront not only non-Western cultures with a historically new situation: They are a new and difficult challenge for all cultures. No culture, religion, or moral system knows a set of rights and duties such as developed in the Universal Declaration of Human Rights. In the Declaration, in contrast to most cultural and religious traditions, the recognition of human dignity is formulated as a claim to be enforced by law. Moreover, this claim recognizes that the individual is entitled to rights not only through membership of a community, but in his or her own individual capacity.

Most important, human rights standards propose that the moral claims that people make vis-à-vis each other are solely based on their humanity. If rights are related to the human being as such, and not given by an authority, they cannot be taken away by whatever authority. They do not have to be deserved. They are not dependent on good conduct or divine grace. They are inherent to the human being because he or she is human. International human rights standards are grounded in the conviction that all human beings have inalienable entitlements to the protection of their life and liberty because of their humanity and not as derivates of a higher order. This notion of human autonomy is certainly not universally shared. Joseph Chan argued that whereas Western liberals ground the right to free speech in personal autonomy, Confucianism accepts the same norm, but grounds this as "a means for society to correct wrong ethical beliefs, to ensure that rulers would not indulge in wrongdoing, and to promote valuable arts and cultures in the long run" (in Bauer & Bell, 1999, p. 237). This constitutes justification of moral standards on instrumental rather than on intrinsic grounds.

If progress is to be made in the implementation of human rights standards, we should get away from the common and convenient approach in which human rights are seen as mainly a problem for non-Western civilizations. It needs to be recognized, however, that this denies that the West has great difficulties with the theory and practice of human rights (see the U.S. reluctance to ratify major human rights treaties). The human rights regime challenges fundamental ways of thinking in all cultural traditions; it reflects a mode of thought that is new to all societies, not just non-Western societies. There is widespread unwillingness to take human rights seriously in the East, West, North, and South. For most communities around the world (whatever their cultural backgrounds), there are serious difficulties in grounding human rights. Human rights pose essential challenges to a Chinese Confucian culture, but equally to a Western consumer culture, to Islamic, as well as to Christian theology. The need of an internal critical discourse on human rights standards is equally strong everywhere (A.An Naim in Bauer & Bell, 1999).

Before 1945, there were human rights declarations such as the Magna Charta of 1215, the British Bill of Rights (1689), the American Declaration of Independence (1776), and the French Déclaration des droits de l'homme et du citoyen (1789). In 1945, this long history of the protection of human dignity acquired a fundamentally new significance. In the first place, the protection of human dignity (earlier mainly a national affair) was put on the agenda of the world community. Thus, the defense of fundamental rights was no longer the exclusive preoccupation of national politics and became an essential part of world politics. The judgment of whether human rights had been violated was no longer the exclusive monopoly of national governments. Earlier concerns about what happened in foreign countries were largely dependent on whether this affected one's politico-economic interests. Such concerns may have been whether one's diplomats would be treated correctly by other countries. There were no standards to treat all human beings decently. There was little or no altruism involved. International concerns were selective and did not imply compassion with humanity as such. Minority treaties under the League of Nations had little to do with respect for rights of minorities, but were inspired by concerns about peace among nations. The unfair treatment of minorities could lead to disturbance of the peace. Concern for citizens of other states was hindered by strict conceptions of state sovereignty, but also by inadequate information. Moreover, how could states have intervened in other countries, whereas in most countries governments routinely violated those rights that later came to be called *human rights*?

In the second place, the enjoyment of human rights was no longer restricted to privileged individuals and social elites. The revolutionary core of the process that began at San Francisco—with the adoption of the UN Charter in 1945—is that "all people matter." There are no longer nonpersons. Basic rights hold for everyone and exclude no one.

The American Declaration of Independence (1776) stated that individuals have inalienable rights that were subsequently recognised in the U.S. Constitution and the Bill of Rights (1789). Slaves were excluded from these rights. Although there were many demands for its abolition (e.g., by Thomas Paine), slavery was only abolished in 1865. Also women were excluded. The right to vote was only extended to women in 1920. There was protest among others from Susan B. Anthony, who wrote in 1873, "The preamble of the Federal Constitutions says, 'We, the people of the United States . . . '. It was we, the people; not we, the white male citizens; The only question left to be settled now is: Are women persons?" (Collins, 1998, p. 340). The French Declaration excluded women, although there were strong demands for equal rights of women at the time. Among the protesting voices was Olympe de Gouge, who issued in 1790 The Declaration of the Rights of Women. The French National Assembly of 1792 refused this declaration. Olympe de Gouge was executed. Vincent Ogé pleaded for rights for mulattos and their inclusion in the National Assembly at Paris. He was executed.

It should also be remembered that the American and French declarations of human rights were written at the time of Western colonialism and they had no provisions for people under colonial rule.

In the third place, the conventional view that individuals can only be objects of international law changed to the conception that the individual is a holder of rights and bearer of duties under international law. The individual can appeal to international law for the protection of his or her rights, but can also be held responsible for violations of human rights standards. The recognition of individual rights under international law was thus linked with the notion that individuals also have duties under international law. This was eloquently expressed in 1947 by Mahatma Gandhi in a letter to the director of UNESCO about the issue of human rights. Gandhi wrote, "I learnt from my illiterate but wise mother that rights to be deserved and preserved came from duty well done." Much more recently (September 1997), the Forum 2000 Congress at Prague (attended by a selection of the world's political, intellectual, and religious elites) focused on the importance of duties by adopting a Universal Declaration of Human Duties.

THE UNIVERSALITY OF HUMAN RIGHTS

Human rights transcend all earlier moral codes because they incorporate *everyone* and thus claim universal validity. This claim has time and again been challenged. Among others are those critics who argue that human rights are an exclusive Western idea. However, the fact that many nations were not present in San Francisco at the founding of the United Nations and did not take part in the UN General Assembly at December 10, 1948, which discussed the Universal Declaration of Human Rights, does not necessarily undermine its universal character. In the years after 1948, all the absent nations when they formulated their national constitutions borrowed concepts and phrases from the Universal Declaration. The universality of human rights is reflected in the basic legal documents of such different countries as Cambodia, Nepal, and South Africa.

In a series of different human rights instruments such as the Universal Declaration of Human Rights (UDHR), the International Covenant on Civil and Political Rights (ICCPR), the African Charter on Human Rights and Peoples' Rights, the Declaration of Basic Duties of ASEAN Peoples and Governments (ASEAN), and the Universal Islamic Declaration of Human Rights (UIDHR), we find striking similarities.

On the principle of equality and the right not to be discriminated against.

In the UDHR Article 1. "All human beings are born free and equal in dignity and rights."

In the ICCPR Article 2.1. "Each Party to the present Covenant undertakes to respect and to ensure to all individuals within its territory and subject to its jurisdiction the rights recognized in the present Covenant, without distinction of any kind, such as race, colour, sex, language, religion, political or other opinion, national or social origin, property, birth or other status."

In the African Charter Article 19. "All peoples shall be equal; they shall enjoy the same respect and shall have the same rights."

In the ASEAN Declaration Article 5.1. "It is the duty of government to ensure a minimum decent standard of living for all the people, reduce the gap in access to goods and services by different economic and social sectors, and equalize wealth, power and opportunities without distinctions based on race, sex, language, religious belief, political conviction, economic or social status, or ethnic origin."

In the UIDHR Article 3. (a) "All persons are equal before the Law and are entitled to equal opportunities and protection of the Law, (c) No person shall be denied the opportunity to work or be discriminated against in a manner or exposed to greater physical risk by reason or religious belief, colour, race, origin, sex or language."

On the principle of security and the right to life:

In the UDHR Article 3. "Everyone has the right to life, liberty and security of the person."

In the ICCPR Article 6. "Every human being has the inherent right to life. . . ."

In the African Charter Article 4. "Human beings are inviolable. Every human being shall be entitled to respect for his life and the integrity of his person. . . ."

In the ASEAN Declaration Article 1 ". . . it is the duty of each government to respect. . . . The right to life, liberty and security of person."

In the UIDH Article 1. "Human life is sacred and inviolable and every effort shall be made to protect it."

On the Right Not to Be Tortured:

In the UDHR Article 5. "No one shall be subjected to torture or to cruel, inhuman or degrading treatment or punishment."

In the ICCPR Article 7. "No one shall be subjected to torture or to cruel, inhuman or degrading treatment or punishment."

In the African Charter Article 5. "Every individual shall have the right to the respect of the dignity inherent in a human being and to the recognition of his legal status. All forms of exploitation and degradation of man particularly slavery, slave trade, torture, cruel, inhuman or degrading punishment and treatment shall be prohibited."

In the ASEAN Declaration Article 1. "It is the duty of each government to respect. . . . The right to freedom from torture, cruel, inhuman and degrading treatment or punishment."

In the UIDHR Article 7. "No person shall be subjected to torture in mind or body, or degraded, or threatened with injury either to himself or to anyone related to or held dear by him, or forcibly made to confess to the commission of a crime, or forced to consent to an act that is injurious to his interests."

On the Right to Freedom of Association.

In the UDHR Article 20.1. "Everyone has the right of peaceful assembly and association."

In the ICCPR Article 21. "The right of peaceful assembly shall be recognized."

In the African Charter Article 10. 1. "Every individual shall have the right to free association provided that he abides by the law."

In the ASEAN Declaration Article 1. It is the duty of every government to respect. . . . The right to freedom of assembly and associ ation, and the other rights and freedoms of individuals and of peoples."

In the UIDHR Article 14. (a). "Every person is entitled to participate individually and collectively in the religious, social, cultural and political life of his community and to establish institutions and agencies meant to enjoin what is right and to prevent what is wrong."

Actually these similarities are not so surprising even if we accept the reality of the world's cultural diversity, because there are remarkably few people who support racism, slavery, or genocide. If one accepts that moral standards are culturally relative, this does not imply that there cannot be universal moral standards or that we could not make moral choices for solutions we can argue to be preferential to other choices. Moreover, the observation that people come to different moral judgments does not necessarily prove that the moral principles that underlie these judgments are fundamentally different. The problem is that cultural relativism tends to insist on cultural differences while discarding cultural similarities.

When people differ about the value of certain customs and practices, they may share the same basic moral premises. The ways in which cultural communities approach the treatment of the deceased, the male–female relations, or the education of children may be totally different. Yet they may be based on the same moral principles. Burying, cremating, embalming, or eating the dead may all be inspired by the same respect for those who passed away.

Most essential for the universal significance of human rights standards is the observation that they constitute the only global moral framework that the international community has at present. This was—after much discussion—clearly confirmed by the 1993 UN World Conference on Human Rights in Vienna. This Conference stated in its unanimously adopted declaration,

> The World Conference on Human Rights reaffirms the solemn commitment of all States to fulfil their obligations to promote universal respect for, and observance and protection of, all human rights and fundamental freedoms for all in accordance with the Charter of the United Nations, other instruments relating to human rights, and international law. The universal nature of these rights and freedoms is beyond question. (United Nations, 1993b, pp. 3–4)

In March 2003, a meeting of Asian NGOs (March 25–28) in Bangkok adopted the Bangkok Declaration on Human Rights, which states among others, "Universal human rights standards are rooted in many cultures. We affirm the basis of universality of human rights which afford protection to all humanity. . . . As human rights are of universal concern and are universal in value, the advocacy of human rights cannot be considered to be an encroachment on national sovereignty."

Although this was an important step, the recognition of universal validity did not resolve the question of the admissible variety of cultural interpretations. Universal validity does not mean that all local forms of implementation are similar. A variety of cultural interpretations remains possible. This has provoked the question of to which degree local cultural interpretations can be accepted. There is increasing support for the view that culturally determined interpretations reach a borderline when they violate the core principles of human rights law. Moreover, this view holds that the admissibility of the interpretation should be judged by the international community and not by the implementing party.

Given the world's diversity of cultures and the fact that human rights will only be taken serious if they are seen as culturally legitimate, the reference in the 1993 Vienna declaration to the need of cultural interpretations makes sense. However, questions remain. What universality is left once cultural interpretations are fundamentally in conflict? For example, in the case of religions that only accept the authority of their sacred texts and authorized interpretations of such texts. If human rights texts prevail over religious texts or the other way around, there may be a non-negotiable conflict. Another problem with the issue of cultural interpretation is posed by the flawed assumption of homogeneous cultures that totally bypasses the existing internal diversity in cultural communities. There are always in all cultures traditionalists versus modernists, for example. The West is often portrayed as a homogeneous cultural entity! But is it? Does the West exist? If so, since when? Is it a reality or merely an ideological by-product of the cold war?

In the early stages of the United Nations, only 13 out of 51 member states perceived of themselves as Western. Only 6 of the 18 members on the Human Rights Commission considered themselves Western. Interestingly the Chinese were in favor of nondiscrimination and equal rights provisions in the UDHR, whereas the United States and the United Kingdom opposed these. Actually, at the time of the League of Nations, Japan wanted to ban racism, but lost to the United States, the United Kingdom, and France.

A troublesome assumption is also the construction of totally distinct value systems between the East and West (e.g., in the idea of a juxtaposition of an Asian collectivism versus a Western individualism). It could be, however, that the West turns out to be less individualistic than some Asian political elites propose. There is more collective social security in the West than in many Asian countries. The common good is important in many Western countries. Actually taxation for the common good is common in the West. One often finds the accusation that Western values lead to crime and drugs abuse. It would also be good to reflect on Asian values and the levels of pollution in Asian cities, the widespread occurrence of AIDS, and booming criminality. Moreover, it may be that so-called *individual rights* like the right to free speech serve collective purposes (like democracy) and that the right to free association represents a claim for community and social solidarity.

It is often said that the human rights tradition is exclusively focused on individual rights. It is certainly true that human rights are to an important extent articulated in the language of a Western individualistic liberal tradition. However, this does not hinder the provision of collective rights, such as the rights of minorities. In the evolution of human rights, the link between individual and collective rights has become stronger. Moreover, individual rights are always tied to the rights of other members of the community and the community at large. As Article 29 of the Universal Declaration of Human Rights provides, "Everyone has duties to the community in which alone the free and full development of his personality is possible."

The real controversy, however, is not between individual versus collective rights, but is about whether people are entitled to being treated decently by their state, society, tribe, clan, family, and partners. Can this entitlement be realized universally so that no one is excluded?

Abdul Aziz Said (1998) wrote, "Human rights may be difficult to define but impossible to ignore" (p. xi). It is indeed true that in the second half of the 20th century human rights have become a reality, but so have their worldwide violation. One could say that after World War II the world community treated itself to a very special gift: the recognition of human dignity as a universal moral and legal claim. It would seem the key challenge for the 21st century to begin to unwrap and enjoy this gift to humanity. In the following chapters, the contribution that communicators could make is explored.

SUGGESTIONS FOR DISCUSSION

Discuss proposals for the promotion, protection, and implementation of the 12 core human rights, particularly in your own local context.

Discuss what kind of individual responsibilities people like yourself have in relation to these 12 core rights.

Discuss the statement by Donnelly (1999) that the place of origin of human rights is irrelevant to their applicability. If it can be argued that this is true for the relativity theory of Albert Einstein, why would it not also be valid for human rights standards?

Discuss to what extent (using concrete examples) the current gobalization of trade supports or hampers the universalization of human rights.

Discuss the problems your own society has in implementing human rights. For example, has your country ratified all the relevant human rights treaties? Does it accept the authority of supranational monitoring (e.g., UN Human Rights Committees) and adjudication mechanisms (e.g., Regional courts/commissions of human rights)?

Discuss relevant, local examples of human rights in conflict.

2

The Standard of Free Speech

The most essential standard in human rights law that relates to information and communication is the entitlement to free speech. As early as 350 BC, the Greek statesman and orator Demosthenes realized the central importance of free speech for human dignity. He expressed this by saying that taking away the freedom of expression is one of the greatest calamities for human beings. For an early record one could also refer to Roman historian Tacitus (55–116), who complimented the emperor Trajan for the felicitous times when one could freely express whatever one wanted to say.

However, the desire to restrict free speech has an equally long history. Greek philosopher Plato, for example, warned against the dangers reading Homer. In his work *The Republic*, he proposed, "Then the first thing will be to establish a censorship of writers of fiction and . . . reject the bad."

It could be argued, however, that a real systematic articulation of the concern began only with the invention and proliferation of the printing press, which almost immediately led to censorship. In 1493, the Inquisition in Venice issued the first list of books banned by the Church. In 1559, the Index Librorum Prohibitorum was made binding on all Roman Catholics and was administered by the Inquisition. Actually the secular powers also took to the example and issued forms of regulation to control expression. The official rationale for this was greatly inspired by Thomas Hobbes' reflections in his book *Leviathan* where he extended the state sovereignty to the opinions and persuasions of the governed: ". . . it is annexed to the Sovereignty, to be the Judge of what Opinions and Doctrines are averse, and what conducing to Peace. . . ." (1968, p. 233)

An example of such sovereign control was the English Regulation of Printing Act for the control of printing and printing presses. This licensing law provided for a system of censorship through licenses for printing and publishing. Against this type of regulation, John Milton published his *Aeropagitica* in 1644. In this famous speech to the Parliament of England on the liberty of unlicensed printing, Milton claimed, "Truth needs no licensing to make her victorious."

In 1695, the Regulation of Printing Act was revoked. Interestingly enough, Milton's plea for freedom of printing did not apply to Roman Catholics because he felt one should not extend principles of tolerance to those who are intolerant. In Sweden in 1766, an order on the freedom of the printing press was enacted as formal law, including the rights of access to public information. The oldest catalogue of fundamental rights (in the sense of human rights and civil rights, which possess a higher legal force) is the Declaration of Rights, preceding the constitution of the state of Virginia, in 1776. Here the freedom of expression was formulated as press freedom, "That the freedom of the Press is one of the greatest bulwarks of liberty, and never be restrained by despotic governments." Following the Anglosaxon tradition, the French Declaration on human and citizen rights (Déclaration des droits de l'homme et du citoyen) was formulated in 1789. This declaration went beyond the Virginia declaration in stating, that the unrestrained communication of thoughts or opinions being one of the most precious rights of man, every citizen may speak, write, and publish freely, provided he be responsible for the abuse of this liberty, in the cases determined by law. Then in 1791, the U.S. Bill of Rights stated in Article I that famous provision that "Congress shall make no law . . . abridging the freedom of speech, or of the press."

In the 19th century, legislation on fundamental rights emerged in many countries, and the freedom of the press became a central issue, primarily in the form of the prohibition of censorship. This was reflected in many national constitutions. Until the 20th century, the concern about freedom of information remained almost exclusively a domestic affair. Interestingly enough, when in the early 20th century the League of Nations focused on the problems of false news and propaganda, it did not address the protection of freedom of expression. The International Federation of Journalists, however, stated the concern about freedom of information in the first article of its statute in 1926. "Its purpose is, notably, to safeguard in all possible ways the liberty of the Press and of journalists which it will endeavour to have guaranteed by law." During World War II, the professional community would continue to express its concern about the freedom of information. At the second congress of the International Federation of Journalists of Allied or Free Countries (IFJAFC) in 1942, a resolution was adopted on the Charter of the Free Press that read in part,

> The Congress recognises, however, that the freedom of the Press is no greater and no less than the freedom of the individual and carries with it the obligations, which the journalist worthy of the name will freely accept and observe, not to publish false or distorted news, not to do anything likely to discredit his profession, his paper, or himself. To this end, Congress urges the universal adoption of a Code of Professional Conduct as has been done by several of its affiliated organizations. (Kubka & Nordenstreng, 1986, p. 83)

When during World War II drafts for a postwar international bill of rights were prepared, the freedom of expression figured prominently. This is the case in the draft prepared by a commission of the U.S. Department of State in 1942: "All persons shall enjoy freedom of speech and of the press, and the right to be informed. . . ." The UNESCO Constitution, adopted in 1945, was the first multilateral instrument to reflect the concern for the freedom of information. The Constitution was largely based on U.S. drafts (Wells, 1987). These drafts included among others a proposal stressing the paramount importance of the mass media and "the need to identify opportunities of UNESCO furthering their use for the ends of peace." To promote the implementation of the concern for the freedom of information, a special division of "free flow of information" was established in the secretariat in Paris.

In 1946, the delegation of the Philippines presented to the UN General Assembly a proposal for a resolution on an international conference on issues dealing with the press. This became UNGA Res. 59 (I), which was adopted unanimously in late 1946. According to the resolution, the purpose of the conference would be to address the rights, obligations, and practices that should be included in the concept of freedom of information. The resolution called freedom of information "the touchstone of all the freedoms to which the United Nations is consecrated."

It described the freedom of information as "the right to gather, transmit and publish news anywhere and everywhere without fetters." Already freedom of information began to shift away from the concern about the individual's freedom of speech to the institutional freedom of news gathering by news agencies.

In 1947, the UN General Assembly adopted additional resolutions that were to be placed on the agenda of the Conference on Freedom of Information. One dealt with measures against propaganda and incitement to war, the other was concerned with false or distorted reports. Already by 1947 the UN had indicated a concern for both freedom and social responsibility in matters of information. In 1948, the UN Conference on Freedom of Information took place in Geneva from March 23 to April 21. Fifty-four countries were officially represented, and on the initiative of the United Kingdom, practicing news people were included in the delegations. The United States was only interested in a convention on news gathering. France was mainly interested in a convention on the international right of correction. The United Kingdom preferred a convention on freedom of information. Eventually only the French text became a convention, but with few ratifications.

In the end, the conference produced numerous resolutions and three draft treaties on Freedom of Information (proposed by the British delegation), on the Gathering and International Transmission of News (proposed by the U.S. delegation), and on the International Right of Correction (proposed by the French delegation). The six Eastern European countries voted against all three conventions, and the United States abstained only from the Freedom of Information convention. This was based on the problems the Americans had with the list of limitations on the freedom of expression (Art. 2), which they found too restrictive. The draft convention on the Gathering and International Transmission of News was modified and subsequently approved by ECOSOC (Res. 152 (VII)) and then discussed at a meeting of the Third Committee of the General Assembly (in New York in April 1949), which decided to join the draft with the draft convention on the International Right of Correction. Then the joint texts were adopted by the UNGA Res. 277 (III)C) in 1949, but not opened for signature. The Right of Correction draft was subsequently separated from the Gathering and Transmission text and opened for signature in 1952. After ratification by six countries, the Convention entered into force on August 25, 1962. In 1993, there were only 11 UN member states that had ratified the Convention.[1]

The third draft Convention on the Freedom of Information was adopted by the UN General Assembly in 1949 (UNGA Res. 277 (III)A) after modification and adoption by ECOSOC and modification by the Third Committee, which abandoned work on the Convention after approval of its preamble and five articles. The Convention was never opened for signature and got lost in protracted ideological confrontation. In 1959, ECOSOC—urged by the United States—drafted a set of principles as the basis for a Declaration on Freedom of Information. In 1960, the General Assembly received the principles, but took no action.

---

[1]At the end of its Resolution 48, the Commission appealed to all states: (a) To ensure respect and support for the rights of all persons who exercise the right to freedom of opinion and expression, including the right to seek, receive, and impart information regardless of frontiers; the rights to freedom of thought, conscience, and religion, peaceful assembly, and association; and the right to take part in the conduct of public affairs, or who seek to promote and defend these rights and freedoms, and, where any persons have been detained, subjected to violence or threats of violence or to harassment, including persecution and intimidation, even after their release from detention, for exercising these rights as laid down in the Universal Declaration of Human Rights, the International Covenant on Civil and Political Rights and other relevant human rights instruments, to take the appropriate steps to ensure the immediate cessation of these acts and to create

At the 1948 conference, there were confrontations between those who advanced a largely liberal-economic position in defense of newspapers and news agencies, and those who challenged this as sanctioning of commercial monopolies and propagandistic practices. Serious objections were made by the Soviet Union against a concern for the freedom of information that was exclusively based on commercial claims. The Soviet Union Minister of Foreign Affairs, Andrei Gromyko, claimed that the proposed freedom of information was in fact the freedom of a few monopolies. The doctrine of the free flow of information obscured, in his opinion, the interests of bankers and industrialists for whom Wall Street represented the summit of democracy. The Soviet Union also claimed that the freedom of information could not mean freedom for fascist propaganda. Other delegations equally stressed the need to prevent the establishment of news monopolies under the guise of freedom. Some nations, such as Yugoslavia, drew attention to the wide disparities in available means of mass communication and claimed that freedom should be linked with the standard of equality.

The key provision on this standard in international human rights law is phrased by Article 19 of the Universal Declaration of Human Rights. The Article reads: "Everyone has the right to freedom of opinion and expression; this right includes freedom to hold opinions without interference and to seek, receive and impart information and ideas through any media and regardless of frontiers."

Over the years, the UN Human Rights Commission has given considerable attention to the freedom of information and stated in 2002 in its Resolution 48 that the Commission is deeply concerned about numerous reports of extrajudicial killings, detention, as well as discrimination, threats and acts of violence and harassment, including persecution and intimidation, often undertaken with impunity, against professionals in the field of information as well as other persons exercising their right to freedom of opinion and expression, including human rights defenders. The Commission also expressed its concern at killings of and attacks on journalists in areas of armed conflict, and it stressed the need

---

conditions under which these acts may be less liable to occur, including by ensuring that relevant national legislation complies with their international human rights obligations and is effectively implemented; (b) To ensure that persons seeking to exercise these rights and freedoms are not discriminated against, particularly in such areas as employment, housing, and social services, and in this context to pay particular attention to the situation of women; (c) To create and permit an enabling environment in which training and professional development of the media can be organized to promote and protect the right to freedom of opinion and expression and can be carried out without threat of legal, criminal, or administrative sanction by the state, and to refrain from the use of imprisonment or the imposition of fines for offenses relating to the media which are disproportionate to the gravity of the offense and which violate international human rights law.

to ensure respect for all human rights and fundamental freedoms as well as international humanitarian law, and to bring to justice those responsible for such attacks. The Commission was especially concerned that for women there exists a gap among the right to freedom of opinion and expression, the right to information, and the effective enjoyment of those rights, and that this gap contributes to inadequate action by governments in the integration of the human rights of women into the mainstream of their human rights activities.

Governments were urged by the Commission to respect freedom of expression in the media and broadcasting and, in particular, to respect the editorial independence of the media and encourage a diversity of sources of information, including through transparent licensing systems and effective regulations on undue concentration of ownership of the media in the private sector, and to refrain from imposing restrictions on the free flow of information and ideas which are not consistent with the provisions of Article 19, Paragraph 3 of the International Covenant on Civil and Political Rights, including practices such as the unjustifiable banning or closing of publications or other media and the abuse of administrative measures and censorship. Because the Commission recognized that effective participation depends on the ability to express oneself freely and the freedom to seek, receive, and impart information and ideas of all kinds, it urged governments to facilitate the effective participation of women at decision-making levels in national, regional, and international institutions, including in mechanisms for the prevention, management, and resolution of conflicts.

The Commission works through a Special Rapporteur on the promotion and protection of the right to freedom of opinion and expression who regularly reports to the Commission. In 2002, Mr. Ambeyi Ligabo submitted such a report in which he noted that a large number of allegations continue to refer to the following situations: internal armed conflict, civil unrest, situations where the legal and institutional protections and guarantees of human rights are circumscribed to a greater or lesser degree, or where the legal and institutional protections and guarantees exist but are not properly implemented. The Special Rapporteur also noted that the communications received are not confined to alleged violations in such situations, but also to alleged violations occurring in emerging or long-established democracies.

The Special Rapporteur underlined that the international community's awareness of the right to freedom of opinion and expression, of its principles, and of the need to secure them in laws and regulations to protect this right and ensure its effective exercise seems to be increasing. However, despite this perceived and welcome increase in consciousness about the importance of the effective exercise of the right to freedom of opinion and expression in ensuring democracy and promoting respect for all human rights, the Special Rapporteur was of the view that, in general, adequate steps toward better protection of this right have not yet been taken universally. This is particularly obvious when analyzing the increasing number of communications sent to the Special Rapporteur, reporting on continuing violations to freedom of opinion and expression in all regions of the world.

A majority of cases received by the Special Rapporteur have continued to relate to violations of the right to freedom of opinion and expression of media professionals. The Special Rapporteur noted that the number of journalists killed, arrested, and imprisoned is still very high, although the number of reported killings of journalists seems to have decreased in 2002, and many journalists working in conflict areas have been specifically targeted by belligerents—killed, wounded, arrested and detained, intimidated, harassed and threatened, prevented from access to certain areas, had their press cards confiscated, and expelled from or forbidden entry to certain countries. Similar violations also occurred, although they seem to be less reported on, in relation to political groups and members of opposition political parties, associations defending various rights and interests, human rights defenders, judges and lawyers, students, academics, trade unionists, persons participating in strikes or otherwise demonstrating, peasants, members of religious and indigenous minorities, authors, cartoonists, and, more generally, all individuals and groups seeking to express their opinions freely and to seek and impart information.

The Special Rapporteur wrote in his 2002 report that, as has been the case in the past in a large number of instances, national security and the argument of necessity continue to be frequently used by authorities in a number of countries to silence and/or take punitive action against those who have exercised their right to freedom of opinion and expression. The arguments of national security and necessity have been supplemented by the argument of the fight against terrorism, which is more and more frequently resorted to by the authorities in many countries to infringe—through, inter alia, the adoption of restrictive laws, arrest, detention, censorship, bans, surveillance of and restrictions on publications or the use of the Internet—the right to freedom of opinion and expression, in particular for journalists, members of political opposition groups and parties, and human rights defenders.

The Special Rapporteur, although, unequivocally condemning terrorism and terrorist attacks, expressed his concerns arising from the recent trend among governments to adopt or contemplate the adoption of counterterrorism and national security legislative or other measures that may infringe on the effective exercise of the right to freedom of opinion and expression. According to the report, national security is prioritized by a number of governments over the protection of human rights and fundamental freedoms. Among the measures taken to curb freedom of information are the (a) adoption of restrictive laws and rules for war reporting and increased resort to propaganda and manipulation of the media by defense ministries during conflicts; (b) severe restrictions on the use of encryption software to protect the privacy of e-mail communications, thus facilitating wiretapping by the authorities; (c) increased legal or regulatory pressures on journalists to reveal their sources of information or hand over to authorities information the latter deem to be related to terrorism or terrorist activities; (d) restriction on access to information in a growing number of areas, in particular by enlarging the categories of information to be protected by secrecy; (e) adoption of rules restricting the coverage of governments' activities and requiring it to be submitted for prior authorization; (f) increased exposure to criminal charges of journalists in case of publication of—even nonconfidential—information regarded by governments as damaging, including in certain cases making it a criminal offense to distribute information about any individual or group implicated in terrorist or subversive activities; and (g) the possibility for a government to take over media outlets in areas where antiterrorism operations are being conducted.

In addition to the formal adoption of laws and regulations specifically targeting the free flow and exchange of information and communications and free expression, more generally, the right to freedom of opinion and expression might be effectively—although indirectly—restricted through various means, such as the bombing of broadcasting facilities and the targeting of journalists by the military in conflict areas; restrictions on the freedom of journalists to access certain conflict areas; or arguments of patriotism and the threat of displeasing majority public opinion to demand complicit silence from journalists and stifle dissent and criticism. The use of such means of pressure lead, more often than not, to self-censorship of media professionals, human rights defenders, or political opponents.

Free speech and particularly the free flow of information also became a recurrent concern with UNESCO. In the debates (of the 1970s) on the Third World demand for a new international information order, the concern became a leading controversial issue.

The UNESCO Mass Media Declaration of 1978 used the concept of a "free flow and wider and better balanced dissemination of information" and also referred to "a new equilibrium and greater reciprocity in the flow of information." In line with the extension of the freedom of information with the notion of balance, a new thinking also emerged that sought to extend the existing provisions into a *right to communicate*. I get back to the discussion on a right to communicate in the final chapter.

In the early 1990s, freedom of information was highlighted on UNESCO's agenda through regional meetings to promote the development of free media. These meetings were held in 1990 in Windhoek, Namibia, and in 1992 in Alma Alta, USSR. At these meetings, the free speech standard was addressed in the context of media independence.

Media independence can be defined as the autonomous control over editorial content by publishers, broadcasters, editors, and journalists. This control implies that the work of collecting, editing, and publishing information is conducted within the framework of editorial aims that are articulated and adopted by the professionals involved and without interference from third parties (public authorities or private-interest groups). Control over editorial content has to be protected against a variety of pressures that are external to the media, including direct and indirect political pressures, the use of financial resources, the control of production and distribution to pressurize the media into serving specific commercial interests, or efforts to use the media to promote sectional sociocultural interests. Control over editorial content also has to be protected against pressures from inside the media, such as efforts by owners, publishers, and managers to make that content subordinate to interests other than the agreed editorial aims.

Although the concept of media independence does not explicitly appear in the body of binding international information law, its importance has been implied in various governmental and nongovernmental documents. Media independence appears explicitly in the UNESCO-supported Declarations of Windhoek, Alma Alta, and Santiago; in resolutions and declarations of the European Ministerial Conference on Mass Media Policy; and in various declarations made by the International Federation of Journalists.

In the Windhoek Declaration, media independence is defined as independence from "governmental, political or economic control" or from "control of materials and infrastructure," which are essential for the production and dissemination of media.

The UNESCO General Conference in its 26th session (Paris, October–November 1991) stated in Resolution 4.3, on the promotion of press freedom in the world, that it noted with interest the Declaration adopted by participants at the Windhoek seminar and invited the director-general to extend to other regions of the world the action taken so far in Africa and Europe to encourage press freedom and promote independence and pluralism of the media. The 28th session of the General Conference (Paris, October–November 1995) underlined the importance of the declarations of Windhoek, Almaty, and Santiago (Resolution 4.6) and endorsed these declarations.

The concept of media independence is complicated because it has two distinct and yet interrelated dimensions. On one level, media independence refers to the absence of external interference (governmental, political, or economic control) and thus primarily to the freedom for media owners to determine and pursue their editorial aims. Obviously this freedom or the lack thereof, affects all those involved with the editorial product from the owner to the junior journalist. This dimension of media independence, however crucial, needs to be complemented by another level of editorial freedom. This second level refers to the freedom of those employed by the owner of the media organization to pursue the agreed-on editorial aims without undue interference. The two levels are interrelated because it is one of the distinctive features of media organizations that all those involved can invoke the constitutional right to freedom of expression. This right applies irrespective of whether the right holders are employers or employees. Following this reasoning, the notion of media independence refers to the application of the classical human rights rule of freedom of speech to *all* those who are professionally involved with the collecting, editing, and publishing of information, background, and comment in the mass media.

Moreover, the media client (the general public) in a democratic society is best served when robust provisions are in place to guarantee maximum protection against both external and internal interference.

The external dimension refers to external independence from interferences by state or private powers with those who own, publish, or manage media institutions. This level of independence requires provisions that address the conflicts of interest that may arise between media organizations and their social context.

The internal dimension refers to the freedom for editors and journalists from undue interference by owners, publishers, and managers. This level of independence requires the negotiation and agreement within the media organization of a common framework within which the editorial aims are pursued.

MEDIA INDEPENDENCE AND THE BROADER CONTEXT

In most countries, media independence is under pressure from a variety of interferences. These may come from public authorities, private interest groups, or individuals. Pressures are exerted on the media by governments that fire prominent journalists who ask awkward questions, advertisers who seek to influence the direction of broadcast programming, or criminals who decide to execute investigative journalists.

In the Eastern European region, countries are passing through transitional phases toward new forms of democratic governance. In all these countries, one finds different stages of the development of media regulation. In some countries, the former regulatory regime still holds; in others, new media legislation was passed or combinations of the old and new legal orders are implemented. In postcommunist countries, state control over broadcasting remains strong. All these experiences imply both opportunities and risks for media independence.

In North America and Western Europe, a public debate has begun in connection with such issues as violence in the audiovisual media and pornographic, extremist, or racist information and opinions in computer networks. In the debate, legislative proposals have been made that amount to threats to the right to free speech.

The economic environment in which today's mass media operate is characterized by industrial consolidation (mergers, acquisitions, the emergence of mega multimedia conglomerates) in some countries and scarcity of basic resources (print, equipment, distribution mechanisms, levels of payment) in other countries. In either case, media independence is under threat.

The worldwide commercialization of the media leads to a variety of linkages between the media and other operators in the market. As a result of such deals (e.g., between TV networks and advertising agencies), the traditional separation of editorial and commercial interests is increasingly under pressure. Large advertisers are acquiring increasing influence on media contents.

In a growing number of countries, labor conditions move toward flexible arrangements. This means that media enterprises hire journalists not as permanent employees, but as freelancers. Given insecure working and financial conditions, this promotes a trend toward sensational, market-oriented reporting undermining the quality of professional work.

The rise of racism in several countries leads to increased pressure on legislators to enact so-called hate speech legislation. However necessary it is to curb expressions in the media that are discriminatory against individuals and groups of individuals, there is a risk of restricting media independence on unconstitutional grounds.

In many countries, laws on defamation continue to exert a chilling effect on the independence of media reporting. With the threat of million dollar lawsuits by would-be plaintiffs, publishers and editors tend toward forms of self-censorship. In some countries, groups of concerned media clients (in particular TV audiences) have confronted the mass media with demands for better quality programming. Also more often rights of reply are being exercised by those critical of media reporting, and in many countries an increase in complaints to Press Councils can be observed. All this represents a much needed development in media awareness and criticism, but it should be carefully monitored lest it slides toward forms of populist censorship and thus unduly affects media independence.

It is also important to note that the professionalization of journalism has achieved different stages in different societies. Strong supportive regulation for media independence can be seriously undermined when professional standards are inadequate and a robust professional style has not yet developed.

MEDIA REGULATION

Media regulation is one of the instruments through which protection against interference can be achieved. Media regulation provides rules, procedures, and institutional mechanisms for relations among the mass media, the political sphere, the market place, and the public.

Existing regulation may provide an effective defense against a variety of pressures on independence, but it may also fail to do so. Existing regulation may even facilitate external pressures on the editorial process by allowing a broad range of free speech restrictions. The assessment of the quality of existing regulatory conditions in relation to media independence starts from the following two considerations:

- The human rights rule—that speech should be free—can be formulated, implemented, and enforced with varying degrees of robustness. The rule can be limited to negative action (e.g., the prohibition of interference with speech) or extended to forms of positive action.
- The human rights rule that speech should be free is not absolute. Even the most robust regulatory process permits exceptions. This raises the question of the balance between the free speech rule and other human rights standards. Although not all restrictions of the free speech rule may erode the effective defense of media independence, they always imply the risk of abuse and may thus facilitate censorship. The analysis will have to distinguish between restrictive measures that can be justified with due regard for the free speech rule and those restrictions that unduly undermine this rule.

Media regulation addresses in all countries the tension between, on the one hand, state and civil society and, on the other hand, the tension among members of civil society.

Civil society tends to strive toward a maximum degree of freedom to express different ideas and opinions, whereas the state seeks to control some of this freedom in its ambition to protect such standards as the integrity of the state, public order, and national security. Also among the members of civil society there are different perspectives on degrees of free speech. Journalists, for example, often claim more freedom of expression than the people in the news they report about find acceptable.

Media regulation occurs both in the sense of the legal regime—with provisions that are legally enforceable, such as constitutional guarantees—and of the self-regulatory regime—with rules that depend on voluntary compliance, such as in professional codes of conduct.

The relative strength of legal and self-regulatory regimes depends not only on the legal status of the rules, but also on the force of procedures and institutional mechanisms for rule enforcement. Moreover, the actual function of the rules as reflected in the jurisprudence that emerges from the jurisdiction of courts and the judgments of self-regulatory bodies has to be taken into account.

THE LIMITS OF REGULATION

There is obviously no guarantee that if the formal conditions for independence are met, the media are also free and pluralistic. The media may have a broad regulatory freedom and—for a variety of reasons—not use it effectively. Countries may also experience an effectively large degree of freedom for the media, whereas they score low on the formal regulatory protection of media independence. The obvious conclusion is that regulatory instruments are an inadequate indicator of media independence.

Constitutions may provide a robust protection for the freedom of expression, but are of little significance if governments do not respect them. The effectiveness of media regulation depends on how the division of political power operates in reality. For example, will presidential decrees overrule existing legislation? In some countries, the executive branch of government effectively erodes constitutional guarantees by a series of administrative decrees that limit the circulation of information and access to official sources of information. Governments may in fact monopolize the means of public information or the technical resources to operate these means. Constitutional protection may not be able to avoid that strong economic pressures are exerted on the mass media through advertisers or sponsors.

Governments may refuse editors and journalists accreditation to press conferences or may freeze their bank accounts. Media independence may also be seriously threatened when journalists are beaten, kidnapped, or killed and governments refuse to investigate such cases. Government pressures may lead to the firing of journalists who are about to expose illegal acts by governments. In many countries, local authorities may use public subsidies, control of printing facilities, and charges of libel to censor and manipulate mass media.

However, there may also be the potential of severe limits to public speech, which are not enforced by governments or courts. In some countries, there are rules against the defamation of the state and president, but courts may give suspended sentences only or presidents may decide to pardon the defendants. There are also situations in which the government may respect the legal guarantees for media independence, but with the increasing privatization and commercialization of the mass media, a small number of owners may control most means of public information and limit the variety of viewpoints available to the public.

It should also be noted that the notion of professional self-regulation is understood and appreciated in different ways in different societies. It is conceived as a supportive mechanism for professional independence, but also as a nuisance or even hindrance.

PROTECTION AGAINST EXTERNAL INTERFERENCE

The basic regulatory instrument to address this protection is the national constitution. Most constitutions provide for freedom of expression as the essential standard in the maintenance and development of democratic societies. However, the constitutional guarantee of freedom from external interference is stated in different ways. Some constitutions use a positive statement, whereas others use a negative formulation. In some constitutions, freedom of expression is an absolute norm, whereas in others the norm is qualified.

Because the exercise of freedom of expression may clash with important national interests (such as national security or public health) or individual rights (such as the right to privacy), most constitutions recognize limitations on the freedom of expression. It is particularly important to describe and compare such qualifiers that justify limitations on constitutional guarantees. If qualifiers are general and open to different interpretations, there is a serious risk that the core of the provision is under threat. Sweeping and malleable exceptions leave a large degree of discretion for government officials and courts of law to judge between permissible and nonpermissible expressions. Therefore, the degree of elasticity of qualifiers can be used as an important indicator for regulatory robustness. Less elasticity means that limitations are stated in limited and specific ways. Qualifiers are elastic in case essential criteria for limitation (such as morality) are not defined in the relevant legal text.

The protection against external interference can also be addressed by common media statutes. Whether such statutes explicitly provide for the independent operation of media or delete such provision can be used as a relevant indicator. In a self-regulatory regime, the rejection of external interference by the professional ethical codes can be used as a relevant indicator.

PROTECTION AGAINST INTERNAL INTERFERENCE

In a self-regulatory regime, the provision on rejection of internal interference by the professional ethical codes can be used as a relevant indicator. In a self-regulatory regime, the adoption of clauses of conscience in the professional ethical codes is a relevant indicator. Clauses of conscience imply that the journalist has the right to refuse an assignment if it proves to breach the journalist's professional ethics or violates his or her moral beliefs. In a self-regulatory regime, the common use by media institutions of editorial statutes can be seen as a relevant indicator. Editorial statutes regulate the internal relationships among editorial staff, advertising and commercial departments, and boards of directors. They generally establish as minimum standards of media independence that:

- the editorial staff controls the moral and intellectual capital of publishing houses and broadcasting stations;
- the editorial council has the right to be consulted on decisions that affect the appointment and dismissal of the editor-in-chief, the definition of editorial policy and content, the personnel policies, and changes of tasks of journalists in the editorial department;
- the editorial council has the right to be heard on matters of grievances concerning editorial policy; and
- the editorial staff has the right to prevent interference of management by third parties on the editorial content.

STATUTORY LIMITATIONS TO FREEDOM OF EXPRESSION

All countries have regulatory instruments that restrict the editorial contents media can disseminate. Such limitations relate to the interests of the state (national security, public order, safety), important social values (racism, obscenity), and individual rights (defamation, privacy).

For example, most countries enact laws that aim to protect the individual from unjustified defamation. Such laws can obstruct media independence when in the balancing of free speech provisions and antidefamation provisions the emphasis is too strong on the latter. Defamation law and jurisprudence can have a chilling effect on media independence if the burden is primarily on the defendant, if the law offers inadequate defence, and if the risks of considerable punishment (prohibitive compensatory payments) lead editors toward the caution of self-censorship. In a landmark U.S. Supreme Court decision (in 1964, *The New York Times v. Sullivan*), the U.S. libel law was constitutionalized. This means that the highest priority is given by courts to the constitutionally protected free speech except in clear cases of intentional harm to the targets of a publication This also implies that courts generally accept a good faith defense on the part of journalists especially in cases where plaintiffs are public persons. It could be argued that such constitutionalization is particularly necessary in countries where existing laws on defamation do not provide a reasonable balance between freedom of expression and the protection of individual rights.Constitutionalizationis not helpful in case (and this prevails in most countries) the constitutional provisions can only be applied in disputes involving state bodies.

Related to regulation on defamation is legislation on hate speech: laws that prohibit group libel, harassment, and incitement. Such regulation is found in criminal codes (with criminal sanctions), civil codes (providing for civil remedies), anti-discrimination acts, ratification of international agreements, and professional self-regulatory instruments. Rules on hate speech can be abused to limit media independence, and the question is whether indeed the justification of banning hate speech is used to suppress speech of one side in a conflict or silence critics of the government.

Access to Public Information

Although the use of this indicator may be contested in terms of its vital significance to media independence, it can be argued that the unhindered access to public records will effectively contribute to independent journalistic investigation of crucial social issues. In any case, the more access is impeded, the more dependent the journalistic work becomes on third parties.

One indicator here is whether media claims to public information are secured by constitutional provision. In some countries, access to information is provided in the Constitution. If this is not the case, the question is whether legal claims to maximum public access to official records and documents have been articulated in special acts.

An important question here is whether such acts limit access to information in ways that hinder media independence. This can be the case when the exemptions are too vague and elastic. An illustration is the frequent use of national security as the justification for restrictions on providing access to public information. In a self-regulatory regime, the pertinent indicator is whether the profession in its code of conduct explicitly demands access to information.

Protection of Professional Secrecy

Media independence can be threatened when editors are forced to identify their sources. This may unduly restrict media independence, and the indicator is whether special regulatory provisions (in the constitution, statutes, self-regulation) are in place that recognize the need for professional secrecy.

Protection of Media Pluralism

This indicator refers to the availability of public support measures to maintain or establish a range of independent media to foster media pluralism. With regard to public support, the question is whether special statutes provide for affirmative action for media independence. In addition to the negative rights (no interference in free speech) provided in most constitutions, some countries have also enacted affirmative legislative instruments to support pluralism and autonomy of the mass media. The indicator is whether national legislations recognize such measures as government subsidies to media that cannot independently survive or other direct or indirect forms of assistance such as tax, postal, or telephone concessionary tariffs.

Protection against Media Concentration

Media independence can be threatened when media markets are too strongly concentrated in the hands of a few controlling players. The indicator on protection against media concentration is the presence of various regulatory constraints on (cross) media ownership.

International Obligations

Although there is no explicit reference in international law to media independence, there are various international and regional instruments that provide for the protection of freedom of expression. These constitutional instruments provide for the right to freedom of expression, for limitations on this right, and for a test on the legitimacy of these limitations.

It is important to establish whether the provisions of international constitutional instruments are directly accessible to those involved with media organizations. For example, this is the case in those countries in which international law supersedes domestic law and citizens have direct access to supranational courts.

The pertinent indicator is whether nations have ratified the relevant treaties (the 1966 International Covenant on Civil and Political Rights [ICCPR], the 1965 International Convention on the Elimination of All Forms of Racial Discrimination [1965], the 1950 European Convention on Human Rights and Fundamental Freedoms, the 1969 American Convention on Human Rights, and the 1989 Convention on the Rights of the Child) and whether they have adopted the provisions on individual complaints and remedies, such as provided in the Optional Protocol to the ICCPR or Article 25 of the European Convention. The Optional Protocol to the ICCPR provides in Article 1,

> A State Party to the Covenant that becomes a party to the present Protocol recognizes the competence of the United Nations Human Rights Committee to receive and consider communications from

> individuals subject to its jurisdiction who claim to be victims of a violation by that State Party of any of the rights set forth in the Covenant. . . .

The European Convention provides in Article 25:

> (1). The Commission may receive petitions addressed to the Secretary General of the Council of Europe from any person, non-governmental organization or group of individuals claiming to be the victim of a violation by one of the High Contracting Parties of the rights set forth in this Convention, provided that the High Contracting Party against which the complaint has been lodged has declared that it recognizes the competence of the Commission to receive such petitions. Those of the High Contracting Parties who have made such a declaration undertake not to hinder in any way the effective exercise of this right.

Characteristics of Current Regulatory Regimes:

- In many countries, constitutional, statutory, or uncodified limitations on freedom of expression are elastic, rather haphazard and random, and ill-defined.
- Countries with robust regimes to protect the media against forms of external interference (by state bodies) do not always provide an equal protection for editors/journalists against forms of internal interference (by media owners, publishers, managers).
- Few countries provide for an explicit prohibition of forms of prior restraint.
- Few countries provide for adequate protection of professional secrecy.
- Although most countries provide for some guarantee of maximum access to public information, only a few countries have a special Freedom of Information Act.
- Few countries provide for affirmative public measures to support media pluralism.
- Few countries have robust provisions on editorial statutes in their self-regulatory regimes.

The six major controversies in connection with the role of media regulation vis-à-vis media independence focus on the issue of whether media independence is promoted or threatened by special constitutional regard for the media, special media statutes, the protection of professional secrecy, rules on media concentration, professional codes of conduct, and public support to media pluralism.

FREE SPEECH IN THE EUROPEAN REGION

Because the European region has a well-established supranational human rights court to address human rights violations and a body of jurisprudence that was built up over the past years, which provides important guidance for thinking about the free speech standard, special attention to the European situation seems warranted. The basic legal instrument is the European Convention on Human Rights and Fundamental Freedoms (ECHR) of 1950.

Article 10 reads.

1. Everyone has the right to freedom of expression. This right shall include freedom to hold opinions and to receive and impart information and ideas without interference by public authority and regardless of frontiers. This article shall not prevent States from requiring the licensing of broadcasting, television or cinema enterprises.

2. The exercise of these freedoms, since it carries with it duties and responsibilities, may be subject to such formalities, conditions, restrictions or penalties as are prescribed by law and are necessary in a democratic society, in the interests of national security, territorial integrity or public safety, for the prevention of disorder or crime, for the protection of health or morals, for the protection of the reputation or rights of others, for preventing the disclosure of information received in confidence, or for maintaining the authority and impartiality of the judiciary.

Of interest in relation to this regional instrument is that a supranational court supervises the implementation of its provisions and thus develops over the years a jurisprudence that helps understand the meaning of the various articles of the Convention. Over the past years a number of cases involving violations of this article have been brought before the Court and through this case law important European jurisprudence on free speech is developing.

From the early 1950s to 1970, there was only one case in relation to Article 10; in the 1970s, three cases; in the 1980s, 12; and since then the caseload is only growing. Between January 1990 and July 1999, the Court handed down some 70 judgments. In 50% of these cases, the Court concluded that there had been a violation of Article 10. Between July 1999 and May 2002, the Court dealt with 44 cases; it concluded in 36 cases that there was a violation of Article 10.

Most cases address forms of direct and indirect interference by state authorities in the freedom of expression. The Court uses as basic rationale in judging forms of state interference that free speech "constitutes one of the essential foundations of a democratic society and one of the basic conditions for its progress and each individual's self-fulfillment." According to the Court, the notion of free speech is applicable not only to "information and ideas that are favorably received or regarded as inoffensive, but also to those that offend, shock or disturb: such are the demands of that pluralism, tolerance and broadmindedness without which there is no democratic society." The Court has repeatedly stated that, in a democratic and pluralist society, free speech is particularly essential to the political debate. "Free elections and freedom of expression, particularly political debate, together form the bedrock of any democratic society" (the *Bowman v. the UK* case of February 9, 1998). In this context the Court stressed the essential role of the media. In the case *Bladet Tromso & Stensaas v. Norway* of May 20, 1999, the Court stated "One factor of particular importance for the Court's determination in the present case is the essential function the press fulfils in a democratic society." The rulings of the European Court can be organized under the following headings.

Political Polemics

The *Janowski v. Poland* case of January 21, 1999: On September 2, 1992, Mr. Janowski—Polish journalist—intervened when he saw two municipal guards ordering street vendors to leave a square in Zdunska. He argued with the guards, telling them they had no legal basis for their action. The Zdunska public prosecutor instituted a criminal proceeding against Mr. Janowski and charged him with having insulted the municipal guards. On April 29, 1993, the District Court convicted Mr. Janowski and sentenced him to 8 months imprisonment suspended for 2 years and a fine plus the court costs. Against his appeal, the Regional Court also found him guilty of having used such insulting words as *oafs* and *dumb*. The European Court found that Janowski had insulted state officials. His remarks were not part of a public discussion, and he was operating as a private person, not as a journalist. Civil servants should allow for criticism, but not to the same extent as politicians. To strengthen their credibility with the general public, it may be necessary to protect them against verbal violence. As the Court states, "it cannot be said that civil servants knowingly lay themselves open to close scrutiny of their every word and deed to the extent to which politicians do and should therefore be treated on an equal footing with the latter when it comes to criticism of their actions." The Court concluded that the Polish authorities did not overstep their margin of appreciation in assessing the necessity of the measures. With 12 votes against 5, the Court held that there had been no breach of Article 10.

The margin of appreciation rule that the Court refers to is intended to leave space to national authorities to judge the pressing need for interference with free speech. The starting point here is the position that "it is in the first place for the national authorities, notably the courts, to interpret and apply domestic law. The Court's rule is limited to verifying whether the interference which resulted from the applicant's conviction of that offence can be regarded as necessary in a democratic society" (*Lehideux & Isorni v. France*). There is no consistency in the application of the margin of appreciation by the Court because there is a certain ambiguity between, on the one hand, a limited role of the Court and, on the other hand a judgment about an essential quality necessary in a democratic society.

Following Bladet Tromso, the Court defines the margin of appreciation in this way:

> According to the Court's well-established case law, the test of "necessity in a democratic society" requires the Court to determine whether the "interference" complained of corresponded to a "pressing social need," whether it was proportionate to the legitimate aim pursued and whether the reasons given by the national authorities to justify it are relevant and sufficient. . . . In assessing whether such a "need" exists and what measures should be adopted to deal with it, the national authorities are left a certain margin of appreciation. This power of appreciation is not, however, unlimited but goes hand in hand with a European supervision by the Court, whose task it is to give a final ruling on whether a restriction is reconcilable with freedom of expression as protected by Article 10.

The margin of appreciation is circumscribed by the need to show a pressing social need and by the essential role of the press in democratic societies, whereas there is a much wider margin for national authorities in relation to matters of public order in situations where "matters liable to offend intimate personal convictions within the sphere of morals or, especially, religion" are at stake (*Wingrove v. UK*, November 25, 1996). With regard to the latter, the Court has argued that

> what is likely to cause substantial offence to persons of a particular religious persuasion will vary significantly from time to time and from place to place, especially in an era characterized by an ever growing array of faiths and denominations. State authorities are in principle in a better position than the international judge to give an opinion on the exact content of these requirements with regard to the rights of others as well as on the "necessity" of a "restriction" intended to protect from such material those whose deepest feelings and convictions would be seriously offended.

There is ambiguity, but also in concrete practice a tendency for the Court to adopt a robust conception for its supervisory task. The problem with this flexible approach to the margin of appreciation is that the Court distinguishes in its protection of Article 10 between different situations without explicit criteria, thus leaving a margin of arbitrariness.

In the field of political polemics, the *Oberschlick v. Austria* (No. 2) case of July 1, 1997, is interesting. The periodical Forum reproduced a speech held on October 7, 1990, by Mr. Jörg Haider, leader of the Austrian Freedom Party. The editor of the magazine, Mr. Gerhard Oberschlick, commented on the speech and called Haider a *trottel*, an "idiot." On April 26, 1991, Mr. Haider brought an action for defamation and insult. On May 23, 1991, the Court found Mr. Oberschlick guilty of having insulted Mr. Haider, and sentenced him to a fine, and ordered the seizure of the relevant issue of Forum. In his application to the European Court, Mr. Oberschlick alleged that his conviction was contrary to Article 10 of the Convention. The Court stated that the use of the word *trottel* should be seen as part of a political discussion in response to Haider's speech. As the Court expressed, "the applicant's article and in particular the word Trottel, may certainly be considered polemical, but they did not on that account constitute a gratuitous personal attack as the author provided an objectively understandable explanation for them derived from Mr. Haider's speech, which was itself provocative." The necessity of interference with the author's freedom of expression was not shown, concluded the Court, and it found that there had been a breach of Article 10.

Racism and Revisionism

The *Lehideux & Isorni v. France* case of September 23, 1998:

On July 13, 1984, the daily newspaper, *Le Monde,* published a one-page advertisement bearing the title "People of France, You Have Short Memories." The text basically called for a more positive attitude toward Marshal Pétain and his role during World War II as French Head of State. On October 10, 1984, the National Association of Former Members of the Resistance filed a criminal complaint against Mr. Lehideux as president of the Association for the Defense of the Memory of Marshal Pétain, Mr. Isorni as the author of the text, and the publication manager of *Le Monde* for publicly defending the crimes of collaboration with the enemy. In the judicial process that followed, the highest French court judged (November 16, 1993) that the text defended a person convicted of collusion with the enemy and concluded that the finding of the lower court in favor of the complainants did not infringe the right to freedom of expression as protected by Article 10 of the European Convention. Mr. Lehideux and Mr. Isorni submitted an application to the European Commission on Human Rights, which found their complaint admissible. The case thus proceeded to the Court, which concluded that the criminal conviction of the applicants was disproportionate and not necessary in a democratic society. According to the Court, there had been a breach of Article 10.

The Court clarified that the protection of Article 10 would not hold if the cruelties of the Nazis had been justified in a publication or if the Holocaust would have been denied. In its *obiter dictum*, the Court said that Article 17 of the Convention takes the protection of Article 10 away from those who deny the Holocaust.

Use of Confidential Documents

The case *Bladet Tromsoe & Stensaas v. Norway* of May 20, 1999: The newspaper, *Bladet Tromsoe*, published some articles on the hunting of seals. In the first article, scientist Lindberg, inspector for the Ministry of Fishing, talked about the unacceptable ways in which the animals are killed. The hunters got an opportunity to do their story. Then the newspaper published the official report by Lindberg for the Ministry. The report was withdrawn from publicity because there were allegations of criminal conduct that needed investigation, and the accusations of Lindberg were not proved. The newspaper and editor, Stensaas, were sentenced for slander.

The European Court expressed the need for careful scrutiny in cases where government interference may discourage the participation of the press in debates on matters of public concern. It confirmed the "watch dog" function of the press even if reputation and name of people are at stake.

The Court's majority confirmed that the seal hunters have a right to protect their name and reputation and to be held innocent until their guilt has been proved in a court of law. However, the allegations were part of the contents of the Lindberg report, and the newspaper had good reason to believe the report was reliable. The Court saw no evidence that the newspaper acted not in good faith. Therefore, the Court concluded that the interference with the applicant's freedom of expression was disproportionate. The Court sentenced the Norwegian government to a compensatory payment of 693,606 Norwegian crowns. As may be expected, the Court's opinions are not without dissent and controversy. In this case, the three dissenting judges argued against the consenting majority. "In our view the fact that a strong public interest is involved should not have the consequence of exonerating newspapers from either the basic ethics of their trade or the laws of defamation." They concluded that the judgment "sends the wrong signal to the press in Europe. . . . Article 10 may protect the right for the press to exaggerate and provoke but not to trample over the reputation of private individuals." The dissenting opinions found the judgment undermines the basic ethics of the profession: to carefully check facts and to not trample over the reputation of private individuals.

Another important case that addressed the use of confidential documents is *Fressoz & Roire v. France* case of February 21, 1999.

Roger Fressoz was former publishing editor of the weekly satirical newspaper, *Le Canard Enchaîné,* and Claude Roire was a journalist with the weekly. On September 27, 1989, *Le Canard* published an article by Claude Roire about the boss of Peugeot at the time of industrial unrest in the motor company. The managing director refused to meet workforce request for a pay raise, and the weekly wrote, "the Peugeot boss has given himself a 45.9% raise over the last two years." The newspaper illustrated the article with a photocopy of his notices of assessment to the tax authorities. Mr. Calvet, the Peugeot boss, began a criminal procedure on the basis of the accusation that his tax forms were stolen.

In a judgment of March 10, 1993, the Paris Court of Appeal sentenced Mr. Fressoz and Mr. Roire to pay fines because they were found guilty of handling photocopies of Mr. Calvet's tax returns obtained through a breach of professional confidence by an unidentified tax official. In the European Court's view, the sentencing of the publisher and a journalist of *Le Canard Enchaîné* violated Article 10 "given the interest a democratic society has in ensuring and preserving freedom of the press." Like in the Bladet Tromso case, the Court argued that, "The most careful scrutiny on the part of the Court is called for when as in the present case, the measures taken or sanctions imposed by the national authority are capable of discouraging the participation of the press in debates over matters of legitimate public concern."

Protection of Journalistic Sources

The landmark case is *William Goodwin v. The United Kingdom* (March 27, 1996).

This case provides the legal basis for the journalistic privilege in Europe. Until then the protection of journalistic sources was only recognized in voluntary professional codes.

Journalist William Goodwin, who worked for *The Engineer,* received confidential information about financial problems at the company Tetra Ltd. He intended to publish an article on this. The company complained that the information in the article originated from a confidential business plan and requested a prohibition to publish the information. A court of law supported the request that was valid for all British media. Moreover, because the judge found that "the interests of justice" are at stake, Goodwin was ordered to reveal his source. Also in appeal the House of Lords confirmed "the importance to the plaintiffs of obtaining disclosure lies in the threat of severe damage to their business." Goodwin got a fine of 5,000 British Pounds for contempt of court and took his case to Strasbourg.

The European Court stated that freedom of expression constitutes one of the essential foundations of a democratic society and confirmed that the protection of journalistic sources is one of the basic conditions for press freedom. The Court finally judged that the disclosure order cannot be regarded as having been necessary in a democratic society. The Court took a principled position in favor of the journalistic privilege and did not make it dependent on certain conditions, such as how information was gathered.

Relevant in the case was the concurring opinion of one judge who suggested that the injunction was an utterly unacceptable form of prior restraint. Even if there had been no injunction, the disclosing order would have been illegitimate.

The Goodwin case is particularly important because the European Convention does not provide for the freedom to gather information. This is a difference with the Universal Declaration on Human Rights and the International Covenant on Civil and Political Rights, which provide for the right to seek information and ideas. The Court strongly concluded that, "Protection of journalistic sources is one of the basic conditions for press freedom. Without such protection, sources may be deterred from assisting the press in informing the public on matters of public interest." Failing this protection, "the vital public-watchdog role of the press may be undermined and the ability of the press to provide accurate and reliable information may be adversely affected." The Court proposed that an order to reveal sources "must be limited to exceptional circumstances where vital public or individual interests are at stake." The Court also proposed that in these cases the national margin of appreciation is restricted because the interests of the democratic society are at stake. The Court saw the legitimate interests of the Tetra company, but considered that they weighed less than the vital public interest in protecting confidential sources.

A relevant dimension of this case was also that the Court made reference to the field of professional self-regulation through codes of conduct. "Protection of journalistic sources is one of the basic conditions for press freedom, as it is reflected in the laws and the professional codes of conduct in a number of Contracting States and is affirmed in several international instruments of journalistic freedoms." Also in the cases *Fressoz & Roire v. France* and *Bladet Tromso*, the Court referred in its argumentation to the ethics of journalism. The reference was used against state interference and in support of professional secrecy (in Bladet Tromso, Goodwin, and De Haes & Gijsels). However, reference to the failure of journalists to heed the provisions of professional ethics has also been used to justify state interference, as in *Praeger & Oberschlick v. Austria* April 26, 1995, where the Court argued that the applicant could not invoke compliance with the ethics of journalism.

Freedom of Expression in Turkey

The complex and tense situation in Turkey has led to several cases involving journalists who wrote about or were in favor of the PKK, the Kurdish Political Party. In most cases, the government was considered guilty of breaching Article 10, but in some cases, the Court also decided that there was hate speech or incitement to violence and thus legitimate interference.

The case of *Zana v. Turkey* of November 25, 1997: Mr. Mehdi Zana, former mayor of Diyarbakir, while serving sentences in the military prison of Diyarbakir, remarked in an interview with journalists: "I support the PKK national liberation movement; on the other hand I am not in favour of massacres." The statement was published in the national daily newspaper, *Cumhuriyet,* on August 30, 1987.

By means of an indictment of November 19, 1987, the Diyarbakir military prosecutor instituted proceedings in the Military Court against Mr. Zana, charging him with supporting an armed organization whose aim was to break up Turkey's national territory. The Turkish National Security Court held in its judgment of March 26, 1991 that Mr. Zana's statement to journalists amounted to a criminal offense.

When the case ended up with the European Court, the judges found Mr. Zana's statement contradictory and ambiguous. "They are contradictory because it would seem difficult simultaneously to support the PKK, a terrorist organization which resorts to violence to achieve its ends, and to declare oneself opposed to massacres." The Court finally judged that the penalty imposed on the applicant could be regarded as answering to "a pressing social need," and consequently there had been no breach of Article 10.

The Court voted 12 against 8. The dissenting opinions found that the restriction imposed by the Turkish government was not necessary in a democratic society. In one opinion, the dissenting judges stated, "Even if one accepts . . . that the maintenance of national security and public safety constituted a legitimate aim for the purpose of taking measures in respect of the statement made by the applicant, his conviction and twelve-month prison sentence cannot, in my opinion, be held to be proportionate to those aims, considering the content of the statement." In the rationale for his dissent, the judge wrote, "The mere fact that in the statement the applicant indicated support for a political organization whose aims and means the Government reject and combat cannot, therefore, be a sufficient reason for prosecuting and sentencing him."

It is interesting to compare the Zana case with the *Incal v. Turkey* case of June 9, 1998. Mr. Ibrahim Incal, lawyer by profession, was a member of the executive committee of the Izmir section of the People's Labour Party, dissolved by the Constitutional Court in 1993. On July 1, 1992, the executive committee decided to distribute a leaflet criticizing measures taken by the local authorities against small-scale illegal trading and the sprawl of squatters' camps around the city. The leaflet concluded with, "The Driving the Kurds out policy forms part of the SPECIAL WAR being conducted in the country at present against the Kurdish people. It is one of the mechanisms of that war, the way it impinges on the cities. Because the methods used are the same, namely enslavement, violence, terror and oppression through compulsion. It is a psychological war." The Izmir security police considered that the leaflet contained separatist propaganda capable of inciting the people to resist the government and commit criminal offenses. A criminal investigation was opened, and Mr. Incal was found guilty by the National Security Court and sentenced to 6 months and 20 days imprisonment and a fine. In a judgment of July 6, 1993, the Court of Cassation upheld the judgment. When the case came to the European Court, the judges observed that interference with the freedom of expression of a politician who is a member of an opposition party, like the applicant, call for the closest scrutiny on the part of the Court.

The Court further stated that the limits of permissible criticism are wider with regard to the government than in relation to a private citizen or even a politician. "In a democratic system the actions or omissions of the Government must be subject to the close scrutiny not only of the legislative and judicial authorities but also of public opinion." The Court was prepared to take into account problems linked to the prevention of terrorism. Here it referred to its judgment in the Zana case. However, the Court judged that Mr. Incal's conviction was disproportionate to the aim pursued and therefore unnecessary in a democratic society. It is interesting that the Court finds contrary to the Zana case that found Mr. Incal cannot be held responsible for terrorism in Turkey.

OPERATIONAL PROCEDURE OF THE EUROPEAN COURT

In its operational procedure, the Court follows the standard practice that it first decides whether there was an interference of Article 10.1 and then examines whether the interference is justified. The questions then asked are:

> Was the interference prescribed by law? What is the basis for the interference in national law? Is the law precise enough? Did the applicant have adequate protection from arbitrary interference?
>
> Did the interference pursue a legitimate aim?
>
> Was the interference necessary in a democratic society? In other words, can the interfering state authority demonstrate that there was a pressing social need for its invention? The contracting states have a certain margin of appreciation in assessing whether a pressing social need exists, but eventually the decision is with the Court.

The question about the pressing need is followed by the question of whether the measures taken by the state are proportionate to a legitimate aim and whether the proposed reasons are relevant and sufficient. In several cases, the Court judged an interference to be not legitimate because the information censored by the state was already available in the public domain anyway.

CHALLENGES FOR THE IMMEDIATE FUTURE

A first challenge addresses an essential and far-reaching element in the Court's jurisprudence, which is its interpretation of the right to receive information. According to the jurisprudence of the European Court, the European citizen has the right to be properly informed. In several opinions, the Court has stated that not only do the mass media have a right to impart information, but they have the task "to impart information and ideas on matters of public interest" and the public has a right to receive such information and ideas. The Court has ruled that the media are purveyors of information and are public watchdogs. This imposes a special public responsibility on the performance of the media. According to the Court, the media of information have a corresponding duty to provide information that properly informs their audiences. This is a vitally important position in view of the increasing commercialization of media and the trend toward trivialization of information provided by them: the sound bites, the info-tainment formats, the mediahypes, which are a provocative challenge to both practitioners and policymakers. The Court's position also deserves to be elaborated. It turns out to be difficult to find more precise formulations than properly informed and even harder to operationalize such formulations. However, it is a task urgently needed and pertinent to the current media climate.

A second challenge deals with the relationship between the European Convention and the European Union. A peculiarity of the European region with regard to human rights is the fact that, although individual EU member states have ratified the ECHR, the EU as an institution has not. This creates a situation in which it is unclear how robust the protection of human rights really is for EU citizens. At the end of 2000, the European Union proclaimed at its meeting in Nice the European Charter on Fundamental Rights. The Charter formulates the freedom of expression in Article 11, "1. Everyone has the right to freedom of expression. This right shall include freedom to hold opinions and to receive and impart information and ideas without interference by public authority and regardless of frontiers. 2.The freedom and pluralism of the media shall be respected." In the commentary on this article, it is stated that restrictions of the right to freedom of expression should not exceed the limitations of the European Convention, Article 10, Paragraph 2. It is regrettable that the Charter only refers to the interference by public authority and effectively excludes the interference from private parties and thus undermines the possible horizontal effect of the Charter. As with the European Convention, the right to seek information is not explicitly mentioned here. It is also unclear whether Paragraph 2 on the pluralism of the media implies a positive duty on the part of governments to promote this media pluralism. It would be a constructive step if the EU decided to ratify the European Convention and if the provisions of the European Charter would be implemented in accordance with the jurisprudence of the European Court.

A third challenge concerns the accession of Eastern European countries. In recent years, Albania, Armenia, Azerbeidjan, Bulgaria, Rumania, Russia, and other Central and Eastern European countries ratified the ECHR, and thus the number of parties to the Convention rose to 43. The newly acceded countries bring different legal traditions and political experiences to the Court's proceedings, and it will be of critical importance that the level of protection secured by the Convention not be lowered. The expanded membership may also confront the Court with more complex cases about situations where gross and systematic violations of human rights take place, and this raises the question of whether the Court is adequately equipped to deal with this growing burden of the caseload.

The fourth challenge regards the horizontal effect of basic rights. In the years ahead, there may be a considerable number of cases in which interferences with the right to freedom of information come from private parties. Will the Court be adequately legally equipped to deal with this? In the case of *Fuentes Bobo v. Spain* of February 29, 2000 (about an employee of RTVE, the Spanish public broadcaster, who criticized his employer and was subsequently fired), the Court concluded that Article 10 also applies to horizontal relations. Therefore, there is a legal precedent, but more work needs to be done as the so-called *Dritt-Wirkung* (or horizontal effect of constitutional rights) remains a controversial issue.

A fifth challenge for the Court is the need to apply in its opinions substantial lines of argumentation and avoid nonsubstantial arguments. In some cases, the Court has introduced peculiar, nonessential arguments that tend to erode the principled nature of these cases. An illustration is the consideration in Paragraph 55 of the Incal case, where the Court refers to the fact that the security police had an opportunity to require changes in the leaflet. Also in the Goodwin case, there is the odd consideration that the interfering party no longer had a claim to the exposure of sources because a judge had already prohibited the publication and thus limited the damage thereof.

A sixth challenge is to the find a balance between the right to free speech and European efforts to secure safety of the Internet in particular for children. The Council of the European Union approved on December 21, 1998, an Action Plan on promoting safer use of the Internet by combating illegal and harmful content on global networks. Whatever the valid intentions behind this Plan, it will imply limits on Internet contents and thus require a careful consideration of the limitation of these limits.

A seventh challenge is the need to make the Court more accessible for European citizens. Given the current caseload, this sounds like an irresponsible proposition. It should be realized, however, that the institution of the Court is a great historical example of how the protection of human rights can become a reality indeed. The ultimate success of the Court's functioning will depend on its concrete effect on the lives of European citizens. It is evident that in this process a great deal could be done by national judicial institutions. In many cases, national courts would have come to different conclusions if they had already introduced in their reasoning the test of the criteria that emerge from the European Court's jurisprudence.

A last challenge is also provided by the need to have robust rules on access to information. Although the Council of Europe has declared work on a legal text on access to information a priority, no concluding document has been produced so far. The European Court has held in the *Guerra & Others v. Italy* case of February 19, 1998, that the Convention does not provide a general right of access to public information, but a specific right to information on environmental hazards.

CONCLUDING NOTE

The right to freedom of expression is interpreted by different schools of thought in conflicting manners. In the line of Platonic philosophical thought, human beings need to be protected against immoral and dangerous ideas, and the sociopolitical elite—whose representatives know what virtue is—is entitled to intervene in the flow of ideas. In the line with the Artistotelian tradition, human beings are free to make their own choices about virtue and truth. The traditions can be summarized as follows: The common good needs protection against immoral ideas versus the common good emerges from free individual choice.

Different interpretations are also to be found between the absolutists like the famous Justice H.L. Black, who said in 1960 about the First Amendment "I take no law abridging to mean no law abridging" and the relativists who accept that there are situations where freedom may be abridged.

Conventionally, the concept of freedom is constructed in a negative sense only. The classical right to freedom of expression is a good illustration. It provides a freedom from interference of the state with the expression of opinions, ideas, and information. Complete freedom, however, also encompasses the freedom to emancipation and self-development. It implies a process of human emancipation.

Conventional human rights conceptions do not provide this positive extension of the basic norm of freedom. The *freedom to* (positive freedom) points to a process of empowerment through which people liberate themselves from all those forces that hinder them in taking decisions concerning their own lives. This interpretation of freedom implies a process of emancipation that should be guided by the basic norm of the sovereignty of individuals and peoples. This concrete activity of human emancipation requires certain social conditions.

The norm freedom in conventional human rights theory is Lockean in nature (i.e., it is intrinsically related to the protection of private property). The primary purpose of the norm is to protect property. In this legal thinking, freedom primarily equates to the autonomy to use your property provided no legal rule is violated. Freedom of the press, for example, is the right to use the press within the limits of the law. There is no social responsibility beyond the limits of the law. If the unhindered expansion of property causes inequalities, then these are necessarily legitimate. Freedom as the right to own and protect the expansion of property does not provide protection for those who do not own property (e.g., a printing press or TV station). The basic assumption of conventional human rights thinking regarding the freedom of information is that freedom of expression as such is given and there should only be protection against the danger of interference by the state. This assumption glosses over the fact that in the reality of unequal societies this freedom does not exist for everyone. In almost every society, individuals and people are silenced.

Therefore, the right to freedom of expression would have to focus on the provision of access to the public expression of opinions rather than on the prevention of restricting opinions. The right to freedom of expression entails the right to the conditions (the means) for the realization of this freedom. If we extend the definition of *freedom* to include the (positive) *freedom to*, then the implication is that the means through which this can be implemented should be available and accessible.

If in a society the access to public media is obstructed for most people due to economic or other constraints, the claim to freedom of expression is invalidated. In the conventional conception, the right to freedom of expression is formulated as a "liberty" and not a "right" in the strict legal sense. It represents a privilege of expression without interference, but does not constitute a claim right (i.e., an entitlement with a corresponding legal obligation). In the strict legal sense, a right implies a situation where a person is entitled by legal process to compel another person to act as prescribed.

In cases where human rights are formulated as liberties (as with the freedom of expression), it is impossible to impose a corresponding duty on an other natural or legal person that can be forced by the subject of a right to implement this right. In fact many crucial human rights are rather liberties, providing certain privileges to its holder with which another person has no right to interfere.

The human rights claim to the protection of free speech is always under threat by efforts to curb the flows of information among people, organizations, and societies. George Orwell once wrote that freedom of expression means that everyone has the right to say things others do not want to hear. This nicely illustrates the complexity of the moral principle. It is undoubtedly natural to silence those who say things one does not want to hear. Certainly in unequal power relations—as obtain in all societies—it demands a good deal of moral maturity to allow dissident voices to speak out.

All forms of communication are under threat of censorship. Each day people become victims of censorship measures. Journalists are killed, writers detained, radio stations blown up, and films prohibited. Less dramatically, but even more frequently, children are silenced by their parents, and employees regularly find their right to free speech restricted. Censorship is common to all types of regimes: authoritarian, totalitarian, or liberal democratic and to all kinds of human relationships. Not only do the creative elites fall prey to censorship, but in fact all those who want to be informed about what happens in the world.

Around the world, governments have undertaken efforts to regulate Internet traffic. Regulatory measures range from laws requiring self-censorship by Internet ISPs (Australia, 1996), obligations for Internet subscribers to register with the authorities (China, 1996), control over individual access (Cuba, 1996), application of laws on pornography and racism to CyberSpace (Germany, 1997), legislation against Internet offences (Japan, 1996), censorship measures (Philippines, 1996; Republic of Korea, 1996), or monitoring of Internet contents (Malaysia, 1996). Worldwide forms of religious and moral censorship are growing among others in the form of *fatwas*. Moreover, free access to a diversity of information sources and creative products is under pressure as a result of the strong trend toward consolidation on the global online market. In all the essential domains of this market, one finds a strong degree of concentration among the key players. These predominantly American commercial players are the manufacturers of ICT tools and appliances, as well as the providers of telecommunication services, access to the Internet, and audiovisual contents. In recent years, several of the key players have consolidated their market position through the conclusion of merger deals. Particularly worrisome is the interest that media giants have in privatization of the airwaves. On February 7, 2001, 37 leading U.S. economists signed a joint letter to the Federal Communications Commission (FCC) proposing that broadcasters be allowed to make radio frequencies the private domain of the largest media companies. The radio frequencies—or the electromagnetic spectrum—are essential for sending and receiving words, images, and data through PCs, cellular phones, radio, and TV. The plan proposed by the economists argues that it would make good economic sense to sell the airwaves to commercial companies and let them sublease this private domain to other interested parties. This privatization scheme once implemented would imply that the radio frequencies are owned and controlled by the largest bidders: an unprecendented opportunity for censorship by such media conglomerates as AOL-Time Warner, Vivendi, and Walt Disney.

Limits to Limitations

As argued earlier, the free speech standard is not absolute, and its exercise can be subjected to limitations. This obviously implies the risk of abuse by those actors (and particularly governments) intent on curbing free speech. Limitations could easily erode the significance of a normative standard. For this reason, a threefold test has been developed in international law to assess the permissibility of limitations. These must be provided by law. They must serve purposes expressly stated in international agreements, and they must be shown to be necessary in a democratic society. The UN Special Rapporteur on freedom of information has expressed concern about the tendency of governments to invoke Article 4 of the International Covenant on Civil and Political Rights in justification of the suspension of free speech. This Article lists the human rights provisions that are nonderogable. This means that under no circumstance, not even in times of war, can they be suspended. The right to freedom of expression is not listed in Article 4. However, the Human Rights Committee, in its General Comment No. 29 (CCPR/C/21/Rev.1/Add.11), has identified the conditions to be met for a State to invoke article 4 (1) of the Covenant to limit certain rights enshrined in its provisions, including the right to freedom of opinion and expression. Inter alia, the measures must be strictly limited in time, provided for in a law, necessary for public safety or public order, serve a legitimate purpose, not impair the essence of the right, and conform with the principle of proportionality. It is the view of the Special Rapporteur that, in many of the cases brought to his attention, all or some of these conditions are not being met, and that the argument of the fight against terrorism is used by governments as an illegitimate justification for the restriction of human rights and fundamental freedoms in general, and the right to freedom of opinion and expression in particular. There are cases where the feeling of insecurity caused by recent terrorist attacks has provided states with an opportunity to adopt such measures that had long been on the authorities' agenda—cases where the argument of national security is used to cover direct attacks against free media, investigative journalism, political dissent, and human rights monitoring and reporting.

In this context, the Special Rapporteur observes, however, that in practice it is quite difficult to monitor the legitimacy, necessity, and proportionality of antiterrorism measures in the absence of a universally accepted, comprehensive, and authoritative definition of *terrorism*. This, on the one hand, leaves ample space for abusive restrictions based more on varying definitions of terrorism that respond to individual states' interests than on a universal concept of what a terrorist act is, and, on the other hand, makes it all the more difficult to monitor and evaluate the necessity and proportionality of such restrictions.

In conclusion, it can be said that in the early 21st century the implementation of the free speech standard is both urgently needed and under great pressure. Finding a balance between its robust application and its justified limitation presents one of the essential challenges for today's democratic societies.

SUGGESTIONS FOR DISCUSSION

Discuss the implications of corporate control over the EMS.

Discuss the pros and cons for the adoption of editorial statutes in news media.

Should journalistic codes of conduct have a clause on conscience?

Discuss the European Court's margin of appreciation with regard to matters involving morals and religion. In such cases, should national authorities have a wider scope for national assessment of the legitimacy of restrictions?

Are current provisions in international human rights law sufficiently robust to counter worldwide occurrence of censorship?

Discuss what forms of censorship threaten the right to freedom of expression in your local context.

3

Media Performance and Human Rights

EDUCATION AND EXPOSURE

The standard of free speech discussed in chapter 2 forms part of the international human rights regime. In addition to the protection of the human right to freedom of information, there is a set of other provisions that have important implications for media performance.

A human rights framework for media performance is given with the preambles of the UDHR and the two international human rights covenants (ICCPR and ICSECR) and in Articles 29 and 30 in the UDHR. These preambles propose a general responsibility to contribute to the teaching of human rights. The UDHR states, "That every individual and every organ of society, keeping this Declaration constantly in mind, shall strive by teaching and education to promote respect for these right and freedoms. . . ." The Covenants provide both "Realizing that the individual, having duties to other individuals and to the community to which he belongs, is under a responsibility to strive for the promotion and observance of the rights recognized in the present Covenant." The reference to *everyone, every organ of society*, and *individual responsibility* would seem to logically imply that media are among those organs and media workers among those individuals who are expected to contribute to the promotion and protection of human rights.

This is particularly important because worldwide there is a tremendous lack of knowledge about the existence of human rights and the possibilities to use them in defense of human dignity. Too many people do not know they are entitled to the protection of fundamental rights. This imposes on the media, as crucial channels of information and knowledge in many societies, a special responsibility to teach and inform people about human rights. In most countries, the media fail to provide this public service. Over many years, I have monitored in various countries what media do in the field of human rights. The overall record is not at all impressive. The Final Declaration of the Vienna World Conference recognized this by stating in Paragraph 39: "Underlining the importance of objective, responsible and impartial information about human rights and humanitarian issues, the World Conference on Human Rights encourages the increased involvement of the media, for whom freedom and protection should be guaranteed within the framework of national law." This reference to national law has been strongly contested from a free speech perspective because often national legislation restricts media independence rather than encourages it, and it would have been more insightful had the world conference referred to principles of international law.

Although formulated in an awkward manner, the statement still recognizes that the human rights ideal represents a moral ideal that most people in the world have no knowledge of. Although the UN Centre for Human Rights and the Division of Human Rights of UNESCO have been active in the field of human rights teaching, this is still a largely underdeveloped area. Particularly in the world's rural areas there is widespread ignorance about human rights legislation and jurisprudence. As a consequence, because rural people lack knowledge as to whether an illegality occurs, they often do not seek legal redress.

Knowledge and awareness of human rights are so essential because, through the awareness that one possesses fundamental rights, the development of self-confidence is encouraged. It is important that poor people know and understand that many of their food, health, habitat, and environmental problems can be translated into human rights problems. This is the beginning of a process in which the victims assert their rights and demand remedies. To recognize that you have rights and others can be held accountable for the infringement of these rights helps establish a basic feeling of human dignity.

However, even if the texts of human rights instruments were widely disseminated, which is not the case, there would still be the problem that so many people could not read them. The availability of the written entitlements would be of little significance for the world's 1 billion illiterate adults or for the 100 million children for whom there are no schools. Even if human rights standards were published and people could read them, it is far from certain they would understand the often technical, abstract, and complex legal language in which they are articulated.

At the International Conference on Human Rights in 1968 in Teheran, participants resolved to call on states to ensure that all means of education be used to provide youth with the opportunity to grow up in a spirit of respect for human dignity and equal rights. As the basis of such education, the conference saw "objective information and free discussion" and urged the use of "all appropriate measures" to stimulate interest in the problems of a changing world. The UN General Assembly also resolved in 1968 to request member states to introduce or encourage the principles proclaimed in the UDHR and other instruments. It called for progressive instruction in the curricula of both primary and secondary schools, and it invited teachers to seize every opportunity to draw the attention of their students to the role of the UN system.

In 1978, UNESCO organized an international congress in Vienna about teaching human rights. A similar congress took place in Malta in 1987. In late 1988, the UN Centre for Human Rights held a seminar on the teaching of human rights in Geneva. In the United Nations (1989) publication *Teaching Human Rights*, it was noted that despite general agreement in principle of the desirability of education of this sort, there remains a marked paucity of practical materials for the purpose.

Crucial to the development of a human rights culture is the internal dialogue about the concept of human rights. All cultural communities have problems with human rights and need to reflect on these. As stated earlier, particularly in the West, there is a tendency to see human rights problems as the exclusive domain of non-Western cultural communities. This is reflected, for example, in the strong emphasis that Western media give to Islamic problems with women's rights. There is also little serious attention paid to the problems that the western community and its different constituencies have with the implementation of social, economic, and cultural rights. The media could offer public fora for reflection on these issues.

A crucial part of human rights teaching by the media has to do with the ways in which the media (and in particular the news media) cover human rights violations worldwide. In terms of professional reporting, most media are, by and large, ill-equipped to adequately deal with human rights violations. The prevailing style of news reporting emphasizes the sensational and focuses on the sound bite. Evidently the standard news values that affect news reporting in general also shape human rights reporting. Human rights reporting typically needs background, context, and in-depth analysis. Because most news reporting favors the incidental event, many chronic human rights violations go unreported. Occasionally violations occur as a sensational event that suits the timing needs of the media, but more often human rights violations are long-term structural processes. News tends to be about short-lived events and not about long-term processes (Van Ginneken, 1998). The media's emphasis on event rather than process tends to hamper a sufficient understanding of what specific violations are really about. As a result, events caused by basic human rights violations (such as in the case of massive poverty) are presented as natural disasters.

There is also the additional problem that the victims of human rights violations are often the forgotten social actors because they do not belong to the world's newsmaking elites. Moreover, as with all other events, media select in biased ways what is newsworthy and what is not; as a result, not all human rights violations are considered equally newsworthy.

Herman and Chomsky (1979) convincingly documented how the U.S. media (in the 1970s) found violations in Cambodia more newsworthy than those in Indonesia and East Timor. If human rights are reported at all, there is a strong tendency to concentrate on the civil and political rights and to ignore the social, economic, and cultural rights. Ovsiovitch (1999) found in his study of human rights reporting in the *NewYork Times*, Time, and CBS (1978–1987) that most references were to civil rights (in particular the integrity of the person) and somewhat less to political rights (in particular political participation). In all three media, there was only marginal attention paid to socioeconomic rights.

It should also be realized that serious reporting of human rights violations is hampered in many countries by forms of state censorship, intimidation from fighting factions, and real dangers for journalists. In case journalists are really committed to human rights reporting and are deeply engaged in human rights concerns, they often meet strong opposition (Van Ginneken, 1998). A final consideration concerns the fact that in most media the area of human rights is not accepted as a special field of reporting. Few, if any media have a human rights *beat*.

Adequate human rights reporting is important because the media are among the few social institutions that can expose violations to mass audiences. Crucial to the protection of human rights is the public exposure of violations. This exposure recognizes the victims as persons or groups that are entitled, under international law, to the protection of their integrity.

It also identifies and may shame the perpetrators so as to deter future violations. Exposure may also relieve some of the burden for the victims and could influence public opinion on human rights matters and educate a general public. In any case, without news reports many victims are simply forgotten.

Beyond the requirement to contribute to the promotion and defense of human rights, there are still more responsibilities for the performance of the media. Article 29 of the UDHR says that everyone has "duties to the community in which alone the free and full development of his personality is possible." The reference to *everyone* obviously includes media professionals. What such duties to the community may imply is suggested in Article 30 of the UDHR. This article warns that "nothing in the Declaration may be interpreted as implying for any State, group or person any right to engage in any activity or to perform any act aimed at the destruction of any of the rights and freedom set forth in the Declaration." Therefore, the media should not engage in types of performance that may undermine the rights and freedoms to which human beings are entitled. The following paragraphs address the essential human rights standards for media professionals.

ON THE FREEDOM OF INFORMATION

The implication of this standard for media performance is the responsibility to secure maximum degrees of free speech in reporting and commenting by the media. It tends to be overlooked that media may be their own worst enemies whenever they give in all too easily to governmental pressures. During the 1991 Gulf War, for example, many news media, among them CNN, raised no fundamental protests about wide-ranging forms of military censorship. During the invasion of Iraq in 2003, media consented with the *embedding* of journalists in sections of the military. It is obvious from the military point of view that news reporting needs some control, but media should not give in to the pressures of censorship, lest they themselves become guilty of violating the free speech standard. Moreover, the media can also, by exercising control over who gets access to them, take away from individuals and groups their right to freedom of speech.

ON THE PROTECTION OF PRIVACY

Article 12 of the UDHR provides that "No one shall be subjected to arbitrary interference with his privacy, family, home or correspondence, nor to attacks on his honour and reputation. Everyone has the right to the protection of the law against such interference or attacks."

If everyone is entitled to this protection, it follows that the media should operate carefully when people's privacy is at stake. This does not mean that media could never interfere with the private sphere or could never attack someone's reputation. The European Court of Human Rights has established in its jurisprudence that certainly in the case of public persons the expectation of privacy protection cannot always be upheld. In past years, many national courts of law have judged that people who are in the lime light of public attention and who lead very public lives will have to accept that there is a limit to their privacy. Yet the problem is that the UDHR refers to *everyone* and does not say that some may be excluded from this provision. The consequence is that one may at least expect from the media that when the editorial choice is made to interfere with someone's private life they have good reasons and accept public accountability for their decision. An escape for media is offered by the word *arbitrary*. This was introduced to refer to forms of interference that lacked justification in terms of valid motives or legal principles. Actually in the preparatory negotiations, before the text of Article 12 was adopted, there was some discussion on how interference should be qualified. Various words were proposed, such as *unreasonable* and *abusive*. *Arbitrary* was eventually preferred and was interpreted as "without justification in valid motives and contrary to established legal principles" (Rehof, 1992, p. 190).

Much discussion also addressed the question of whether attacks against honor and reputation should be included. Some delegates considered this provision so general and the terms so vague that they feared this might cause unwarranted violations of the right to freedom of expression. In the debate the Cuban representative, for example, stated that some reputations might be justifiably attacked (Official Records). Several delegates offered arguments to delete all qualifications, such as arbitrary and unlawful, because these were adequately addressed in Article 27 of the Declaration. The final version of Article 12 was adopted by 29 votes in favor, 7 against, and 4 abstentions.

The protection of privacy became a binding norm in international human rights law through its codification in the ICCPR, Article 17. This article states, "1. No one shall be subjected to arbitrary or unlawful interference with his privacy, family, home or correspondence, nor to unlawful attacks on his honour and reputation. 2. Everyone has the right to the protection of the law against such interference or attacks."

This article seeks to establish that there is legal redress against violations. The right to privacy has a positive obligation on the part of state parties to act toward the effective protection of their citizens. It reinforces the sovereignty of the individual over a person-bound sphere of no intrusion, which is inherent in the person and therefore moves with the person to sites such as the workplace. The mention of correspondence implies that the provision also regards the right to the protection of confidential communications.

The privacy standard obviously needs balancing against other norms such as the right to seek information. This is further complicated by the recognition that the protection of privacy can also imply the right not to know. This is relevant in the context of genetic information and people's right not to know that they are certain to develop some hereditary disease.

Despite these complications, a robust formulation of the standard is needed in the light of a growing violation of people's privacies in public communication. It has become common in many countries to obtain imagery of people without their consent and use this for entertainment purposes. An example is the use by TV stations of video material taken from rescue or emergency services. Privacy is also massively under attack in countries where electronic surveillance of people is widely spread. In several countries, governments are preparing legislation to prohibit the encryption of telecommunication and data traffic. This action against secret encoding of electronic communications facilitates for police forces the interception of communications by criminals. However, one of the results will be that people can no longer protect their private use of electronic communication.

ON DISCRIMINATION

In the UDHR, Article 2 provides, "Everyone is entitled to all the rights and freedoms set forth in this Declaration, without distinction of any kind, such as race, colour, sex, language, religion, political or other opinion, national or social origin, property, birth or other status."

Furthermore, according to the Declaration, no distinction shall be made on the basis of the political, jurisdictional, or international status of the country or territory to which a person belongs, whether it be independent, trust, nonself-governing, or under any other limitation of sovereignty. The essential principle here is equality. Differential treatment of people based on the features of persons or groups conflicts with the basic notion of human dignity. Article 2 is intended to provide a general protection against discrimination.

The equality standard enters international law for the first time with the UN Charter. The earlier Covenant of the League of Nations (1919), for example, did not provide this protection. The Preamble of the UN Charter states, ". . . the equal rights of men of women and of nations small and large. . . ." During the drafting work, discussion focused among others on the grounds of discrimination. One of the controversies was: Should political opinion be included? Also notions such as status, property, and birth were objects of dissenting opinions. The phrasing "without distinction of any kind, such as . . ." implies that the enumeration should not be read as exhaustive.

One of the most important treaties to codify the nondiscrimination standard is the Convention on the Elimination of All Forms of Racial Discrimination (1965). The most contested (and for media most pertinent) provision of this Convention is found in Article 4, which concerns the dissemination of ideas based on racial superiority. The Race Convention has been ratified by an overwhelming majority of UN member states. Article 4 of the International Convention on the Elimination of All Forms of Racial Discrimination makes it obligatory for states to provide penal sanctions for incitements to racial discrimination. This goes beyond the mere prohibition of such incitements. However, the Convention provides for due regard to the free speech standard of the UDHR.

Article 20.2 of the International Covenant on Civil and Political Rights provides for the incorporation into domestic law of the prohibition of the dissemination of ideas based on racial superiority and the incitement to racial hatred or advocacy of national or religious hatred. The formulation is that "Any advocacy of national, racial or religious hatred that constitutes incitement to discrimination, hostility or violence shall be prohibited by law." This calls for the prohibition of discriminatory statements, but does not necessarily make them a criminal act. During the preparatory negotiations for the Covenant, some of the discussion (in both the Third Committee of the General Assembly and the Commission on Human Rights) dealt with the fear that a provision prohibiting advocacy of hatred could be detrimental to free speech. Among the objections raised was the argument that governments could abuse the prohibition to impose prior censorship against expressions by certain social groups. Those arguing in favor stated that governments should prohibit expressions that incite to violent acts. It was also argued that legislation provides no solution for problems of national, religious, or racial hatred.

Other important provisions against discrimination are found in the Convention on the Elimination of All Forms of Discrimination Against Women (1979). Article 5 of this Convention demands the elimination of stereotyped representations of roles for men and women and prejudices based on the idea of the inferiority or superiority of either of the sexes.

The human rights standard of equality is extended to take into account the real inequalities that prevail in most societies. It is essential to recognize that the realization of basic human rights in situations of social inequality may demand the unequal treatment of unequals and may thus require preferential measures for the large group of the *information-poor*. In the real world, some individuals or groups have more access to information and means of communication than others, and some are capable of silencing others very effectively. It needs to be acknowledged that social inequality exists on many different levels. Beyond rights to political equality, rights to informational and cultural equality should be taken equally seriously.

The standard of equality implies that there is equal entitlement to the conditions of self-empowerment. Among the essential conditions of people's self-empowerment are access to and use of the resources that enable people to express themselves, share these expressions with others, exchange ideas with others, inform themselves about events in the world, create and control the production of knowledge, and share the world's sources of knowledge. These resources include technical infrastructures, knowledge and skills, financial means, and natural sources. Their unequal distribution among the world's people obstructs the equal entitlement to the conditions of self-empowerment and should be considered a violation of human rights.

The equality standard has important implications for media performance. People have the right to the protection by law against prejudicial treatment of their person in the media. This right to be treated in nondiscriminatory ways implies that reporting by the media should refrain from the use of images that distort the realities and complexities of people's lives, fuel prejudice by discriminatory descriptions of people and situations, and neglect the dignity and ability of opponents in national, racial, or ethnic conflicts.

Again, among free speech advocates, there is often the fear that these provisions can be abused. This is a legitimate concern. In the end, courts of law establish, nationally and regionally, when these protective provisions interfere in unacceptable ways with the free speech standard.

ON THE PRESUMPTION OF INNOCENCE

The UDHR states in Article 11, "Everyone charged with a penal offense has the right to be presumed innocent until proved guilty according to law in a public trial at which he has had all the guarantees necessary for his defense."

The right to the presumption of innocence as provided in Article 11 of the Universal Declaration of Human Rights and in Article 14 of the International Covenant on Civil and Political Rights guarantees that people accused of a criminal offense are presumed innocent until proved guilty in a public trial. Presumption of innocence is a general standard found in many different societies. It protects the accused against prejudgments about the outcome of a trial. According to the jurisprudence of the European Court of Human Rights, the standard serves to impose the burden of proof on the public prosecutor. The rule applies primarily to public authorities, but it would seem sensible to extract implications for communicators. This is all the more pertinent because news media worldwide tend to deal rather carelessly with people who are accused of criminal acts, particularly if their crime has a sensational dimension. Of course, there are different professional traditions in reporting crime and, as a result, varying degrees to which the accused are exposed. This ranges from mere initials to complete identity descriptions inclusive of a photo. In all such cases, there is the considerable risk that the public has already judged the accused before he or she appears before a court of law, and certainly in cases where the defendant is found *not guilty* a lot of damage to name and reputation has been wrought by publications. If the media were to apply this standard strictly, they would have to use a large measure of caution in relation to the criminal cases and the people about which they report.

ON THE PROHIBITION OF PROPAGANDA

Article 20.2 of the ICCPR imposes an obligation on states to incorporate the prohibition of war propaganda into domestic law. The formulation is, "Any propaganda for war shall be prohibited by law." However, the text does not say what kind of law this should be. There must be a prohibition, but states are free to choose the legal means they find appropriate. There was a lot of discussion in the Third Committee of the General Assembly, and the final text remained controversial. It was adopted by 52 votes in favor and 19 votes against. There were 12 abstentions, and Australia, Belgium, Luxembourg, the Netherlands, New Zealand, and the United Kingdom made reservations.

One problem was that *war* was not defined. The discussions, however, clarified that reference was made to *war of aggression*. Concerns were also expressed about the use of *propaganda* because it could be abused by governments to limit free speech.

When media become part of propaganda campaigns, there is the great risk that they violate the prohibition of propaganda for war. During the 1991 Gulf War and more recent international conflicts, several times the international newsmedia crossed the borderline among mere disinformation, incidental distortions, and intentional propaganda.

This happened when the language and imagery used in the newsmedia presented the war as inevitable and morally justified. Major international news media were engaged in the effort to sell the morality of the war effort. In the language employed by news media deceptive concepts were introduced to hide the reality of the war. Civilian killings became *collateral damage*, and saturation bombing became *laying down a carpet*. The battlefield was made to look more innocent as a *theatre*.

ON THE PROHIBITION OF GENOCIDE AND INCITEMENT TO GENOCIDE

Article 3 of the 1948 Convention on the Prevention and Punishment of the Crime of Genocide declares that among the acts that shall be punishable is "direct and public incitement to commit genocide." Article 4 states that "Persons committing genocide or any of the other acts enumerated in article 3 shall be punished, whether they are constitutionally responsible rulers, public officials or private individuals." In conflict situations, we may find that news media are complicit in the dissemination of messages that incite to genocide.

One of the world's most critical problems is the alarming and worldwide increase of ethnic conflicts. What is most troublesome in the rise of ethnic conflicts is that most are characterized by the exercise of gross violence against civil populations. Contrary to classical warfare between armies, violence now increasingly targets civilians of the fighting parties. At the dramatic core of ethnic conflicts is the grand-scale perpetration of crimes against humanity. As the term suggests, these are *criminal* acts that render their perpetrators enemies of the human species. Crimes against humanity transgress taboos that apply in most cultures, such as the murder or torture of defenseless men and women and the killing of children. Among the crimes against humanity—as defined by international law—are murder and extermination of civilian populations, genocide, and apartheid.

A well-known example of a serious violation of the genocide standard was the situation in Rwanda. In 1994, in just a few months, some 500,000 to 1 million Tutsis were killed by Hutus. Radio Télévision Libre des Milles Collines (the Hutu extremist radio and TV station) played an essential role in the massacre by repeatedly broadcasting messages in which Tutsis were slandered, ridiculed, and depicted as despicable. The Hutu militia were informed by the station where Tutsis—who were referred to as *cockroaches*—were hiding so they could be murdered. The Hutus were made to believe that the Tutsis deserved to be eliminated, and this led to a horrifying bloodbath. The Hutu radio/TV station was founded in 1993 as a private station supported by members of President Habyarimana's family, army commanders, and leaders of the Hutu militia. Its programs transmitted information to paramilitary groups and security forces, publicly broadcasted names of individuals who were considered "traitors deserving to die," and guided the killers to churches where Tutsis had taken refuge. The hate propaganda was so effective that neighbors who had been living in peace together for many years, got killed by people they considered to be friends. Ordinary people turned into crazed killing machines because they were made to believe that it was a dangerous and hideous enemy who lived next door. In 2003, the Rwanda Tribunal in Arusha sentenced the two founders of the station to life imprisonment on the basis of inciting people to commit genocide.

Genocide and other crimes against humanity are motivated and justified through elimination beliefs: ideas and convictions that present the (violent) elimination of a target group as necessary, desirable, and legitimate. Such elimination beliefs were decisive in the Rwandan genocide: The Hutus killed the Tutsis because they believed the Tutsis deserved to die.

In elimination belief the other is dehumanised and one's own superiority is emphasized. The threat *the other* poses is concrete, and the only effective means to escape this is his elimination. The actual killings are preceded by the dissemination of this elimination belief.

Although crimes can be committed without apparent motivation, the exercise of gross violence at a grand scale—as in crimes against humanity—needs motivating beliefs. To get people to commit such crimes, they need to believe that the violent acts are right. In situations where crimes against humanity are committed, one usually finds a systematic distribution of hate propaganda and disinformation preceding the actual criminal acts of violence. The purpose of this is the promotion and justification of the social and/or physical elimination of certain social groups. Members of such groups are often first targeted as socially undesirable. They are publicly ridiculed, insulted, and provoked (often in the media); when the harassments are put into acts the victims are finally beaten up and killed. In the propagation of elimination beliefs, the other is dehumanized, whereas the superiority of one's own group is emphasized. The propagandists convincingly suggest to their audiences that the "others" pose fundamental threats to the security and well-being of society and that the only effective means of escaping this threat is the elimination of this great danger. The use of violence in this process is presented as inevitable and thus not only acceptable, but absolutely necessary.

The elimination beliefs that motivate people to kill each other are not part of the human genetic constitution. They are social constructs that need social institutions for their dissemination. Such institutions include religious communities, schools, families, and the mass media. Because crimes against humanity are unthinkable without elimination beliefs, the institutional carriers of such beliefs should be seen as enemies of the human species. This implies that all those who propagate beliefs in support of genocide, through whatever media, have to be treated as perpetrators of crimes against humanity.

For the prosecution of crimes against humanity, there is an important historical precedent in the acts of the post-World War II International Military Tribunal (IMT) at Nuremberg. Before and during World War II, Nazi politics aimed at the active persecution and extermination of Jews used for the realization of these goals the instruments of propaganda. In 1946, the IMT condemned racist propaganda as a crime against humanity. In doing so, the IMT recognized the genocidal potency of this sort of propaganda. The IMT also determined the individual liability for the dissemination of racist propaganda and sentenced to hang Nazi propagandist, Julius Streicher, for spreading eliminationist ideology. Streicher—member of the Nazi party since 1921—had been editor and publisher of "Der Stürmer" (a fervent anti-Semitic weekly) between 1923 and 1945 and had incited his German audience for 25 years to eliminate Jews. Streicher preached the total extermination of Jews and described them as vermin that deserved to be eliminated. The important aspect of his death sentence was that the IMT judged incitement to genocide, not exclusively the execution thereof a crime against humanity. Strangely enough, however, the Tribunal acquitted radio propagandist, Hans Fritzsche, who was a high officer of the Propaganda Department during the war. He was in charge of the daily press releases as well as the broadcasting of anti-Semitic messages by radio, and as such contributed in important measure to the dissemination of eliminationist beliefs. Although Fritzsche had actively mobilized for Hitler (and the Nazi politics aimed at the active persecution and termination of Jews), the IMT did not link this with complicity to genocide. The Tribunal did find sufficient proof of Fritzsche's knowledge that the information he distributed was false. According to the Tribunal, he wanted to promote support for the war, but his propaganda was not intended to incite the Germans to crimes. Only the dissenting Soviet judge in the IMT considered Fritzsche guilty of crimes against humanity by spreading anti-Semitic propaganda. In the case of Streicher, the judges found clear evidence of his intent to incite active persecution of Jews. In Fritzsche's case, they judged this was not proved beyond reasonable doubt. The Soviet judge based his dissenting opinion on the function propaganda had during the Nazi regime—the realization of Nazi goals. These included the full and obedient acceptance of fascist crimes by the German population. In this propaganda, Fritzsche played a crucial role as chief of radio in Goebels' Ministry for Propaganda (and radio was considered by the Nazis as an effective medium). Even in his last radio broadcast on April 7, 1945, he pleaded to continue the Nazi activities underground. According to the Soviet judge, Fritzsche was an active member of a criminal organization and was fully responsible for supporting genocidal politics.

Already in 1948, the UN International Law Commission was asked to draft a statute for a permanent international criminal court for gross violations of human rights. It lasted until 1989—largely as a result of the East/West cold war—for UN member states Trinidad and Tobago to reopen the debate on such a court. In 1996, the international community finally began to take this matter seriously and the UN General Assembly decided on a concrete agenda for the establishment of an international criminal court. In July 1998, an international diplomatic conference that was convened by the United Nations (in Rome) produced a treaty establishing the permanent International Criminal Court (ICC). The ICC deals with war crimes and crimes against humanity. In accordance with existing treaties, the Court will have the mandate to prosecute those who incite to genocide by propagating elimination beliefs. In 2003, the ICC was established in the Hague and began its work, although several countries, among them the United States, refused to acknowledge the authority of the Court. The crucial element in the success of the ICC will be the readiness of national governments to cooperate in the arrest and prosecution of perpetrators under their jurisdiction.

A difficult question concerns which actors should be prosecuted: only the elite decision makers or also the lower level executors? The IMT of Nuremberg was confronted with lower ranking officials who claimed they had only executed orders given by their superiors. The court established this rule: "the fact that the Defendant acted pursuant to order of his Government or of a superior shall not free him from responsibility." The Tribunal asked whether the defendant did have the choice to act differently (Roht-Arriaza, 1995). This raises a host of challenging questions to judge the degree of culpability and complicity in media organizations for the dissemination of elimination beliefs.

One of the problems that needs to be addressed is whether the prohibition of incitement constitutes an invitation to censorship by governments. The prohibition certainly raises the question of how the right to free speech can be given its due weight. The problem is complicated because those who propagate hate speech do not commit physical acts of violence. They disseminate information and opinions. Even if the messages they distribute contain incitement to hate, the content is *speech*. The incitement to genocide is speech, hate speech, and albeit offensive and unpalatable; as such it is protected by the fundamental human right to freedom of expression. Therefore, the difficulty is that if the free speech rule is accepted as fundamental, the implication is that its coverage should be broad and the prohibition of this speech needs a robust justification. To deal with this, various approaches are possible. One is to provide the proof that inciting speech leads to actual harm. The decisive criterion here is whether violent acts can be directly linked to the incitement. In this approach, incitement follows the *Oxford Dictionary* (1964) definition, in which to incite means to urge a person to do something (*Oxford Concise Dictionary*, 1964). This approach is not satisfactory if incitement is seen as the effort to urge people to believe something. In a different approach, the question is whether there is the systematic and intentional dissemination of ideas and opinions that propagate the belief that a group deserves to be eliminated from social life. In this approach, it is not relevant whether incitement indeed leads to acts of elimination because it can be argued that the historical record demonstrates beyond reasonable doubt that elimination beliefs constitute a grave and imminent danger in a society. Once people believe that *the other* is such an evil that he deserves to die, the torturing and killing of the victims will soon follow. In yet another approach, courts of law have reasoned that the rationales for the protection of free speech are destroyed by hate speech. These rationales are the search for truth, support for democracy, and fostering of individual autonomy. However good this sounds, the hate propagandist could argue that it is precisely hate speech that is necessary to uphold these values. A more promising approach would take as a starting point the observation that human rights claim universal validity. Everyone can claim the right to freedom of expression. At the same time, everyone needs to recognize that everyone else also has this right. To incite to acts that undermine or nullify this right is unacceptable. The propagandist who incites through elimination beliefs to silence others—often in the extreme sense—denies them their right to freedom of expression. Herewith the propagandists lose the claim to this right. One can only demand the right to freedom of expression as long as one recognizes and respects that others have the same right. The basic ground to claim a right is the recognition of similar claims made by others. This reciprocity is basic to human rights because these rights are always exercised in relation to others. When this reciprocity is denied, human rights can legitimately be restricted. This is an important argument because claims to freedom of expression cannot be restricted on the basis of the contents of expressions. Free speech implies that expressions may have undesirable, objectionable, or immoral contents.

Finally, it needs to be observed that hate speech is usually not propagated in a climate of freedom of expression. It is not correct to assume that hate speech is made possible because a society permits free speech. Incitement to hate and violence tends to occur in situations where media employees are under a great deal of pressure from governing elites and cannot freely express their opinions. In those cases, media professionals often operate under far-reaching and systematic state censorship. Although it appears logical to fight hate speech with the restriction of freedom of expression, it would be better to expand the freedom and independence of media workers.

ON THE PUBLIC EXPOSURE OF PRISONERS OF WAR

International humanitarian law can be described as human rights for times of armed conflict. An important instrument in humanitarian law is the Third Geneva Convention relative to the treatment of prisoners of war (August 12, 1949). In this Convention, we find the prohibition to expose prisoners of war to public curiosity. News media violate human rights when they publish pictures of captured prisoners of war and thus expose them to public curiosity. In various recent armed conflicts, this standard was violated in most of the world's news media. Well-known examples of such violations were the pictures of the Al Qaeda suspects in Quantanamo Bay and in Afghanistan, the TV station Al Jazeera showing British soldiers taken captive, and the video fragments of Iraqi military taken as prisoners of war that were broadcast around the world by Western media.

ON THE RIGHTS OF WOMEN

In 1979, the UN General Assembly adopted the Convention on the Elimination of All Forms of Discrimination against Women (UNGA res. 34/180), which entered into force in 1981. Article 5 of the Convention provides that "States Parties shall take all appropriate measures to modify the social and cultural patterns of conduct of men and women, with a view to achieving the elimination of prejudices and customary and all other practices which are based on the idea of the inferiority or the superiority of either of the sexes or on stereotyped roles for men and women." In Article 10, which addresses education, there is a strong plea for the elimination of any stereotyped content of the roles of men and women at all levels and in all forms of education.

The implementation body for the 1979 Convention on the Elimination of Discrimination Against Women is the Committee on the Elimination of Discrimination Against Women. Although the Committee was initially not authorized to receive individual communications, this has recently changed. It was decided at the UN World Conference on Human Rights in 1993 that the CEDAW "should quickly examine the possibility of introducing the right of petition through the preparation of an optional protocol to the Convention. . . ." The UN World Conference on Human Rights in 1993 reaffirmed that the human rights of women are an integral and indivisible part of universal human rights. In a series of working group meetings, the text of the 21-article protocol was subsequently prepared, debated, and accepted.

On October 6, 1999, the UN General Assembly adopted an Optional Protocol to the Convention (UNGA res.54/4). This Protocol—entered into force in December 2000—enables the Committee (CEDAW) to process individual complaints about violations of the Convention.

The key issue for media performance is obviously that the Convention addresses, among the causes of discrimination against women, stereotyped gender images. In a formal sense, women are gaining more rights through the Convention and the Optional Protocol. However, this does not mean that in actual daily practice the quality of their lives is improving accordingly. On an international level, it was noticeable during the 1990s that women's groups played a significant role in a series of world conferences, such as the 1995 UN Social Summit and more particularly in the same year's Fourth World Conference on Women in Beijing. Yet lofty ideas about the need for less gender-biased media contents and for more prominent decision-making positions for female communicators are not easily translated into operational effects. Few women have attained decision-making positions in the media industry, and gender-based stereotyped representations still abound in the media around the world. This is strikingly clear in entertainment and advertising.

Women's struggle for human rights in the media is made complicated because they often find themselves being accused of procensorship positions. As Margaret Gallagher (2001) observed, often women speaking from a feminist perspective are pushed into convenient niches such as conservative censorship supporters. They often find themselves in the company of questionable parties: "The shadowy presence of such unwanted company is just one of those things that can make it extraordinarily difficult to explain to media practitioners that feminist advocacy and monitoring have nothing to do with censorship, but everything to do with freedom" (p. 19).

As Gallagher commented,

> One of the biggest challenges for media advocates is to make clear what lies behind the concept of fair and diverse media por-trayal, to explain that it is not just a matter of substituting a "positive" image for a "negative" one, however these might be defined. Media people have to grasp the complex problems and limitations in typical media representations of gender, to understand that these are deeply embedded social practices and interpretations, and the part they themselves play in constructing those representations. (p. 20)

The Fourth Conference on Women in Beijing (September 4–15, 1995) gave in its Declaration and Program of Action special attention to this issue of images in the media by stating in the Platform for Action, Paragraph #118 on violence, "Images in the media of violence against women, in particular those that depict rape or sexual slavery as well as the use of women and girls as sex objects, including pornography, are factors contributing to the continued prevalence of such violence, adversely influencing the community at large, in particular children and young people." Paragraphs 234 to 245 deal exclusively with concerns about women and the media. The proposals for action address the need to increase the participation and access of women to expression and decision making in and through the media and new technologies of communication, as well as the promotion of a balanced and nonstereotyped portrayal of women in the media.

On the European regional level, the Committee of Ministers of the Council of Europe adopted on September 25, 1984, a recommendation (No R(84) 17) on Equality between Women and Men in the Media. Among the measures proposed are:

> Encouraging adoption by the media organisations of positive action programs to improve the situation of women, particularly at decision-making levels and in technical services;
>
> Developing channels of education and training facilities for women in the new media technology;
>
> Ensuring application of the principle of equal treatment;
>
> Encouraging the presence of women in an equitable proportion in media supervisory and management bodies;
>
> Encouraging wider participation by women in talks and discussions broadcast by the media;
>
> Ensuring that in media publicity campaigns sponsored by public authorities, the dignity of women is safeguarded and a positive image of them is projected and also that the factual reality of relationships between women and men based on partnership is reflected without any sexual stereotyping and that any exploitation of the bodies of women and men to draw attention to goods and services is barred;
>
> Encouraging awareness in the media and among the general public of the problems of equality between women and men in the media,

in particular by the nationwide organisation of meetings and events on this question.

Another recommendation (No R (90)4) adopted on February 21, 1990, by the Committee of Ministers addressed the Elimination of Sexism from Language. The recommendation encourages the use of nonsexist language in the media.

ON CHILDREN'S RIGHTS

As observed earlier in this book, the core element of the international human rights regime is that fundamental rights and freedoms are considered universally valid for everyone. In short, the human rights regime that emerged after World War II represents the moral standard that *all people matter*. This inclusive conception of human rights is a novelty in the history of international law because until 1945 there were always social groups excluded from the protection of the dignity and worth of the human person. However significant this change was, for some time in the early stages of the new regime there remained a category that was not included in all people: children. This changed on November 20, 1989, when the UN General Assembly (in UNGA res. 44/25) unanimously adopted the Convention on the Rights of the Child. With this Convention, children also became subjects of international law in their own right.

Article 2 of the Convention recognizes that "States Parties shall respect the rights set forth in the present Convention to each child within their jurisdiction without any discrimination of any kind . . . ." The Convention concluded a process that began with the preparations for the International Year of the Child in 1979. Although there had been declarations on the rights of children by the League of Nations in 1924 and by the United Nations in 1959, it was felt by some Member States that these rights should be brought under the authority of binding international law.

It is important to observe that the Convention today is ratified by the majority of the member states of the United Nations. The five basic principles of the Convention are non-discrimination, the best interests of the child, the right to life, survival and development and the views of the child. The latter principle is evidently essential to the field of information and communication because it expresses the notion that children have the basic right to be listened to and to have their views taken seriously.

In line with this principle, the Convention has the following important provisions in the field of information and communication:

Article 12.1. "States Parties shall assure to the child who is capable of forming his or her own views the right to express those views freely in all manners affecting the child. . . ."

Article 13.1. "The child shall have the right to freedom of expression; this right shall include freedom to seek, receive and impart information and ideas of all kinds, regardless of frontiers, either orally, in writing or in print, in the form of art, or through any other media of the child's choice."

Article 14.1. "States Parties shall respect the right of the child to freedom of thought. . . ."

Article 16.1. "No child shall be subjected to arbitrary or unlawful interference with his or her privacy, family, home or correspondence, nor to unlawful attacks on his or her honour and reputation."

Article 16.2. "The child has the right to protection of the law against such interference or attacks."

Article 17. "States Parties recognize the important function performed by the mass media and shall ensure that the child has access to information and material from a diversity of national and international sources, especially those aimed at the promotion of his of her social, spiritual and moral well-being and physical and mental health. To this end, States Parties shall:

Encourage the mass media to disseminate information and material of social and cultural benefit to the child and in accordance with the spirit of article 29;

(a) Encourage international co-operation in the production, exchange and dissemination of such information and material from a diversity of cultural, national and international sources;

(b) Encourage the production and dissemination of children's books;

(c) Encourage the mass media to have particular regard to the linguistic needs of the child who belongs to a minority group or who is indigenous;

(d) Encourage the development of appropriate guidelines for the protection of the child from information and material injurious to his or her well-being, bearing in mind the provisions of articles 13 and 18."

Article 29.1. "States Parties agree that the education of the child shall be directed to:

(a) The development of the child's personality, talents and mental and physical abilities to their fullest potential;

(b) The development of respect for human rights and fundamental freedoms, and for the principles enshrined in the Charter of the United Nations;

(c) The development of respect for the child's parents, his or her own cultural identity, language and values, for the national values of the country in which the child is living, the country from which he or she may originate and for civilizations from his or her own;

(d) The preparation of the child for responsible life in a free society, in the spirit of understanding, peace, tolerance, equality of sexes, and friendship among all peoples, ethnic, national and religious groups and persons of indigenous groups."

As with all human rights, the key issue regarding children's rights is obviously their implementation. This continues to represent the weakest element in the international human rights regime. As with all human rights conventions, also for the Convention on the Rights of the Child, the institutions and procedures for serious enforcement are largely ineffective.

In 1991, States Parties to the Convention elected for the first time the monitoring body for the Convention: the Committee on the Rights of the Child. The Committee which consists of 10 experts, meets three times a year to examine the implementation reports that are submitted by States parties that have accepted the duty (Article 44 of the Convention) to regularly report about the steps they take to implement the Convention. However important the work of the Committee is, its powers to enforce the standards of the Convention are severely limited. Moreover, the Convention does not provide for individual complaints about violations from children or their representatives.

When children's information rights are summarized, the following program of action emerges: The mass media should disseminate information and material of social and cultural benefit to the child. This implies that the mass media should have particular regard to the linguistic needs of the child who belongs to a minority group or who is indigenous; that they should develop respect for human rights and fundamental freedoms, and for the principles enshrined in the Charter of the United Nations, and should prepare the child for responsible life in a free society, in the spirit of understanding, peace, tolerance, equality of sexes, and friendship among all peoples, ethnic, national, and religious groups, and persons of indigenous groups.

It is difficult to see how the expanding volumes of commercial messages directed at children contribute to their social and cultural well-being. By and large, children receive more material about life in the shopping mall than about life in a free and responsible society. The media teach them the *pester power* they can use to get their parents to buy consumer goods for them. This is a different process indeed from teaching them tolerance, equality of sexes, and friendship among all peoples, ethnic, national, and religious groups, and persons of indigenous groups.

Additionally the Convention's legal entitlements to the protection of privacy and free speech for children are of great importance. Actually they are particularly relevant and challenging in a time of increasing concern about the contents of such advanced media as the Internet. However understandable such concerns are, they tend to be debated and acted on without serious consideration of the child's right to freely seek and receive information and the right to respect for his or her privacy.

A particularly difficult problem in relation to children's rights is the matter of content (e.g., on the Internet) that is legal and yet harmful to children (e.g., adult pornography that could be seen by children). It is contested whether one should monitor or regulate content that falls under the protection of free speech, although when viewed by minors it may create harm.

In the European region, provisions on the protection of children have been formulated in a series of legal instruments. The European Convention on Transfrontier Television of the Council of Europe, adopted on October 3, 1989, provides in Article 5, Paragraph 2, "All items of program services which are likely to impair the physical, mental or moral development of children and adolescents shall not be scheduled when, because of the time of transmission and reception, they are likely to watch them." In the amendment of the Convention on June 30, 1997, extra provisions were adopted on the protection of minors.

The European Broadcasting Union (1992) issued Guidelines for Programmes when dealing with the portrayal of violence and dealt extensively with programs for children and young people. Among other provisions, there is a warning to take care not to cause anxiety and undesirable tension nor to incite aggressive behavior. The guidelines also say that in news reports attention should be given to the likely impact, particularly on children viewing alone, of coverage of violence and its consequences. Programs should take care not to undermine the moral development of minors.

In 1995 at the first World Summit on Television and Children (Melbourne, Australia), a Children's Television Charter was presented by Anna Home of the BBC. The revision of this Charter was adopted in Munich in May 1995 and reads among others, "Children should have programs of high quality which are made specifically for them, and which do not exploit them. These programs, in addition to entertaining, should allow children to develop physically, mentally and socially to their fullest potential." Futher, "Children's programs should promote an awareness and appreciation of other cultures in parallel with the child's own cultural background."

On July 5, 1996, the Asian Summit on Child Rights and the Media (in Manila) adopted the Asian Declaration on Child Rights and the Media. The Ministers of Information, Education, Welfare and Social Development from 27 countries in Asia adopting the declaration resolved that all media for or about children should protect and respect the diverse cultural heritage of Asian societies; be accessible to all children; all media about children should adopt policies that are consistent with the principles of nondiscrimination and the best interests of children; address all forms of economic, commercial, and sexual exploitation and abuse of children; and protect children from material that glorifies violence, sex, horror, and conflict. All media for children should support their physical, mental, social, moral, and spiritual development; it was also resolved that opportunities should be provided for children in creating media and express themselves on a wide range of issues relating to their needs and interests.

From October 8 to 12, 1997, the first All Africa Summit on Children's Broadcasting was held in Accra, Ghana. The delegates to the summit adopted the Africa Charter on Children's Broadcasting. Article 1 provides that,

> Children should have programs of high quality, made specifically for them and which do not exploit them at any stage of the production process. Children should be allowed to have a say in the initial stages of production of the programs being produced for them. These programs, in addition to being entertaining, should allow children to develop physically, mentally and socially to their fullest potential.

In May 1998, the International Federation of Journalists issued guidelines for journalists on child rights and the media. Among other provisions, the guidelines propose to strive for standards of excellence in terms of accuracy and sensitivity when reporting on issues involving children; avoid the use of stereotypes and sensational presentation to promote journalistic material involving children; give children, where possible, the right of access to media to express their own opinions without inducement of any kind; avoid the use of sexualized images of children; and not make payment to children for material involving the welfare of children.

On December 21, 1998, the Council of the European Union approved an Action Plan on Promoting Safer Use of the Internet by combating illegal and harmful content on global networks. The plan proposes a series of initiatives (between January 1, 1999, and December 31, 2002) with a budget of 25 million Euro. The objectives of the Plan are to incite industrial actors and users to develop and implement adequate systems of self-regulation, to strengthen developments by stimulating application of technical solutions, to alert and inform parents and teachers, and to foster cooperation and exchange of experiences and best practices. The four main action lines proposed are: (a) creating a safe environment through industry self-regulation, (b) developing filtering and rating systems, (c) encouraging awareness actions, and (d) additional actions to evaluate the impact of community measures, assess legal implications, and coordinate with similar international initiatives.

HUMAN RIGHTS AND CORPORATE RESPONSIBILITIES

The implementation of human rights, as Hossain (1997) rightly observed, requires good governance. "Governments as well as powerful corporations must adhere to respect human rights and be accountable for their conduct measured by human rights standards" (p. 20).

Jagersw suggested that if human rights are to be effectively protected, obligations for TNCs can no longer be ignored (in Addo, 1999, p. 269). The issue of human rights with regard to private actors becomes more important now that public services are often performed by private actors. Once such formerly state-owned institutions like the postal services are privatized, the obligation to ensure that the human right to privacy is not violated does not change. The serious obstacle here is that increasingly governments are (often voluntarily) losing the regulatory instruments to control the powerful corporations, and global governance is increasingly the arena of private business actors. However, the trademark of these actors is often the refusal of public accountability for their conduct.

Many of the operations of TNCs across the globe have human rights dimensions. The commercial activities of a growing number of TNCs affect such issues as global warming, child labor, genetically manipulated food, or financial markets.

Following widely accepted policies of liberalization and deregulation, the reach and freedom of TNCs have considerably expanded without a concurrent development of their social responsibility. However, TNCs increasingly face public challenges to their moral conduct through incidents such as the Union Carbide gas leak in Bhopal, the Exxon oil spill in Alaska, or Shell's behavior in Nigeria. Large international firms have confronted in recent times demonstrations of public moral indignation about their conduct. For some corporate actors, this has meant that they cannot ignore the moral quality of their performance. One finds more and more reports and debates about the requirement of good corporate governance, which refers to the need for more transparency and accountability of business firms toward their shareholders. The business publication *Fortune* has—after the ENRON scandal—repeatedly suggested that new forms of good corporate governance are essential to the restoration of investor and public confidence in the corporate sector.

The World Business Council for Sustainable Development promotes the notion of corporate social responsibility (CSR) and proposes that this means that management acts responsibly in its relationships with all stakeholders who have a legitimate interest in the business. CSR is seen as ethical behavior of companies toward society. According to the World Business Council, the ultimate goal of CSR is to create maximum shareholder value. This implies that CSR is not primarily a moral concept, but a long-term economic strategic notion. A lack of CSR may damage a company's image and have detrimental financial effects. Among companies that take this seriously, one observes a trend to look at the social (and environmental) consequences arising from business decisions, and therefore they enter into dialogue with interested social parties. Companies also begin to say that compliance with human rights standards is good for business. It makes them look good for consumers. It helps avoid legal cases, enhance risk management, and increase worker productivity. The organization Human Rights Watch has proposed in a statement to the United Nations to view the development of guidelines as a first step in the process to develop binding human rights standards for corporations. It believes "that there is a need for binding standards to prevent corporations from having a negative impact on the enjoyment of human rights. Such standards should not just be limited to transnational corporations but should apply to any corporation: local, national, or transnational."[1]

The UNDP Human Development Report 1999 also argues that TNCs are too important for their conduct to be left to voluntary and self-generated standards (UNDP, 1999).

The protection of human rights implies that states should stop private parties from violating their citizens' human rights. The Maastricht Experts Meeting Guidelines on Violations of Economic, Social and Cultural Rights (1997) provided: "The obligation to protect includes the States' responsibility to ensure that private entities or individuals, including transnational corporations over which they exercise jurisdiction, do not deprive individuals of their economic, social and cultural rights."

International human rights law does indeed provide for an obligation on the part of states to ensure that private business respects human rights. This is part of the indirect accountability of states. There are, however, also direct obligations for commercial companies.

---

[1]Statement by Human Rights Watch to the UN Sub-Commission on the Promotion and Protection of Human Rights' Working Group on the Working Methods and Activities of Transnational Corporations, July 31, 2001.

There is the obligation for all parties (as the Preamble of the UDHR states) to promote human rights. This means to publicize and disseminate human rights principles and standards, explain them, help others to understand them, and use whatever influence one has to protect human rights. The Committee for the ICESCR has been outspoken about the inclusion of private actors in the protection of human rights. The Committee has among others pointed to the need for the right to privacy to be protected from violations by private entities.

The Committee has taken the position that the rights it is responsible for do indeed apply to private parties, just like the tripartite ILO Declaration on Principles Concerning Multinational Enterprises and Social Policy (1977) refers in Article 8 to the need to respect human rights for all parties (government, employers, and trade unions) and mentions among others the right to freedom of expression. Private industry has a clear preference for forms of self-regulation, such as voluntary codes of conduct without binding sanction mechanisms. There are various preemptive moves of business toward self regulation, such as the adoption of the Business Charter for Sustainable Development by the International Chamber of Commerce in 1991. Another example was the establishment in 1995 of the World Business Council for Sustainable Development. In 1997, the World Federation of the Sporting Goods Industry and the International Council of Toy Industries adopted codes on working conditions particularly regarding children. Products should have a certification that guarantees that no child or slave labor was used in its production. The 1994 Trading Charter of the Body Shop states that the company aims to ensure that human rights will be respected throughout its business activities. Many such voluntarily adopted ethical guidelines tend to be restricted to issues such as the environment and child labor and do not include human rights such as the right to strike.

THE UNITED NATIONS AND CORPORATE BUSINESS: THE GLOBAL COMPACT

In the 1990s, a trend developed toward partnership between the United Nations and big business. One of the illustrations is the decision of UNESCO to allow Disney to use the UNESCO logo for its Youth Millennium Dreamer Award in 2000.

It is ironic that over the past 10 years the UN has moved all the time closer to the major transnational corporations that have consistently tried to weaken the impact of the UN system.

On January 31, 1999, at the World Economic Forum at Davos, UN Secretary General Kofi Annan said in his address, "Our challenge is to devise a compact on a global scale to underpin the new global economy and lay the foundation for an age of global prosperity." He proposed a Global Compact with principles covering human rights, labour standards, and the environment, and he asked businessmen to ensure that human rights, decent labor, and environmental standards be upheld by their businesses. A few months after his speech, a delegation of the International Chamber of Commerce entered into discussion with the Secretary General, and several companies agreed to cooperate with the UN. Among them were Alcatel, Allied Zurich Investor, Norsdk Hydro, Rio Tinto, Royal Dutch Shell, Unilever, and Siemens. The Global Compact was launched with UNEP, ILO, and UNHCHR in July 2000. Now WHO, UNICEF (cooperating with McDonalds for the world's Children's Day), and UNESCO are partnering with businesses. On human rights, the Global Compact states that businesses should support and respect the protection of internationally proclaimed human rights and should make sure that they are not complicit in human rights abuses.

There is a whole set of problems implied in the project of the Global Compact. Among the companies that join the partnership with the UN are known violators of human rights such as Nike, Shell, Rio Tinto, Bayer, and DuPont. A letter signed by Instituto del Tercer Mundo, Institute for Policy Studies, Third World Network, and other NGOs like the International Baby Food Action network expressed strong disappointment at seeing the name of UNHCR associated with that of Unocal Corporation and with Nestlé as members of the Business Humanitarian Forum (BHF). The arrangement with the BHF allows Unocal, a company currently being sued for alleged human rights abuses in Burma, to enjoy the benefits of associating itself with the UN without actually taking steps to protect human rights. Among the other partners are firms like Disney and McDonalds, which can hardly be considered credible human rights protectors. The International Chamber of Commerce plays an important role in the Global Compact on behalf of business and has routinely opposed UN proposals for the regulation of TNCs. It is unclear why the UN should team up with organizations that have completely different goals and aspirations. The Global Compact suggests that the interests of the United Nations and corporate business are compatible. The UN and business organizations, however, have completely different aspirations. Whereas the UN stands for humanitarian values, the business firms represent commercial values.

The UN Secretary General appears to be partnering with the representatives of neoliberal globalization, which implies enormous suffering for millions of people around the world and against which there is increasing resistance among civil society organizations. Whereas the UN Sub-Commission for the Promotion and Protection of Human Rights recognizes that the World Trade Organization (WTO) is a nightmare for developing countries, the UN Secretary General wants a partnership with the major supporters of the WTO. This suggests that it should be possible for the UN system to put a human face on economic globalization as if it only needs to be tinkered with by applying some social values and for the rest is a benign system.

There is a strong feeling of resentment about the Global Compact among developing countries in the UN and a great deal of distrust among civil society organizations. The Global Compact is about partnership, but why should the UN want to partner with business? There should obviously be cooperation and consultation, but partnership is for the UN risky business. Projects like the Global Compact project the image that the UN supports the neoliberal variant of globalization and provides legitimacy to transnational business. In the Guidelines for Cooperation between the UN and the Business Community, the Secretary General (July 2000) stated that the UN business partners must demonstrate responsible citizenship. It is confusing that the Secretary General identified business firms as citizens. Behind the Global Compact is the contested belief that free open markets are to benefit the world's people and solve the world's worst crises of hunger, poverty and environmental degradation. Whatever the intentions behind the Global Compact are, the UN system does not have the capacity to monitor whether a TNC complies with human rights obligations. Another problem is that within the United Nations a whole set of legal standards has been adopted that are largely ignored by corporations. Concrete implementation of these standards is the core problem of international human rights law. It is at least dubious whether this is helped by adopting a set of general nonenforceable principles. There is no monitoring or enforcement mechanism foreseen in the Compact. There is nominal commitment to the principles, but no control over their implementation. On the part of the business community (through the ICC and other spokespeople), it is clear that companies do not want binding prescriptions for their conduct. Because the Global Compact consists of voluntary and nonenforceable principles, which are much weaker than already established standards of international human rights law, the whole project could undermine all the earlier UN efforts.

The Sub-Commission on the Promotion and Protection of Human Rights (a body of the UN Human Rights Commission) has a working group on transnational corporations and human rights. In 1999, the Working Group began work on a code of conduct on corporations and human rights that was approved for further development in 2000. The Working Group wants to see the Code eventually as a binding instrument. The U.S. administration opposes this and has proposed the dissolution of the Sub-Commission.

For media professionals, the relationship between corporate business and human rights is relevant for the following reasons. Business conglomerates in various market sectors have become—in national economies and in the world economy—crucial social actors. Their activities not only impact economic developments, but they also have political, social, and cultural effects. As such they constitute topics of essential interest to professionals in the field of news production. As important players in world politics, corporate interests also influence policy directions in the field of communication and information. Moreover, for many media professionals, media business corporations are their employers.

Professionals who are active in national and international news media could contribute significantly to the protection of human rights by systematically exposing the human rights record of leading TNCs (e.g., by publicly exposing corporations that manufacture goods or services that inflict considerable harm against human beings, such as torture instruments).

Regular media monitoring of the human rights conduct of business could follow the guidelines implicit in the various reports by Special Rapporteurs for the UN Commission on Human Rights (Addo, 1999). This would mean that essential features for assessment would be the variables *degree*, *conditions*, *type*, and *proximity*.

The variable *degree* means inquiring whether violations are sporadic and random or systematic and planned. The variable *conditions* refers to the assessment of violations as the direct result of an activity or as a result of ineffective and incompetent conduct. The variable *type* questions whether political, civil, social, economic, or cultural rights are violated. The variable *proximity* raises the question about the measure of involvement of a company in human rights violations. Was the firm directly involved or were the violations perpetrated by subsidiaries or joint venture parties?

For this kind of monitoring, the checklist of human rights principles that Amnesty International (1998) produced to improve the ability of corporations to promote human rights could also be used. These principles include: developing an explicit company policy on human rights; providing effective training for their managers and their staff in international human rights standards, preferably with input and assistance from appropriate nongovernmental organizations; consulting nongovernmental organizations, including Amnesty International, on the level and nature of human rights abuses in different countries; and establishing a clear framework for assessing the potential impact on human rights of all the company's and its subcontractors' operations. News media could use this checklist to assess the quality of human rights protection in individual corporations.

This assessment should obviously also apply to the leading international media conglomerates. Among the questions to be asked could be the following: Do media corporations violate human rights (directly or indirectly)? Do media corporations impede the protection of human rights? Do media corporations promote the protection of human rights? Do media corporations have a human rights policy? Do they have a human rights policy unit to monitor, report, and troubleshoot human rights issues?

The monitoring should recognize that media corporations can also be victims of human rights violations. In this context, the observation of Addo (1991) is important:

> Most legal jurisdictions recognise the entitlement of corporations to rights of property, to a fair trial, to privacy or to some form of freedom of expres-

> sion." This should be taken seriously because, "In getting corporations to appreciate the value of human rights, especially in seeking to give credibili ty to corporate duties in the field of human rights, it is also important to recognise the corresponding claims and entitlements of these corporations. Such an approach will give the corporations a stake in the human rights regime on which one can build a relationship of co-operation in the effective protection of human rights. (p. 192)

The practice of the European Court of Human Rights provides many illustrations of the application of the human rights standard of free speech to corporations. In many cases, the Court has accepted complaints from corporations that stated their human right to freedom of expression was violated. A famous case was *Sunday Times v. UK* (1979), in which the newspaper successfully fought an injunction against it because of a publication contested in United Kingdom courts.

This obviously raises the question of the entitlement of corporate entities to human rights protection. Human rights can be claimed by everyone, but does this include other subjects than individual persons? In 1886, the U.S. Supreme Court in the *Santa Clara County v. Southern Pacific Railroad* case took the landmark decision that private corporations are natural persons with all the rights and privileges of human beings. In line with this decision, mega media conglomerates may view themselves as entitled to the same free speech rights as the members of their audiences. This has produced an ongoing debate on the freedom of so-called *commercial speech*. Despite the corporate entitlement to individual rights, in many countries commercial and professional advertising has been excluded from free speech protection. Only in the past few decades has the U.S. Supreme Court begun to reconsider this traditional exclusion (Barendt, 1989) and offered arguments in defense of the freedom of commercial speech. For example, in the case of *Virginia State Board of Pharmacy v. Virginia Citizens Consumer Council* (1976), where the Court stated that the interest of consumers "in the free flow of commercial information . . . may be as keen, if not keener by far, than his interest in the day's most urgent political debate." In the jurisprudence of the European Court of Human Rights, there is a noticeable trend towards the inclusion of commercial speech under the protection of Article 10 of the European Convention, with the observation that commercial ideas are entitled to less protection than political speech. This means there is a difference when the balancing test is applied to the question of whether expressions are justly regulated. For both political and commercial speech, the ultimate test is whether government has a compelling interest in restricting a publication. In the case of commercial speech, the interpretation of what may constitute a compelling interest (e.g., consumer protection) tends to be much broader than with political speech. In many countries, it has now been found that there are no constitutional (fundamental rights) objections against restricting commercial speech about dangerous products such as cigarettes.

CORPORATE OWNERSHIP

International human rights law does not contain any specific and direct provisions that address the issue of the ownership of information and communication institutions. There are no standards that regulate the possible monopolization or oligopolization of the production and/or distribution of information–communication goods and services. However, there is a multitude of provisions on the diversity of cultural contents, the diversity of information sources, the social function of information, the equitable sharing of information and knowledge, and the specificity of cultural goods and services as more than mere consumer goods. It is difficult to see how the human rights standard of cultural diversity can be combined with a cultural market that is monopolized or oligopolized by a few mega cultural industries. Rather the implications of current human rights provisions seems to point toward the need for a variety of independent producers and distributors of information-communication goods and services and a balanced mixture of privately owned, commercial corporate actors and publicly owned, not-for-profit institutions. It is interesting to note that, contrary to the free speech provisions in the UDHR and ICCPR, the European Convention refers in Article 10 to the freedom expression as freedom from "interference by public authority." This issue was discussed earlier by those who drafted Article 19 of the UDHR. They preferred to not limit the interference to public parties. Several delegations at the time expressed concern that private media control could limit free speech as much as state interference could.

CONCLUDING OBSERVATION

The total of human rights standards creates a code of conduct for the professionals who own and manage media and for those who work in these media. Such a code of conduct is often strongly contested by media professionals on the basis that such moral standards limit their right to free speech and can easily be abused by those people who want to curtail the media. This fear is not without ground. The defense of free speech and the respect for other human rights standards are not always easy to reconcile. A classic case is the confrontation of free speech with hate speech. In discussions on media and human rights there is a tendency to focus exclusively on the importance of the free speech standard. It needs to be realized however that this standard is part and parcel of a broader package that inevitably sets limits to the exercise of the freedom of expression. It remains an urgent challenge for communicators to implement these limitations with due regard to the free speech standard.

SUGGESTIONS FOR DISCUSSION

The human rights standards mentioned in this chapter could be seen as core elements of a code of conduct for media performance:

Discuss the contents of this code.

Discuss how this code could be applied to media practice and media policymaking.

Discuss whether this code could be applied across cultural borders? What kind of variations may be necessary in different cultural settings?

Discuss concrete examples of ways in which the media in your local context can contribute to the creation of a human rights culture.

In 1997, a Universal Declaration of Human Responsibilities has been proposed by the InterAction Council, a body consisting of former heads of state and government. (Kung & Schmidt, 1998). In Article 14, the Declaration provides, "The freedom of the media to inform the public and to criticize institutions of society and governmental actions, which is essential for a just society, must be used with responsibility and discretion. Freedom of the media carries a special responsibility for accurate and truthful reporting. Sensational reporting that degrades the human person or dignity must at all times be avoided."

Discuss how realistic the responsibility that the Declaration proposes is in the light of the worldwide commercialization and concentration of the news media?

Discuss the issue of criminal culpability of journalists in the context of hate speech, and discuss the pros and cons of international prosecution of media propagandists.

In 1998 and 1999, the Western allies proposed action in Bosnia against radio, TV stations, and newspapers that distributed propagandistic messages that undermined peacekeeping and that threatened the safety of the NATO peacekeeping forces. Discuss the argument that such action violates the human right to freedom of expression.

Discuss whether corporations should be held responsible for human rights violations?

How can the implementation of corporate human rights responsibility be monitored.

Who should monitor this? Business? Government? Citizens?

Are self-regulatory instruments adequate to secure that transnational corporations comply with human rights standards?

Discuss what journalists could do to SECURE that transnational corporations comply with human rights standards.

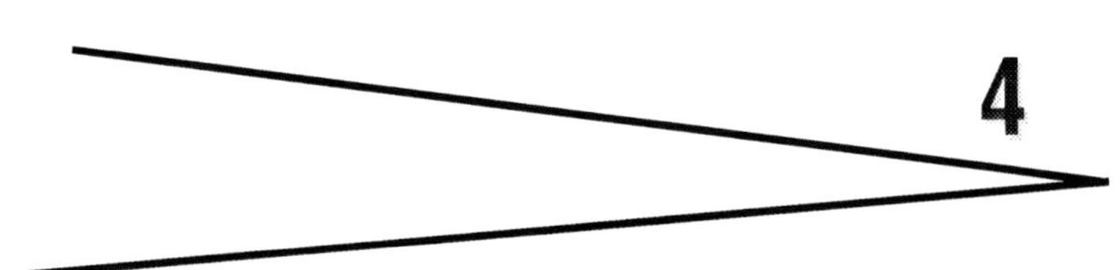

4

Cultural Human Rights

SIGNIFICANCE OF CULTURAL RIGHTS

Although the public focus is often on civil and political rights, the international human rights regime has also adopted social, economic, and cultural rights as fundamental entitlements of individuals and communities. Professionals working in the media should be especially aware that the international community has established human rights standards with regard to culture.

The recognition of cultural rights raises complex questions that need serious debate. Such issues address among others the collective nature of cultural rights. Rights to language and religion are enjoyed in communities. They cannot be implemented by protecting individual rights only. In international law, there has been an evolution from an exclusive emphasis on sovereign nation–states to individuals, nonstate social groups (peoples), and humankind. However, there is still a strong tendency to give priority to individual rights, and states tend to be against the recognition of the collective rights of minorities because governments usually favor assimilation over cultural autonomy.

Even more than in other domains, the weakness of enforcement in international human rights is a serious problem for cultural rights. The mechanisms for the enforcement of cultural rights are soft and urgently need to be strengthened.

At the present time, serious attention for the protection of cultural rights is especially pertinent. Among others the arguments for this position are the following:

- Around the world we find today a rapid commercialization, consolidation, and globalization of the cultural industries. A worldwide process of cultural erosion is reinforced by international trade agreements that perceive of independent cultural policies as unfair barriers to international trade. As media become industrial conglomerates, they move ever farther away from service to the common good toward service to commercial imperatives. Their essential mission is to produce material that attracts large audiences that can be sold to advertisers. This poses a serious risk to the diversity of cultural production and the independent creativity of cultural workers as the interests between independent knowledge production and conglomerate political or economic interests conflict with each other. Commercial imperatives do not likely cater to the linguistic needs of ethnic minorities or indigenous groups.
- The dominant variant of globalization is steered by a neoliberal, commercial agenda. This globalization-from-above—despite the occasional recognition of local varieties such as the Indian vegetarian Burger or Chinese rock on MTV—promotes a uniformity that is fatal for the cultural diversity on which multicultural and multilingual societies are based. Moreover, the neoliberal definition of citizenship prioritizes civil and political rights (as fundamental conditions for the creation of individual wealth) over economic, social, and cultural rights.
- The primary messages of the global media conglomerates are of a commercial nature. They are the key vehicles in shaping societies in which people worldwide are better informed about consumer goods than about the environmental consequences of the global rate of consumption. Worldwide advertising has become ubiquitous. In many countries, there are hardly any advertising-free zones left. Despite all political declarations on the emergence of a global information society, it seems more realistic to expect a global billboard society. Whatever its local variation, advertising proclaims to the world a single cultural standard for its audiences: Consumption fulfills people's basic aspirations, and fun shopping is an essential cultural activity. It subjects the world's cultural differences to the dominance of a consumption-oriented lifestyle. People's fundamental cultural identity is to be a consumer.
- Cultural self-determination is particularly sought after by minorities and is particularly desired by the world's indigenous people as a key element in their social empowerment.
- There is currently a growing—predominantly commercial—interest for those cultural rights that deal with the protection of

intellectual property. In this context, the UN Sub-Commission on Human Rights has called attention to the possible conflict between international trade provisions (such as provided in the World Trade Organization's [WTO's] Agreement on Trade-Related Intellectual Property Rights [TRIPS] of 1993/1994) and the implementation of cultural human rights. It has pointed to the possibility that trade rules limit the control by indigenous people over their cultural heritage.

The shift from the protection of intellectual property as a human right to its protection as a trading right relates to the increasing commercial significance of intellectual property. In 1947, intellectual property constituted less than 10% of U.S. exports, and by 1994, this was over 50% (Shiva, 2001). In 1999, U.S. exports of intellectual property amounted to some $80 billion. It is ironic that, with the shift to the trading perspective, the enforcement of IPR protection becomes robust and effective.

- Around the world, culture is subject to a process of commodification, which basically threatens cultural rights. This process is manifest in the international political trend to refuse a special position for cultural goods and services in international trade. Current negotiations in the WTO favor the rejection of a cultural exemption clause and prefer to see culture as any other tradeable commodity. The products of the mind are seen as ordinary tradeable goods and services that can be sold and bought in the marketplace. Their users are consumers and not participants. In this commercial conception, culture becomes a spectacle like the Disney theme parks, where people are spectators and not citizens. In a human rights framework, culture is a lived experience and a social process.

CULTURAL RIGHTS IN INTERNATIONAL LAW

During the discussions preceding the adoption of the UN Charter (1945), several Latin American states proposed the inclusion of cultural rights. This was not successful at the time, but in 1948 the Universal Declaration of Human Rights referred to cultural rights in Articles 22 and 27. Article 22 states that everyone is entitled to realization of the economic, social, and cultural rights indispensable for his dignity and the free development of his personality. Article 27 provides "Everyone has the right freely to participate in the cultural life of the community."

In 1966, the International Covenant on Economic, Social and Cultural Rights (ICESCR) was adopted by the UN General Assembly, and cultural rights were provided in Articles 1 and 15. Article 1 provides that "All peoples have the right of self-determination. By virtue of that right they freely determine their political status and freely pursue their economic, social and cultural development." Article 15 says that the States Parties to the present Covenant recognize the right of everyone:

> (a) To take part in cultural life;
> (b) To enjoy the benefits of scientific progress and its applications;
> (c) To benefit from the protection of the moral and material interests resulting from any scientific, literary or artistic production of which he is the author.

For the protection of these provisions, the UN Educational, Scientific and Cultural Organization (UNESCO) became the key specialized UN agency. Over the past decades, UNESCO produced several relevant instruments that address cultural rights. In 1995, UNESCO also received the report from the World Commission on Culture and Development, "Our Creative Diversity," which proposed an agenda for action on cultural rights. On November 2, the 31st General Conference of UNESCO adopted the UNESCO Universal Declaration on Cultural Diversity. As the UNESCO Director-General Koichiro Matsuura declared at the time of its adoption

> This is the first time the international community has endowed itself with such a comprehensive standard-setting instrument, elevating cultural diversity to the rank of "common heritage of humanity"—as necessary for the human race as bio-diversity in the natural realm—and makes its protection an ethical imperative, inseparable from respect for human dignity.[1]

Article 5 of the Declaration provides that,

> Cultural rights are an integral part of human rights. The flourishing of creative diversity requires the full implementation of cultural rights.. All persons have therefore the right to express themselves and to create and disseminate their work in the language of their choice, and particularly in their mother tongue; all persons are entitled to quality education and training that fully respect their cultural identity; and all persons have the right to participate in the cultural life of their choice and conduct their own cultural practices. . . .

[1]The web site for the Declaration is http://www.unesco.org/confgen/press_rel/021101-_clt_diversity.shtml.

The Declaration continues to state in Article 7 that all cultures should be able to express themselves, make themselves known, and have access to the means of expression and dissemination. Article 8 addresses cultural goods and services and demands special attention "to the diversity of the supply of creative work, to due recognition of the rights of authors and artists and to the specificity of cultural goods and services which . . . must not be treated as mere commodities or consumer goods."

Added to the Declaration is an Action Plan for its implementation. It proposes among others to:

- preserve the linguistic heritage of humanity;
- promote digital literacy and mastery of the new Information and Communication Technologies (ICTs);
- promote access to new ICTs in developing countries and countries in transition;
- support the presence of diverse contents in the media and emphasize the role of public broadcasting;
- increase the mobility of creative artists;
- help enable the cultural industries of developing countries;
- involve civil society in the elaboration of social policies that aim at the preservation of cultural diversity.

Within the international human rights regime, the following essential cultural rights have been identified.

THE RIGHT TO CULTURE

Several factors explain the emergence of cultural rights in the post-World War II era. There was the rise of postcolonial states who sought their identity in the light of both imposed colonial standards and their own traditional values. The issue of cultural identity came up particularly strong in the process of decolonization. The newly independent states saw the affirmation of their cultural identity as an instrument in the struggle against foreign domination. In their earlier battle with colonialism, cultural identity played a significant role in motivating and legitimizing the decolonization movement.

The proliferation of the mass media offered possibilities of unprecedented cultural interaction as well as risks of cultural uniformity. The spread of a consumer society—largely promoted by the mass media—raised serious concerns about the emergence of a homogeneous global culture.

The adoption of the right to culture as part of the human rights system with its inclusive emphasis on rights for everyone implied a shift away from an elite conception of culture to a view of culture as common heritage. Actually, the UNESCO Declaration on Race and Racial Prejudice (1978, General Conference Res. 3/1.1/2) founded the right to culture on the notion of culture as common heritage of mankind, which implies that all people "should respect the right of all groups to their own cultural identity and the development of their distinctive cultural life within the national and international context" (Article 5).

In 1968, a UNESCO conference of experts considered the question of cultural rights as human rights (Paris, July 8-13, 1968). The conference concluded, "The rights to culture include the possibility for each man to obtain the means of developing his personality, through his direct participation in the creation of human values and of becoming, in this way, responsible for his situation, whether local or on a world scale." The Intergovernmental Conference on the Institutional, Administrative and Financial Aspects of Cultural Policies (convened by UNESCO in 1970) decided that the right to participate in the cultural life of the community implies a duty on governments to provide the effective means for this participation. A series of regional conferences on cultural policies (in 1972, 1973, and 1975) provided important inputs for the formulation of a UNESCO Recommendation on "Participation by the People at Large in Cultural Life and Their Contribution to It," which was approved on November 26, 1976. The Recommendation aims to "guarantee as human rights those rights bearing on access to and participation in cultural life" and proposes that member states "provide effective safeguards for free access to national and world cultures by all members of society," "pay special attention to women's full entitlement to access to culture and to effective participation in cultural life," and "guarantee the recognition of the equality of cultures, including the culture of national minorities and of foreign minorities." Regarding the mass media, the Recommendation states that they "should not threaten the authenticity of cultures or impair their quality; they ought not to act as instruments of cultural domination but serve mutual understanding and peace." The Recommendation is especially concerned about the concentration of control over the means of producing and distributing culture and suggests that governments "should make sure that the criterion of profit-making does not exert a decisive influence on cultural activities." There was strong Western opposition to various elements of the Recommendation, such as the mention of commercial mass culture in a negative sense and the use of the term people at large. In the preparatory meetings and during the UNESCO General Conference, several Western delegations expressed their concern that the Recommendation, if implemented, would restrict the free flow of information and the independence of the mass media. The strongest opponent was the United States.

> The USA asserted a belief from the outset that access to and participation in cultural life were not fit subjects for international regulation, took minimal part of the drafting process, sent no delegation to the intergovernmental meeting, urged the General Conference to turn down the proposed text and,

> after its adoption, announced that it had no intention of transmitting the Recommendation to the relevant authorities or institutions in the USA. (Wells, 1987, p. 165)

The Recommendation used a broad notion of culture, which it saw as an integral part of social life and one of the principle factors in the progress of mankind. Culture "is not merely an accumulation of works and knowledge which an elite produces, collects and conserves . . . but is . . . the demand for a way of life and the need to communicate."

The main line of thought in the Recommendation was reinforced by the 1982 World Conference on Cultural Policies held in Mexico City. The Declaration on Cultural Policies adopted by the Conference reaffirmed the requirement that states must take appropriate measures to implement the right to cultural participation. In Recommendation 28 on cultural rights, the conference participants claimed that governments should take measures "to strengthen the democratization of culture by means of policies that ensure the right to culture and guarantee the participation of society in its benefits without restriction." An assessment of the implementation of the recommendation on participation in cultural life in 1985 to 1986 showed that little had been done by many states and these issues remained relevant.

In summary, it can be established that the recognition of the human right to culture implies participation in cultural life; protection of cultural identity; need to conserve, develop, and diffuse culture; protection of intellectual property rights; recognition of linguistic diversity; and access to science and technology. Each of these themes is treated in the following paragraphs.

THE RIGHT TO PARTICIPATE FULLY IN CULTURAL LIFE

Participation in cultural life has raised difficult questions about the definition of communities, the position of subcultures, the protection of participation rights of minorities, the provision of physical resources of access, and the links between cultural access and socioeconomic conditions. Underlying some of these difficulties is the tension between the interpretation of culture as public good or private property. These interpretations can be mutually exclusive when, for example, historical works of art disappear in the vaults of private collections. The right to freely participate in the cultural life of one's community recognizes that a society's democratic quality is not merely defined by civil and political institutions, but also by the possibility for people to shape their cultural identity, realize the potential of local cultural life, and practice cultural traditions.

Participation rights also entail people's right "freely to participate in the cultural life of the community, to enjoy the arts and to share in scientific advancement and its benefits" (Article 27 of the UDHR). The participation claim requires the creation of social and economic conditions that will enable people "not only to enjoy the benefits of culture, but also to take an active part in overall cultural life and in the process of cultural development." The Unesco Recommendation on Participation by the People at Large in Cultural Life and their Contribution to It (1976, 19th session of the General Conference), which articulates this requirement, also provides that "participation in cultural life presupposes involvement of the different social partners in decision-making related to cultural policy. . . ." Participation extends beyond public participation in media production or media management into the areas of public decision making. This means that political practices should provide for people's participation in public policy making on the management of a society's cultural resources.

People have the right to participate in public decision making on the preservation, protection, and development of cultural expressions. This means there should be ample scope for public participation in the formulation and implementation of public cultural policies.

THE RIGHT TO THE PROTECTION OF CULTURAL IDENTITY

The protection of cultural identity became an especially hot issue during the 1970's debates on cultural imperialism. In 1973, the Non Aligned Summit at Algiers stated that "it is an established fact that the activity of imperialism is not limited to political and economic domains, but that it encompasses social and cultural areas as well, imposing thereby a foreign ideological domination on the peoples of the developing world."

Cultural domination and the threat to cultural identity was also treated by the UNESCO appointed MacBride Commission. The Commission saw cultural identity "endangered by the overpowering influence on and assimilation of some national cultures though these nations may well be the heirs to more ancient and richer cultures. Since diversity is the most precious quality of culture, the whole world is poorer" (International Commission, 1980, p. 31).

In its recommendations, the Commission focused on the establishment of national policies "which should foster cultural identity. Such policies should also contain guidelines for safeguarding national cultural development while promoting knowledge of other cultures" (International Commission, 1980, p. 259). No recommendation was proposed on what measures the world community might collectively take. The Commission proposed the strengthening of cultural identity and promoted conditions for the preservation of the cultural identity, but left this to be implemented on the national level.

A decade later, the South Commission addressed the issue of cultural identity. According to its report, the concern with cultural identity "does not imply rejection of outside influences. Rather, it should be a part of efforts to strengthen the capacity for autonomous decision-making, blending indigenous and universal elements in the service of a people-centred policy" (South Commission, 1990, p. 132). The Commission urged governments to adopt Cultural Development Charters that articulate people's basic rights in the field of culture. Cultural policies should stress the right to culture, cultural diversity, and the role of the state in preserving and enriching the cultural heritage of society (South Commission, 1990, p. 133).

The notion of cultural identity remains a topic for much discussion. Unresolved questions are among others: How can a society protect cultural identity and at the same time maintain social cohesion? Is cultural identity a barrier or a condition for cultural diversity?

THE RIGHT TO THE PROTECTION OF NATIONAL AND INTERNATIONAL CULTURAL PROPERTY AND HERITAGE

This cultural right is particularly relevant in times of armed conflict. It also implies the recognition of the intellectual property of indigenous people.

The UN General Assembly adopted in 1973 a resolution (UNGA Res. 3148 (XXVIII) on the preservation and further development of cultural values. The resolution considers the value and dignity of each culture as well as the ability to preserve and develop its distinctive character as a basic right of all countries and peoples. In the light of the possible endangering of the distinctive character of cultures, the preservation, enrichment, and further development of national cultures must be supported. It is important that the Resolution recognizes that "the preservation, renewal and continuous creation of cultural values should not be a static but a dynamic concept." The Resolution recommended to the Director General of UNESCO to promote research that analyzes "the role of the mass media in the preservation and further development of cultural values." The Resolution also urged governments to promote "the involvement of the population in the elaboration and implementation of measures ensuring preservation and future development of cultural and moral values."

A specialized instrument on the protection of the world cultural heritage was adopted by the 17th session of the UNESCO General Conference in 1972. This was the Convention for the Protection of the World Cultural and Natural

Heritage. The text noted that the world's cultural heritage is threatened, that this impoverishes the world, and that effective provisions are needed to collectively protect the cultural heritage of outstanding universal value. In the Convention, the international protection of the world cultural heritage is understood to mean "the establishment of a system of international co-operation and assistance designed to support States Parties to the Convention in their efforts to conserve and identify that heritage."

On the protection of cultural property, the world community has also adopted—through UNESCO—other agreements such as the Hague Convention for the Protection of Cultural Property in the Event of Armed Conflict (1954), the Convention on the Means of Prohibiting and Preventing the Illicit Import, Export and Transfer of Ownership of Cultural Property (1970), and the Convention on the Protection of the World Cultural and Natural Heritage (1972). In 1973, the UN General Assembly adopted on its agenda the issue of restitution of works of art to countries that are victims of expropriation. UNGA Res. 3187 (XXVIII) of December 18, 1973, sees prompt restitution of works of art as strengthening international cooperation and as a just reparation for damage done. To implement this, UNESCO established the Intergovernmental Committee for Promoting the Return of Cultural Property to its Countries of Origin or its Restitution in Case of Illicit Appropriation. Throughout the 1980s, the UN General Assembly stressed the issue, commended the work of UNESCO done in this field, and called on member states to ratify the relevant Convention. In 1986, the General Assembly proclaimed that the 1988–1997 period would be the World Decade for Cultural Development. The following objectives were formulated for the Decade: acknowledgment of the cultural dimension of development, enrichment of cultural identities, broadened participation in cultural life, and promotion of international cultural cooperation (UNGA Res. 41/187 of December 8, 1986).

Other approaches of the world community to the protection of cultural property include the safeguarding of traditional culture and folklore. In 1989, the General Conference of the UNESCO adopted a recommendation that stressed the need to recognize the role of folklore and the danger it faces. Folklore is defined as the totality of tradition-based creations of a cultural community. The recommendation urges measures for the conservation, preservation, dissemination, and protection of folklore.

The UN Draft Declaration on the Rights of Indigenous Peoples (1994) refers explicitly to the cultural property of indigenous peoples. Article 12 states,

> Indigenous people have the right to practice and revitalize their cultural traditions and customs. This includes the right to maintain, protect and develop the past, present and future manifestations of their cultures, such as archaeological and historical sites, artefacts, designs, ceremonies, technologies and visual and performing arts

and literature, as well as the right to restitution of cultural, intellectual, religious and spiritual propert taken without their free and informed consent or in violation of their law, traditions and customs.

THE RIGHT TO PROTECTION OF MORAL AND MATERIAL INTERESTS OF WORKS OF CULTURE

This cultural right puts the protection of intellectual property in the context of other human rights such as freedom of expression, the right of access to information and knowledge, and the right to the protection of cultural identity.

International rules for the protection of intellectual property rights find their origin in the 19th century. From its beginnings, this protection has been inspired by three motives. The first motive was the notion that those who invested in the production of intellectual property should be guaranteed a financial remuneration. With the establishment of the first international treaties on intellectual property protection (the Paris Convention for the Protection of Industrial Property of 1883 and the Berne Convention for the Protection of Literary and Artistic Works of 1886), a monetary benefit for the creator was perceived as a necessary incentive to invest in innovation and creativity. During the 1928 revision of the Berne Convention, the notion of moral rights was added to the entitlement to economic benefits. The introduction of the moral value of works recognized that they represent the intellectual personality of the author. Moral rights protect the creative work against modification without the creator's consent—they protect the claim to authorship and the right of the author to decide whether a work will be published. Early on in the development of intellectual property rights (IPRs), it was also recognized that there is a public interest in the protection of intellectual property. As a common principle it was recognized that IPRs promote the innovation and progress in artistic, technological, and scientific domains, and therefore benefit public welfare. The U.S. Constitution, for example, articulates this as follows: "to promote the progress of science and the useful arts, by securing for limited time to authors and inventors the exclusive rights to their respective writings and discoveries." The protection of intellectual property rights is in fact a delicate balancing act among private economic interests, individual ownership, moral values, and public interest.

With the increasing economic significance of intellectual property, the global system of governance in this domain has moved away from moral and public interest dimensions and emphasizes in its actual practice mainly the economic interests of the owners of intellectual property. Today such owners are by and large no longer individual authors and composers who create cultural products, but transnational corporate cultural producers. The implication is that

IPR arrangements tend to favor institutional investment interests over the interests of individual authors, composers, and performers.

The recent tendency to include intellectual property rights in global trade negotiations demonstrates the commercial thrust of the major actors. Copyright problems have become trade issues, and the protection of the author has conceded place to the interests of traders and investors. This emphasis on corporate ownership interests implies a threat to the use of intellectual property for the common good and seriously upsets the balance between the private ownership claims of the producer and the claims to public benefits of the users. The balance between the interests of producers and users has always been under threat in the development of the IPR governance system, but it would seem that the currently emerging arrangements provide benefits neither to the individual creators nor to the public at large.

Its key beneficiaries are the transnational media conglomerates for which the core business is the production and distribution of content. Several of their recent mergers are in fact motivated by the desire to gain control over rights to contents, such as are, for example, invested in film libraries or collections of musical recordings. German media tycoon Leo Kirch made much of his enormous fortune through the acquisition of rights to content. Kirch bought from United Artists/Warner Brothers the rights to some 100 successful American TV programs. He holds rights to over 50,000 hours of TV series such as "Baywatch" and owns copyrights to 16,000 film titles, which he bought from Columbia Pictures, Paramount, and Universal. He also acquired the Pay-TV rights to Disney films. The British music company EMI owns the copyrights to over 1 million of the world's most popular songs.

Recent developments in digital technology, which open up unprecedented possibilities for free and easy access to and utilization of cultural contents, have also rendered the professional production, reproduction, and distribution of content vulnerable to grand-scale piracy and made the content owners concerned about their property rights and interested in the creation of a global enforceable legal regime for the protection of their rights.

However, protecting intellectual property is not without risks. The protection of intellectual property also restricts access to cultural resources because it defines these as private property and tends to facilitate monopolistic practices. The granting of monopoly control over inventions may restrict their social utilization and reduce the potential public benefits. The principle of exclusive control over the exploitation of works someone has created can constitute an effective right to monopoly control, which restricts the free flow of ideas and cultural expressions. In the current corporate battle against piracy, it would seem that the key protagonists are generally more concerned about the protection of investments than about the moral integrity of creative works or the quality of cultural life in the world.

With the currently emerging protection of IPRs, a few megacompanies become the global gatekeepers of the world's cultural heritage. At the same time, the small individual or communal producers of literature, arts, or music hardly benefit from international legal protection. Most of the collected money goes to a small percentage of creative people (some 90% goes to 10%), and most artists that produce intellectual property receive a minor portion of the collected funds (some 90% share 10%). Most of the money goes to star performers and best-selling authors. The media industry does not make money by creating cultural diversity because it gets its revenues primarily from blockbuster artists. If there was more variety on the music market, for example, the smaller and independent labels would become competitive to the transnational market leaders. Although this would fit into the conventional thinking about free markets, the industry in reality prefers consolidation over competition.

It becomes increasingly clear that the drive to protect media products against unauthorized reproduction leads to an increasing level of restrictions on reproduction for private purposes.

The leading musical recording companies, which are part of large media conglomerates such as Bertelsman, Sony, Vivendi, and Warner Music, battle against the downloading and sales of illegal CDs. They do this through sectoral organizations such as the International Federation of Phonograph Industries (IFPI). In many countries, however, such as China, people cannot buy CDs, DVDs, or computer software because current IPRs make these items too expensive. As a result, many Chinese resort to piracy. In many Western countries, it remains a contested issue whether free downloading really damages sales. There are studies that show that Napster users (the peer-to-peer music sharing system that is now part of the Bertelsman empire) buy more CDs than other consumers (Jupiter research).

The prevailing system often works to the disadvantage of smaller parties in the market. The Recording Association of America has effectively lobbied for a bill (effective since October 20, 2002) that imposes a fee for all Webcasters that stream music to their audiences. The bill is to be retroactive from 1998. The law implies that the fee is based on the numbers of listeners. The result will be that the fee exceeds the revenues for most Webcasters and they will be forced out of business. The fee is not like the normal royalty fee, which amounts to 3% of revenues. The same fee is not imposed for broadcast radio stations because the powerful National Association of Broadcasters stopped this.

The currently most important arrangement on intellectual property rights, the Trade-Related Intellectual Property Rights Agreement (1993), which is administered by the World Trade Organization, conflicts with the notion of protection of intellectual property as a human right because it favors corporate interests over everybody's interests. It prevents the sharing of benefits of arts, science, and technology by all people. "TRIPS prevents government action for sharing benefits of biodiversity and ensuring such utilization is sustainable and conserves biodiversity in an equitable manner since it obliges states to protect patent monopolies" (Shiva, 2001, p. 102). Contrary to the TRIPS Agreement, the Convention on Biological Diversity (signed in 1992 during the Earth Summit in Rio de Janeiro) protects human rights more adequately.

The rules on intellectual property rights as formalized in the TRIPS transform people's common heritage into exclusive, private (corporate) property. A case in point is the world's biological systems, which are common heritage, but which through technological innovations (e.g., in biotechnology) are now becoming private property.

In today's global rules on intellectual property rights, the biotechnology industry is allowed to commercialize and privatize the biodiversity of the Third World countries. This industry uses the genetic resources of Third World countries as a free common resource and then transforms them in laboratories into patentable genetically engineered products. In the process, the industry manipulates life forms that are common heritage. Hence, plants and animals were formerly excluded from the domain of intellectual property rights, but biotechnology has changed this. Life can now be the object of ownership. This has many perplexing implications, one of which is that thousands of years of local knowledge (about life organisms) are devalued and replaced by the alleged superior knowledge of Western scientists and engineers. Against this development, a human rights-based intellectual property right would search a robust implementation of the protection of the rights of indigenous peoples as proposed in the Draft Declaration on the Rights of Indigenous Peoples. Article 29 of this instrument states that, "Indigenous peoples are entitled to the recognition of full ownership, control and protection of their cultural and intellectual property. They have the right to special measures to control, develop and protect their sciences, technologies and cultural manifestations, including human and other genetic resources, seeds, medicines, knowledge of properties of fauna and flora, oral traditions, literatures, designs and visual and performing arts."

An attempt to change the current system of IPR protection could begin with the critical analysis of its essential assumptions. These are that (a) culture can be legitimately appropriated for private commercial purposes, (b) that without protection there would be no cultural production, and (c) without royalties there would be no other sources of revenues. These assumptions are seriously flawed.

Culture cannot be privately owned in such a way that access, use, and adaptation can be commercially controlled. Cultural products are developed in dynamic social processes and as such are always the result of what predecessors have done and of a great variety of inputs. Most creative work is in fact the reordering of already existing work. Intellectual production is typically a collective effort, and it makes little sense to single out a few stakeholders as the only beneficiaries.

Against the claim that there would be no cultural production without adequate ownership protection, it can be argued that artists do in fact have other ways to make money than from royalties (e.g., live performances). Moreover, the argument is thinly based on the expectation that cultural production is motivated mainly by monetary interests and not primarily by the drive to create and innovate.

There are also strong arguments in favor of the abolition of the system of IPR protection.

- The system makes access too expensive and thus prohibitive for the world's majority.
- It stifles creativity because of its concentration on a limited number of star cultural producers. Once the IPR system has gone, there will be space for a greater number and variety of creative artists.
- It poses a serious threat to the public domain. Increasingly freely available cultural products (which are in the public domain, meaning there are no longer copyrights claims against users, as in the case of works by Shakespeare or Mozart) are stored in digital format and deposited in electronic databanks. Such databank collections are entitled to copyright protection; as a result, public access is restricted.
- A system that legally recognizes the individual appropriation of creative work is a fairly recent Western invention. It does not suit the traditions of many other parts of the world, where intellectual and artistic achievement is primarily seen as a collective effort.

Because the likelihood of an abolition of the system of IPR protection is slim indeed, given the enormous interests and powerful actors in the game, the international community should at least try to perceive of intellectual property rights as basic human rights.

Intellectual property rights are recognized as human rights in Article 27:2 of the Universal Declaration of Human Rights. This should shape the political framework for all parties involved—producers, distributors, artists, and consumers. If this were done, the context for the protection of intellectual property rights would be made up of: the right to full participation in cultural life for everyone, the right of affordable access to information for everyone, the recognition of moral rights of cultural producers, the rights of creative artists, the diversity of cultural production, and the protection of the public domain.

Because human rights always imply responsibilities, it would make sense to follow Larry Lessig's 1998 proposal to add to copyright a copyduty. As he wrote, "We may well see the day when our students are taught not of 'copyright' but of 'copyduty'—the legal duty of copyright holders to assure public access."

A human rights-based international agreement on intellectual property rights would recognize the needs of all people, common rights (TRIPS recognizes in its Preamble IPRs only as private rights), the sharing of benefits. Its primary purpose would be societal rather than commercial, and intellectual property rights would be seen as freedom rights more than restrictive proprietary rights. In the initial conception of protection of intellectual property as a human right, the restriction on the use of such property was seen as only temporary. This monopolization was seen as socially acceptable because the product would be returned to the public domain. Current efforts to extend the duration of copyright protection point in the direction of an almost unlimited restriction. A good example provides the so-called Mickey Mouse Protection Act (Lawrence Lessig). Every time the rights to Disney studio contents (such as Mickey Mouse) are about to expire, the U.S. Congress extends these rights. In 1998, the Disney company mobilized an effective campaign to lobby for the adoption of the Copyright Extension Act. The bill provides that exclusive rights of corporations to their copyrighted properties would be for 95 years instead of the 75 years under present legislation. Copyrights held by individuals are extended from 50 to 70 years after the death of the author. Under the present law, the copyright protection on Mickey Mouse would end in 2003, on Goofy in 2007, and on Donald Duck in 2009. At that point in time, they would enter the public domain. Opponents of the Act (among them Nobel Prize laureates Milton Friedman and Kenneth Arrow, and organizations such as the Free Software Foundation) protested that the extension was not in the public interest. On January 15, 2003, the U.S. Supreme Court rejected their arguments and declared the extension legally admissible.

A human rights approach would give full meaning to the so-called fair use doctrine. In a general sense, fair use, which is an important provision in U.S. copyright law, claims that the use of a copyrighted work for purposes like criticism, comment, news reporting, teaching, or research should not be considered an infringement of copyright protection.

The fair use doctrine is under serious threat through the use of advanced technologies, which allow rights holders the control over access by third parties of works in digital form. The use of protective technologies (such as encryption, copy protection codes) strengthens the monopoly control of IPR owners. Because consumers are likely to develop and apply circumvention technologies to undermine this control, the U.S. administration and U.S. motion picture industry have effectively lobbied the WIPO (World Intellectual Property Organization) to incorporate in the 1996 WIPO[2] Copyright Treaty the following Article 13:

[2]World Intellectual Property Organization

> Contracting Parties shall provide legal protection and effective legal remedies against the circumvention of effective technological measures that are used by authors in connection with the exercise of their rights under this Treaty or the Berne Convention and that restricts acts, in respect of their works, which are not authorized by the authors concerned or permitted by law.

In the United States, this provision was enacted in the 1998 Digital Millennium Copyright Act (DMCA), which went much further than the WIPO agreement. The DMCA prohibits the manufacture, sale, or import of technologies that can be used to circumvent protective technologies. This could make it impossible for people who buy perfectly legal items to make extra copies for private use (e.g., the extra CD or DVD in the car or second home). It may also become impossible to play a copyrighted item—legally acquired—on different platforms (not your CD player, but your PC).

The DeCSS case demonstrates where this could lead to. In 1999, Norwegian teenager, Jon Johansen, was arrested on the accusation of creating a circumvention technology to crack the protection code for DVDs. Contrary to most media publicity, cracking the DVD encryption was not his individual effort, but the effort of the MoRE group that authored DeCSS. This is a software application to decrypt DVD movies that can be used among others to play DVDs on Linux-operated computers. When the magazine *Computer 2600* reported about this (and offered a link to the program), the publisher was successfully sued by the Motion Picture Association of America. In 2003, a Norwegian court declared Jon Johansen not guilty.

Because the erosion of the fair use principle has far-reaching implications for people's access to culture, information, and knowledge, the international community should be challenged to issue a strong statement on the need to protect the public dimension of intellectual property rights. The author André Gide articulated the human rights dimension of intellectual property rights aptly with the sentence, "Everything belongs to he who makes good use of it."

THE RIGHT TO USE ONE'S LANGUAGE IN PRIVATE AND PUBLIC

This cultural right recognizes that linguistic rights are a critical part of cultural rights. The language we speak and, in particular, our mother tongue is a crucial part of who we are as individual persons. For a minority group, the loss of language means that the existence of the group is under threat—because this leads to assimilation with the group whose language one speaks.

The most far-reaching Article in (binding) human rights law granting linguistic rights is Article 27 of the International Covenant on Civil and Political Rights (1966): "In those states in which ethnic, religious or linguistic minorities exist, persons belonging to such minorities shall not be denied the right, in community with other members of their group, to enjoy their own culture, to profess and practice their own religion, or to use their own language."

Initially this article was seen as referring to individuals and not to collectives, which did not do much good to immigrant communities that were not seen as minorities. This changed with an interpretation of the article provided in a General Comment on Article 27 adopted by the UN Human Rights Committee on April 6, 1994. The Committee sees the article as offering protection to all individuals on the State's territory or under its jurisdiction, meaning also to immigrants and refugees.

The UN Draft Universal Declaration on Rights of Indigenous Peoples formulates language rights strongly and explicitly and requires the state to allocate resources. Yet the fate of the Draft is still unsure—the latest version was completed July 25-29, 1994, and forwarded to the UN Sub-Commission on Prevention of Discrimination and Protection of Minorities, which in its turn submitted it to the UN Commission on Human Rights for discussion in February 1995. Work on it is on going, and major changes can still be expected. There is some suspicion that indigenous peoples may be left without adequate influence on them.

In connection with the recognition of their linguistic human rights, the Draft Declaration also provides in Article17 that indigenous people "have the right to equal access to all forms of non-indigenous media." In addition, "States shall take effective measures to ensure that State-owned media duly reflect indigenous cultural diversity."

A World Conference on Linguistic Rights was held in Barcelona in June 1996. It was organized by the International PEN Club and a European Union-funded center for linguistic legislation based in Catalonia. A draft Universal Declaration of Linguistic Rights was approved, and UNESCO submitted the Declaration to national governments for endorsement and refined the text in collaboration with relevant associations. The text is a comprehensive document covering conceptual clarification, rights in public administration, education and the media, culture, and the socioeconomic sphere.

Although the document stresses the rights of what it calls linguistic communities (roughly corresponding to territorial minorities) to their mother tongue, and to proficiency in an official language, it is of little help to nonterritorial and immigrant minorities.

The UNESCO Declaration on Cultural Diversity has some references, but does not highlight the language issue. In Article 5, it provides that "All persons have therefore the right to express themselves and to create and disseminate their work in the language of their choice, and particularly in their mother tongue. . . ." In the Action Plan, Item 5 proposes "Safeguarding the linguistic heritage of humanity and giving support to expression, creation and dissemination in the greatest possible number of languages," and Item 6 states "Encouraging linguistic diversity—while respecting the mother tongue—at all levels of education, wherever possible, and fostering the learning of several languages from the youngest age." Item 10 recommends "Promoting linguistic diversity in cyberspace. . . ."

SHARING BENEFITS FROM SCIENCE AND TECHNOLOGY

The right of access to technology is provided in Article 27.1 of the Universal Declaration of Human Rights, where it is stated that "Everyone has the right to . . . share in scientific advancement and its benefits." This right is inspired by the basic moral principle of equality and the notion that science and technology belong to the common heritage of humankind.

Up until 1968, there was no serious debate in the international community about the relation between scientific and technological development and the protection of human rights. At the Teheran International Conference on Human Rights (1968), the following statement was adopted: "While recent scientific discoveries and technological advances have opened vast prospects for economic, social and cultural progress, such developments may nevertheless endanger rights and freedoms of individuals and will require continuing attention." The Conference recommended in Resolution XI "that the organizations of the United Nations family should undertake a study of the problems with respect to human rights arising from developments in science and technology." The UN General Assembly followed this recommendation and asked the Secretary General (UNGA res. 2450 of December 19, 1968) to focus in this study particularly on:

> (a) Respect for the privacy of individuals and the integrity and sovereignty of nations in the light of advances in recording and other technologies; (b) Protection of the human personality and its physical and intellectual integrity, in the light of advances in biology, medicine and biochemistry; (c) Uses of electronics which may affect the rights of persons and the limits which should be put in such uses in a democratic society; (d) More generally, the balance which should be established between scientific and technological progress and the intellectual, spiritual, cultural and moral advancement of humanity.

On the basis of this study and various related reports, the Commission on Human Rights gave considerable attention to the issue in its 27th session in 1971 and focused particularly on;

> (a) Protection of human rights in the economic, social and cultural fields in accordance with the structure and resources of States and the scientific and technological level they have reached, as well as protection of the right to work in conditions of the automation and mechanization of production; (b) The use of scientific and technological developments to foster respect for human rights and the legitimate interests of other peoples and respect for generally recognized moral standards and standards of international law; (c) Prevention of the use of scientific and technological achievements to restrict fundamental democratic rights and freedoms.

In the years 1971 to 1976, a series of reports was produced dealing with the problems of privacy protection, use of observation satellites, automation, procedures of prenatal diagnosis, introduction of chemicals into food production, deterioration of the environment, and the destructive power of modern weapons systems.

In resolution 3062B (December 18, 1972) the General Assembly asked the Commission on Human Rights to look at the possibility of an international legal instrument that would address the issue of strengthening human rights in the light of scientific and technological developments. In 1973, the General Assembly (UNGA res. 3150) called on States to further international cooperation to ensure that scientific and technological developments are used to strengthen peace and security, the realization of people's right to self-determination, and respect for national sovereignty, and for the purpose of economic and social development. The Secretary General was invited to report on these matters. This report (presented in 1975) addressed the harmful effect of automation and mechanization on the right to work; the harmful effect of scientific and technological developments on the right to adequate food; and problems of equality of treatment in relation to the impact of scientific and technological development on the right to health. The report also analyzed the deterioration of the environment, the problem of the population explosion, and the special problem of the impact of atomic radiation on public health. Then on November 10, 1975, the General Assembly resolved to adopt the Declaration on the Use of Scientific and Technological Progress in the Interests of Peace and for the Benefit of Mankind (UNGA res. 3384).

The key principles of the Declaration are:

- International cooperation to ensure that the results of science and technology developments are used to strengthen international peace and security promote economic and social development, and realize human rights and freedoms.
- Measures to ensure that science and technology developments satisfy the material and spiritual needs of all people.
- A commitment by States to refrain from the use of science and technology developments to violate the sovereignty and territorial integrity of other States, interfere in their internal affairs, wage aggressive wars, suppress liberation movements, or pursue policies of racial discrimination.
- International cooperation to strengthen and develop the scientific and technological capacity of developing countries.
- Measures to extend the benefits of science and technology developments to all strata of the population and protect them against all possible harmful effects.
- Measures to ensure that the use of science and technology developments promotes the realization of human rights.
- Measures to prevent the use of science and technology development to the detriment of human rights.
- Action to ensure compliance with legislation, which guarantees human rights in the conditions of science and technology developments.

In September 1975, a meeting of experts took place in Geneva that recommended the establishment of an international mechanism for the assessment of new technologies from the point of view of human rights. This form of technology assessment would include the evaluation of possible side effects and long-range effects of technological innovations and would weigh the advantages of such innovations against disadvantages. The General Assembly did not act on this recommendation and merely asked the Commission on Human Rights to follow the implementation of the Declaration with special attention. Since 1982, the Secretary General reports on the implementation of the provisions of the Declaration to the General Assembly. Over the following years, the General Assembly and the Commission on Human rights adopted a series of resolutions that by and large endorse the principles of the Declaration.

Among them is a resolution (1986/9) adopted by the Commission on Human Rights on "Use of Scientific and Technological Development for the Promotion and Protection of Human Rights and Fundamental Freedoms." The Resolution calls on States "to make every effort to utilize the benefits of scientific and technological developments for the promotion and protection of human rights and fundamental freedoms."

Over the years, the UN agency UNESCO has been particularly concerned with the human and cultural implications of science and technology developments. In a series of meetings of experts, UNESCO addressed problems related to the effects of science and technology on local cultures. In 1982, a seminar was convened by UNESCO in Trieste (under the auspices of the International Institute for the Study of Human Rights) to study the consequences of science and technology developments, particularly in the fields of informatics, telematics, and genetic manipulation, for human rights. The principles set forth in the UDHR, Articles 23 and 26, and the Convention against Discrimination in Education, (1960), as well as provisions in the two main human rights covenants and the Convention on the Elimination of All Forms of Discrimination against Women (1979), are part of the preamble preceding the 1989 UNESCO Convention on Technical and Vocational Education (which entered into force in 1991). The Convention provides for the right to equal access to technical education and pays special attention to the needs of disadvantaged groups.

PARTICIPATION IN TECHNOLOGY CHOICE

The idea of human rights has to extend to the social institutions (the institutional arrangements) that would facilitate the realization of fundamental standards. Human rights cannot be realized without involving citizens in the decision-making processes about the spheres in which these rights are to be achieved. This moves the democratic process beyond the political sphere and extends the requirement of participatory institutional arrangements to other social domains. The human right to democratic participation claims that technology choices should also be subject to democratic control. This is particularly important in the light of the fact that current political processes tend to delegate important areas of social life to private rather than public control and accountability. Increasingly large volumes of social activity are withdrawn from public accountability, democratic control, and participation of citizens in decision making.

The implication of the human rights regime is that people have the right to participate in public decision making on the choice, development, and application of information and communication technology. This means that there should be ample scope for public participation in the formulation and implementation of public technology policies and the adoption of technical innovations, which have significant human rights implications. From a human rights perspective, broad public deliberation on the costs and benefits of the artificial evolution of posthuman intelligence standards is highly desirable.

SCIENCE AND TECHNOLOGY REPORTING FROM A HUMAN RIGHTS PERSPECTIVE

For journalists there is a need to understand the human rights aspects involved in reproductive technology, the transplantation of organs and tissues, the possibilities of genetic manipulation, questions concerning the mentally ill and euthanasia, exploring modalities of artificial intelligence, developments in nanotechnology and robotics, and the combination of these various technologies. The assessment of new technologies from the point of view of human rights includes the evaluation of possible side effects and long-range effects of technological innovations, and it weighs the advantages of innovations against disadvantages. Human rights-based assessments of science and technology should be made on the basis of the considered opinions of experts and laymen representing the interests of all people as well as future generations.

THE HUMAN RIGHTS MANDATE OF THE ACADEMIC COMMUNITY

With regard to the general duty under international law for everyone to respect and promote human rights, one could argue for a specific professional responsibility for members of the academic community. At the core of the scientific attitude is the demand of accountability for choices made in the scientific enterprise. Whenever human rights abuses take place, there is no neutral ground for scientists. They are either accomplice (by intent or default) or opponent. After the bombing of Hiroshima and Nagasaki, scientists cannot escape from the cui bono question (i.e., whose interests are served by scientific progress?). This is particularly important because scientific achievements can be used to deprive individuals and peoples of their human rights and fundamental freedoms. The development and use of science can contribute to or interfere with the enjoyment of human rights. Against the option of compliant silence, scientists have the opportunity to raise a critical voice. The fact that the scientific community is perceived as representing a respectful moral authority adds to its responsibility.

> In a world increasingly shaped by the omnipresent communication media, I believe that scientists must make themselves heard, on pain of becoming accomplices to the perpetuation of morally unacceptable situations . . . it is also vital that they should speak out in time. . . . Scientists in the last analysis have at their command no more than the force of the word, and they

> should not hesitate to make their voices heard, soberly and rigorously in keeping with the spirit of the scientific enterprise but strongly and courageously as the quest for truth demands. (Address by the UNESCO Director General Federico Mayor to the Annual Conference of the American Association for the Advancement of Science, Chicago, February 7, 1992)

It is also part of the professional ethics of the scientist to realize that the independent search for clarification and understanding is only possible if human rights and freedoms in the conditions of scientific developments are guaranteed.

The media and communication research community has historically been linked—especially through the International Association for Media and Communication Research (formerly known as the International Association for Mass Communication Research [IAMCR], established in 1957)—with a crucial human rights concern of the international community: the protection of the freedom of expression and opinion. The first IAMCR president, Fernand Terrou (the French delegate to the UN conference on freedom of information in 1948), and the third president, Jacques Bourquin, were actively involved in the drafting of Article 19 of the Universal Declaration of Human Rights in 1948. Both made important contributions to the definition and later codification of the international right to freedom of information. In the early development of the Association, the concept of the freedom of information was a crucial moving force despite ideological differences.

As Santoro (1992) documented in his extensive study of the early history of the Association, the concept of freedom of information became especially prominent under the presidency of Jacques Bourquin. During the first General Assembly of the IAMCR at Milan in 1959, President Terrou addressed the need to review the basic right to freedom of information. He pointed to the risk of proclaiming that the freedom of information is exclusively based on a natural individual right without taking into account the conditions under which this right should be exercised. He argued that this could create a gap between basic principles and social reality, resulting in the erosion of the principles.

President Terrou also stressed the need to harmonize legislation on the freedom of information. President Bourquin saw it as his first task to contribute to the internationalization of the debate on the freedom of information.

In a modest way, throughout the history of the IAMCR there has been a series of situations in which members of the community made a contribution to the promotion of basic rights and freedoms. This can be illustrated by the input into the debates of the UN Committee on Freedom of Information of the Commission on Human Rights, the work done by the UNESCO expert panel, the submissions to the MacBride commission, and the contributions for the UNESCO World Communication report.

The VIIth General Assembly of the International Association for Mass Communication Research, convened in Constance from September 1-4, 1970, expressed the sympathy of its members to journalist victims of their duty and to those who are accomplishing dangerous missions to inform the public opinion. The Assembly also extended its gratitude to the organizations and authorities that give their attention to this situation and asked the United Nations:

> to undertake without delay a new codification of the rights and duties of journalists working in foreign countries and, in general, to those who have to carry on their offices under exceptional conditions, to follow, to this end, the propositions elaborated by the professional organizations concerned; and to take the necessary steps so that said regulations be carried out with efficacity, as only this application can ensure the information of worldwide opinion, which is the condition for the respect of the principles of the Charter.

The General Assembly held at Leicester in 1976 passed two resolutions in connection with human rights concerns. Resolution 1 stressed the need to establish international communication policies in the service of democratic development, particularly in the Third World; confirmed the support for UNESCO's concern with "the universal right to communicate" and its promotion of world communication policies as a means to overcome underdevelopment and undemocratic practices; and condemned those institutions and nations with vested interests that resulted in obstacles being placed in the way of freedom of communication and communication research.

Resolution 2 recommended that the executive board of the IAMCR should: "take action in order to foster the study of measures allowing a real and genuine right to communicate useful and trustworthy information between the various parts of the world, including the socalled Third World." In 1992, the Association took active part in the NGO contributions to the Conference on Security and Cooperation held in Helsinki, Finland. The World Press Freedom Committee (WPFC) proposed to this meeting that it should endorse a Charter for a Free Press. This Charter found its origins at the 1987 Voices of Freedom conference on problems of censorship in London (January 16–18). This conference was a joint initiative of the WPFC with the International Federation of Newspaper Publishers (FIEJ), the International Press Institute (IPI), the Inter American Press Association (IAPA), North American National Broadcasters Association, and the International Federation of the Periodical Press. The principles of the Charter were endorsed in a series of CSCE related meetings such as the 1989 London Information Forum, the CSCE Parallel Round Table on Media Issues in Moscow in September 1991, and the CSCE seminar on democratic institutions at Oslo in November 1991. The International Federation of Journalists was asked to support the adoption of the

Charter by the CSCE Helsinki meeting in 1992. In its response to this request, the IFJ Bureau wrote,

> The Bureau believes that although the Charter contains some general points with which we can certainly agree, it does not fully represent the views of working journalists, it is not sufficiently up to date, and it fails to address some practical and serious problems facing the emerging independent media within the CSCE region. . . . The Bureau noted that the primary groups supporting the WPFC in the January 1978 meeting from which the Charter is drawn were publishers and media employer organisations. . . . Of course, the IFJ does not oppose the World Press Freedom Committee Charter, but as it stands we feel strongly that it needs accompanying text which will provide, with greater clarity, respect for the rights and independence of working journalists. The Bureau believes that additional material drawing on the Windhoek Declaration which was adopted by the UNESCO General Conference in November 1991, gives a more balanced approach, particularly on the question of journalistic independence from either political or commercial pressure.

The IFJ Bureau, in a letter to all member unions, asked their support for the submission of a recommendation on press freedom to the CSCE delegates in Helsinki. This recommendation stressed that an independent press should be free from governmental, political, or economic control. "By a pluralistic press, we mean the end of monopolies of any kind and the existence of the greatest possible number of newspapers, magazines and periodicals reflecting the widest possible range of opinion within the community." On the occasion of International Press Freedom Day (May 3, 1992), the Director General of UNESCO issued a declaration in which he expressed his hope that the CSCE in Helsinki would adopt the WPFC Charter for a Free Press. In his address to the CSCE on May 13, 1992, the Director General reiterated his hope that the CSCE would adopt the Charter.

In a statement to the delegates on behalf of the WPFC, Leonard Marks referred to the UNESCO support as he said, "We are very pleased that UNESCO is helping show the way. The Director General of UNESCO, Federico Mayor, should be congratulated for his leadership and vision" (May 13, 1992). The Helsinki delegates were invited to add their names to the "Honor Roll of Freedom" by endorsing the Charter. The Helsinki meeting did not adopt the Charter and referred the media matter to a later CSCE seminar.

At the time of the Helsinki summit, some nongovernmental organizations (among them the IAMCR) had been actively lobbying to persuade the delegates that on such essential matters as freedom of information there should be a wide consultation with pertinent nongovernmental organizations before policy positions were formally adopted. In a letter to the UNESCO Director General, IAMCR President Hamelink noted "with grave concern the reference to the Charter for a Free Press" in the Declaration on the occasion of International Press Freedom Day. The IAMCR stressed the need for consultation with the NGO community in such delicate matters as freedom of information. This position was also clearly reflected in a set of recommendations from an IAMCR expert seminar held in April 1992 at Tampere and Helsinki. These recommendations were forwarded during a press conference to CSCE delegates. In June 1993, the UN World Conference on Human Rights took place. To that conference, the IAMCR has contributed a statement that resulted from an expert meeting held in Bratislava on the eve of the diplomatic conference. This seminar, made possible by the IAMCR sections on Law and International Communication, produced the Bratislava declaration on the Right to Communicate that as part of the NGO forum was fed into the diplomatic conference. The Bratislava Declaration recommended the thorough identification and review of the existing catalogue of communication and information provisions in international law to preserve what has proved successful, but also to examine ways to improve these protections. It also proposed that Article 19 of the Universal Declaration of Human Rights, as qualified by Article 29 of the UDHR, and Articles 19 and 20 of the International Covenant on Civil and Political Rights, Article 10 of the European Convention on Human Rights and Fundamental Freedoms, and all similar documents, be reviewed to affirm and strengthen the Right to Communicate as an inalienable right of individuals and peoples and as a fundamental instrument in the democratization of society. The Declaration also recommended the acceptance of the First Optional Protocol to the International Covenant on Civil and Political Rights, allowing individual complaints of violations of the Covenant. It supported the establishment of a Special Rapporteur on freedom of expression. In the independent daily newspaper of the World Conference "Terra Viva," IAMCR President Hamelink wrote that the work of the Special Rapporteur should be assisted by the pertinent non-governmental organizations in the field of communication and information. He also said to expect that IAMCR would work toward the realization of these recommendations (during and beyond Vienna) in full cooperation with various UN agencies, the Council of Europe, and NGOs such as Article XIX.

In a document submitted to one of the Preparatory Conferences for Vienna, in Geneva in April 1993, the IAMCR president urged the World Conference to seriously address the need for a robust human rights regime in the field of information provision. The supporting argument for this position referred among other considerations to the following. The world political arena has failed to establish a solid human rights regime in the field of information provision. Human rights basically mean that all people matter. If people would indeed matter in the field of information provision, it would be a fair expectation that the governing arrangements in this field should reflect people's needs and interests. However, most arrangements (internationally, regionally, or nationally) that govern the provision of information do not reflect the interests of their largest client community: the world's people. Communication politics everywhere operate as if people did not matter. They are addressed as consumers, markets, and constituencies, but seldom as citizens. The document also emphasized the need to improve the capacity of the information providers to contribute to the protection and promotion of human rights. Here the rationale was that on both the national and international levels, the effectiveness of human rights enforcement is directly related to the quality of information provision about human rights standards and procedures. The political will required for a successful enforcement of human rights needs the mobilization of public opinion. This begins with the provision of information to people. To perform the task of information providers adequately, the information professionals need to be fully informed and sufficiently skilled.

The Bratislava exercise was part of the policy decision by the IAMCR General Assembly 1992 (in Brazil) that the Association should be more engaged in debate and analysis on the issue of the contribution of communication and media research to public life. In line with this decision, the IAMCR continued to be actively involved with the CSCE process. For example, for the CSCE Free Media seminar in Warsaw in November 1993, a joint statement was prepared together with the International Federation of Journalists and Article XIX. The General Assembly in 1994 at Seoul, South Korea, debated a resolution on the fatwa against S. Rushdie and other authors, and it decided almost unanimously to adopt the condemnation of religious censorship.

At Portoroz (Slovenia) in 1995, the Association decided to establish a Human Rights Committee. Since 1995, the Association has developed no significant activity in the field of human rights.

ENFORCEMENT OF CULTURAL RIGHTS

A special problem with the enforcement of economic, social, and cultural rights is the standard by which their implementation is measured. Article 2.1 of the ICESCR requires State Parties "to take steps, individually and through international assistance and co-operation, especially economic and technical, to the maximum of its available resources, with a view to achieving progressively the full realization of the rights recognized in the present Covenant." This standard of progressive realization is much more complicated to monitor and less compelling than the requirements the International Covenant on Civil and Political Rights imposes on State Parties in Article 2.1: "Each State Party to the present Covenant undertakes to respect and ensure to all individuals within its territory and subject to its jurisdiction the rights recognized in the present Covenant."

The measurement of progressive realization demands the collection of comparative, statistical data over time and is complicated by the notion of "to the maximum of available resources." In recent discussions on this issue, a shift from this approach to a violations approach has been argued.

Against the argument that cultural rights are not justiciable (mainly defended by Western governments), a growing number of NGOs put pressure on the UN to adopt an Optional Protocol that would provide an individual right to complain and seek redress.

THE ISSUE OF JUSTICIABILITY

This issue refers to the question of whether cultural rights are legally enforceable and can be made subject to normal court proceedings. The opponents of justiciability of cultural rights often use the argument that civil and political rights, on the one hand, and social, economic, and cultural rights, on the other hand, are fundamentally different. The argument suggests that civil and political rights can be immediately implemented without recourse to material resources, whereas the economic, social, and cultural rights would need such resources and therefore can only be progressively realized.

However, it can be argued that all human rights require legal protection against forms of (public and private) interference as well as constructive social programs for their realization and therefore require material resources. Moreover, to justiciability, usually the following criteria are applied:

1. A legal rule is being violated.
2. There is a victim/there are victims of the violation.
3. There is a perpetrator/there are perpetrators.
4. Legal redress is a possible option: there are legal provisions in such fields as education and health, which can be routinely adjudicated in court proceedings.

These criteria apply to situations in which cultural rights are violated, and one must therefore conclude that cultural rights are indeed justiciable.

To strengthen the enforcement of cultural rights, a first major step would be the establishment of an Independent Ombuds Office for Cultural Rights. The inspiration for such an Office comes largely from a recommendation made by the UNESCO World Commission on Culture and Development chaired by Javier Pérez de Cuéllar in its 1995 report, "Our Creative Diversity." The Commission recommended the drawing of an International Code of Conduct on Culture and, under the auspices of the UN International Law Commission, the setting up of an "International Office of the Ombudsperson for Cultural Rights" (World Commission, 1995). The Commission stated,

> Such an independent, free-standing entity could hear pleas from aggrieved or oppressed individuals or groups, act on their behalf and mediate with governments for the peaceful settlement of disputes. It could fully investigate and document cases, encourage a dialogue between parties and suggest a process of arbitration and negotiated settlement leading to the effective redress of wrongs, including, wherever appropriate, recommendations for legal or legislative remedies as well as compensatory damages. (p. 283)

For the Ombuds Office to be effective, independence from both governmental and business interests as well as adequate financing would have to be secured, and both are difficult to achieve. Obviously an office that operates from a nongovernmental background would have few possibilities for effective remedies in the sense of compensation or other sanctions. Yet the question is whether this is the most important feature. Amnesty International cannot hand out prison sentences to those who violate human rights. However, its politics of shame is certainly effective in providing a good deal of protection for victims of human rights violations. Ideally, one would like to see the establishment of an institution that is fully independent, receiving funding from both governments and industries, and developing a strong moral authority on the basis of its expertise, track record, and quality of the people and organizations that form its constituency.

The Ombuds Office would ideally be supported by a global effort of a nongovernmental organization for the protection of cultural rights. Therefore, the proposal made by human rights expert Peter Baehr (1999) deserves wide support:

> The lack of large, active organizations in the field of economic and social rights, that generate reliable information, is a serious deficiency. If a complaints procedure on economic, social and cultural rights were to be adopted, this would call for an active role by NGOs, either by introducing complaints themselves or by providing relevant information. The establishment of an Amnesty International for economic, social and cultural rights is urgently needed. (p. 39)

SUGGESTIONS FOR DISCUSSION

Discuss the advantages and disadvantages of a world in which we all speak English (or at least various forms of English).

Discuss the impact of cultural globalisation on cultural rights.

Discuss the risk of cultural ghettoization; explore how a balance can be struck in your society between cultural rights for ethnic minorities and social cohesion.

Discuss the desirability of an Amnesty International for cultural rights.

Discuss whether technology should be common heritage or private property.

Discuss modes of people's participation in technology choice. What do you do if people make stupid choices?

5

Human Rights in the Information Society

THE INFORMATION SOCIETY?

It has become common practice to describe modern society as *information society*. This concept refers in a general sense to increases in available volumes of information, the significance of information processing in evermore societal domains, and the fact that information technology provides a basic infrastructure on which societies become increasingly dependent.

The concept is popular, and in 2003 a UN World Summit was dedicated to the Information Society (World Summit on the Information Society, December 2003 in Geneva). Yet the concept is also flawed and contested. Its meaning has been seriously challenged, and it has even been suggested in academic literature that the notion bears no relation to current social realities. For some observers, the reference to *society* raises the good old sociological questions of power, profit, and participation: Who controls the information society? Who benefits from it? Who takes part in it? For others it is questionable whether one can adequately describe societies with one encompassing variable; even if this were possible, it can be questioned whether information is a more precise category than money, crime, or aggression. In any case, it should be noted that societies pursue different paths of development; if one insists on the reference to information, the plural notion of *information societies* should be used. The *information society* means different things to different people: more telephones, more money, more regulation, or more empowerment. For all participants in the debate, there is the feeling that important social and technical developments pose difficult questions and societies are struggling to find adequate answers.

There are undoubtedly informational developments in modern societies, and through interaction with other social developments these have an impact on how the future of such societies shape up in different ways dependent on different historical circumstances. This notion refers to the growing significance of information products (such as news, advertising, entertainment, scientific data, etc.) and information services (such as provided by the World Wide Web); to the increasing volumes of information that are generated, collected, stored, and made available; to the essential role of information technology as the backbone of many social services and as the engine of economic productivity; and to the input of information processing into transactions in trading and finance. The societal confrontation with informational developments occurs in different ways, at different levels, at different speeds, and in different historical contexts. Societies design their responses to these developments through policies, plans, and programs both as centrally steered initiatives and as decentralized activities on national and local levels. Most of these initiatives are driven by economic motives and are strongly technology-centric. The actors involved are both public institutions and private bodies, and increasingly they operate through public/private partnerships. Societies may respond to informational developments with both legal arrangements and self-regulatory agreements.

In much of the current literature, it is suggested in utopian scenarios that these developments have positive effects, whereas negative effects are highlighted in dystopian scenarios. In both cases, the analysts are driven by a deterministic perspective on social development: Technological innovations have a direct impact on social processes. There is no space for serious reflection on the myriad complex ways in which technology and society are dialectically interlinked. This is particularly serious since these informational developments often take place in the context of an uninhibited technological euphoria, propose political claims that are difficult to empirically substantiate, and ignore in their singular emphasis on information the more important social process of communication. Societies and informational developments interact with each other in many different ways. We can differentiate between the following four dimensions to these interactions.

There is a technological dimension to the interaction. Technology obviously plays a vital role in informational developments. The scope, volume, and impact of these developments is, to a large extent, shaped by technological innovations and the opportunities they create. The interaction is a process in which social forces and interests contribute to the shaping of technological innovations. With this dimension, issues are posed about the control over technology, the access to and benefit from technology, and the social risks that innovations and their applications entail.

There is also a cultural dimension to the interaction. The ways in which societies deal with the provision and processing of information are determined by cultural perspectives. Information contents are cultural products. Information is part of a society's cultural fabric. Among the important issues of this dimension are the sharing of knowledge and protection of cultural identity.

There is a sociopolitical dimension to the interaction. Information and information technologies have an impact on a society's development, progress, and political system. Among the important issues are freedom of political speech, protection against abusive speech, and information needs of societies.

There is an economic dimension to the interaction. Worldwide information markets have emerged. Economic interests are at stake in the protection of ownership claims to content. There are issues of corporate social responsibility and self-determination in economic development.

VISIONS WITHOUT CRITICAL ANALYSIS

In the context of a widespread technology euphoria, it is quite common to find in the context of information society debates the following expectations. Through harnessing the potential of information and communication technologies, new and better responses to poverty reduction, equity, and social justice can be found. Knowledge and information constitute one of the fundamental sources of well-being and progress. There is great untapped potential of ICT to improve productivity and quality of life. The benefits of the information society should extend to all and should be development-oriented. In building an information society, it should be ensured that women can equally benefit from the increased use of ICTs for empowerment and fully participate in shaping political, economic, and social development. The information society should be oriented toward eliminating existing socioeconomic differences in our societies.

All the buzzwords from past decades are back: *democracy*, *diversity*, *capacity*, *participation*, *gender*, *bridging the gap*. Such inspirational language! However, the nagging question is, why such aspirations have so far not been taken seriously by the international community. Why has the international community been unwilling—in past decades—to engage in real efforts to implement what it preaches?

This is all the more problematic because the socioeconomic and political conditions under which these claims should become reality are not at all encouraging. As a matter of fact, they are less amenable to the solution of the digital divide through the development of telecom infrastructures or the access to knowledge than the conditions that prevailed during the time of the earlier UN efforts. By way of illustration, one can cite the case of global and equitable access to knowledge. This laudable proposition is in the early 21st century seriously hampered by the emergence of a strict regime for the protection of intellectual property rights in recent WTO negotiations.

Before making all these gratuitous statements on the potential of the information society, information and communication technologies, and knowledge, it would be wise to analyze why at present the world is not an inclusive community, why there is no sustainable development, why there is no global transparent and accountable governance, why citizens can not participate on an equal footing in their societies. There is much discussion on governance of the information society. Again the rhetoric sounds good. *Multistakeholder*, *participatory*, *democratic*, and *transparent* are the buzzwords. Yet why would global governance of the information society have all the characteristics that other domains of such governance do not have? Why would governments that have so easily used notions like the *war on terrorism* to abuse people's fundamental civil and political rights be trusted to want such *people-centered* governance? Why would major global corporations suddenly yearn for greater transparency to the public and more accountability?

The aspiration to solve the digital divide offers a good illustration of a vision without analysis. There is a tendency to treat this issue mainly as a matter of the globally skewed distribution of information and communication resources. This isolates the digital divide from the broader problem of the development divide. In reality the digital divide is not more than one of the many manifestations of the unequal allocation of both material and immaterial resources in the world, both between and within societies.

If this core problem is not resolved—and this needs the political will that is presently not present in the international community—solemn debates on the digital divide are conveniently distracting smoke-screens.

The most fashionable political claim refers to the inclusive and democratic nature of the information society. Although many governments would seem to prefer intergovernmental arrangements for future global governance, other stakeholders propose different approaches. For example, there is the proposal for a tripartite approach. In this type of governance representatives from governments, the private sector, and civil society would come together in policymaking forums. This would by and large follow the example of trilateral negotiations as applied by the International Labour Organization (ILO). The decision-making labor conferences are attended by delegations from governments, employers, and employees. This can be defended with the argument that all three parties have considerable interests at stake with regard to the outcome of international negotiations. On a more fundamental, political level, however, there is a serious problem. The involvement of citizens in political decision making is obvious. The whole democratic system is built around the fundamental interests of citizens. The involvement of citizens' elected representatives is also logical whenever direct democracy is practically not feasible. However, what could be the argument to involve the private sector? There are enough arguments of convenience one could think of, but are there any fundamental arguments? It would seem almost impossible to argue for a legitimate claim by private business actors to political participation.

The choice for a bilateral global governance system would be easier to defend. This system implies that the currently prevailing arrangement by which formal negotiations are reserved for governments only develops into a form of governance that reflects the system of national parliamentary democracies. Following the democratic tradition, the most legitimate form would be a bilateral, parliamentary type arrangement. The typical parliamentary structure is made up by a government that executes programs and decisions in the public realm and a parliament that controls executive power. The parliament stands for such basic democratic features as accountability, transparency, and social participation. On the world level there is at present a type of government in the form of the General Assembly of the United Nations: the combined national Member-States represented by their diplomatic delegates. There is however no controlling power on behalf of the international public interest. Therefore, ideally in the long run a Parliamentary Assembly (PA) should be created to complement the General Assembly. The members of this PA would be nationally elected, much like the members of the European Parliament, currently the only international body that is democratically elected. The construction of a global parliamentary system would offer the business community sufficient means to defend their cause either through the channels of political lobbying or through direct participation in the PA whenever members from business communities were elected to this body.

THE OBSTACLES

Informational developments raise urgent human rights concerns, and critical analysis should focus on the obstacles that obstruct the world community's constructive engagement with these concerns. In addition to the weakness of the formal enforcement mechanisms, which was discussed in chapter 1, the following contextual conditions impede an effective implementation of human rights standards:

a. The widespread lack of knowledge across the world about the existence of human rights. There are many commendable efforts in the field of human rights education, but at present the commitment of resources to such efforts is insufficient.

b. The current worldwide suspension of fundamental human rights under the guise of the war on terrorism or the protection of national security.

c. The lack of political will to commit adequate resources to the realization of human rights.

d. The widening development divide between and within societies and the common refusal of policymakers to see the digital divide and its resolution as part of the lack of political will to resolve the wider problem.

e. The existing and expanding international regime for the protection of intellectual property rights that hampers equitable access to information and knowledge.

f. The trend to subject cultural goods and services to the rules of the WTO regime and to refuse exemption of culture from international trade policies that threaten cultural diversity.

g. The appropriation of much of the world's technical knowledge under corporate ownership and the refusal by technology owners to agree on fair standards of international technology transfer.

h. The monopolized or oligopolized corporate control over the production and distribution of information-communication goods and services.

i. The worldwide proliferation of market-driven journalism, which underinforms, if not disinforms, audiences around the world about matters of public interest.

j. The limited perspective on human rights as mainly or even merely individual rights. This ignores that people communicate and engage in cultural practices as members of communities and hampers the development of indigenous sources of information and knowledge.

What is particularly worrisome in present debates on informational developments and human rights is the singular emphasis on information.

INFORMATION

Essential to the notion of informational developments is obviously information itself. Here we confront the problem that much thinking about information is based on a series of popular myths.

For example, more information is better than less information, more information creates more knowledge and understanding, open information flows contribute to the prevention of conflicts, more information means less uncertainty and more adequate choices, if people are properly informed they act accordingly, more information equals more power, and once people are better informed about each other they will understand each other and be less inclined to conflict. All of these are attractive assumptions, but none is necessarily true.

Most assumptions about the role and effects of information and knowledge are based on seriously flawed Pavlov-type cause-effect models. In such models information and knowledge are conceived of as key variables in social processes; depending on how they are manipulated, certain social effects occur. Social science research has taught us, however, that information and knowledge sharing do not occur in the linear mode of simple stimulus/response models that propose linear, causal relations between information/knowledge inputs and behavioral outputs. These processes are more complex, involve feedback mechanisms, and somewhere between the message and the receiver there are intervening black box variables that may create both predictable, expected and desirable as well as unpredictable, unexpected and undesirable effects.

An attractive line of thought proposes that once people are better informed about each other, they will know and understand each other better and be less inclined to conflict. However, deadly conflicts are usually not caused by a lack of information. In fact they may be based on adequate information that adversaries have about each other. As a matter of fact, one could equally well propound the view that social harmony is largely due to the degree of ignorance that actors have with regard to each other. Many societies maintain levels of stability because they employ rituals, customs, and conventions that enable their members to engage in social interactions without having detailed information about who they really are. There may indeed be conflict situations because adversaries have so much information about each others' aims and motives. There are situations in which more information is not better than less information. If we all had detailed information about other people with whom we live and work, the chance of raging civil war would be great.

The expectations about the power of information neglect that conflicts often address real points of contention and may be based on the antagonistic interests of fundamentally divergent political and economic systems. If disputes are about competing claims to scarce resources (as often is the case), it is unlikely that distorted or insufficient information is the crucial variable or that correct information could resolve the conflict.

It may even be that more information about the adversary leads to more conflict. During the cold war, the critical nuclear stability between the United States and the Soviet Union was maintained because both superpowers lacked information about the exact location of their nuclear submarines. This ignorance provided a powerful deterrent against a first strike. Therefore, it can be argued that a functional level of secrecy can be helpful in containing potential conflict.

Moreover, in situations of conflict, the problem is often the abundance of information rather than the dearth of it. The overload of messages may seriously impede rational decision making because the means through which humans cope with information (selective filtering, stereotyped perception, and simplistic structuring) may reinforce misperceptions and ambivalent interpretations. It is also highly questionable whether people will revise their opinions from earlier held opinions on the basis of new information. In reality, people tend to be unwilling to accept disconfirming information if this violates a fostered opinion they hold. People are rather insensitive as to whether the assumptions on which they base their judgments are sufficiently solid. They are usually overconfident that they are correct. Beliefs change slowly and are resistant to contradictory information (Hamelink, 1988).

A popular assumption claims that information equals power. However, information becomes a source of power only if the necessary infrastructure for its production, processing, storage, retrieval, and transportation is accessible, and when people have the skills to apply information to social practice and participate in social networks through which information can be used to further one's interests. The assumption proposes that if people were unable to exercise power, it was because they were ill informed and ignorant. However, too often people knew precisely what was wrong and unjust, and they were well informed about the misconduct of their rulers. Yet they did not act, and their information did not become a source of power because they lacked the material and strategic means for revolt.

It is also common to follow a core observation from the Constitution of UNESCO: War begins in the minds of men, and therefore the minds of men need to be influenced through the mass media. The implied suggestion is obviously that if the mass media can influence the minds of men in negative ways, the media can also—through positive messages—develop a culture of peace. However, the suggestion that war begins in the minds of men is misleading. Wars among members of the human species start with the material, physical fact of their bodies. The human life form is—like other life forms—constantly involved in a struggle for life. Inevitable components of that struggle are aggression, violence, and war. Greek philosopher Heraclitus called war the *father of all things*: It is the permanent human condition. Centuries later Emmanuel Levinas wrote that the human being is locked up into the state of war.

In the struggle for life, most animals are restrained by their instincts. The human being, however, has inadequate instincts and must hope that rational considerations put limits to the struggle. Because the human being fails so often in this effort, his or her competition and aggression tends to be exercised with a violence that knows little or no restraint.

Given this analysis, people's minds and hearts are obviously not irrelevant factors, but merely addressing mental variables is not likely to prevent or resolve conflicts that are about material, physical resources. The most lethal conflict of the 21st century is likely to be about drinking water, which is rapidly becoming a scarce resource. Information campaigns directed at people's minds and hearts will do little to make the conflict less violent.

Finally, the claim that more information is better than less information seems to be inspired by the assumption that information is benign. This does not take into account the human proclivity to use information in destructive ways. As human history demonstrates time and again, the more knowledge human beings acquire, the greater the destruction they cause. One dramatic illustration is the case of nuclear technology.

WHAT HAPPENED TO COMMUNICATION?

It is striking that in most of the preparatory documents and discussions for the UN World Summit on the Information Society (2003, Geneva), the word *communication* has little presence. In complex modern societies, however, the resolution of the most urgent social problems requires the capacity to communicate more urgently than the capacity to inform. It is a disturbing prospect that as the human capacity to process and distribute information and knowledge expands and improves, the capacity to communicate and converse diminishes. More and more people are worldwide interconnected through high-speed, broad-band digital networks. However, *connecting* is not the same as *communicating*. The real core question is how to shape *communication societies*. This is particularly urgent in relation to the protection of human rights. The possibility of compassionate behavior can only be realized when we do this universally. This is the real meaning of universalism. It does not imply that everybody in all the world's different cultures should follow under all circumstances the same moral rule, but it points out that we can only leave the universe of inhumanity behind us under the condition that all people participate. The institution of human rights poses the challenge that a more humane future can only be realized if the effort is universal. This kind of universalization of human rights requires an intensive and permanent intercultural and interreligious dialogue. As Dianne Otto (1997) proposed, human rights have to be seen not as a civilizing mission, but as a process of constant transformative dialogue. Particularly in the context of current globalization processes, which concur with processes of regional and local sociocultural diversification, there is a growing need to search for common ground in the interpretation of human rights standards. As Freeman (2000) rightly observed "The need to interpret human rights principles requires dialogue" (p. 55).

DIALOGUE

To solve the world's most pressing problems, people do not need more volumes of information and knowledge—they need to acquire the capacity to talk to each other across boundaries of culture, religion, and language. Dialogue is absolutely essential and critical to the global encounter between civilizations. The plea for dialogue sounds obvious and facile. In reality, however, the dialogue is an extremely difficult form of speech. In many societies, people have neither time nor patience for dialogical communication. Dialogues have no short-term and certain outcome. This conflicts with the spirit of modern achievement-oriented societies. Moreover, the mass media are not particularly helpful in teaching people the art of conversation. Much of their content is babbling (endless talking without saying anything), hate speech, advertising blurbs, sound bites, or polemical debate. The requirements for a meaningful dialogue begin with the need for the internal dialogue. This implies that all participants question their own judgments and assumptions. The critical investigation of our own assumptions is a major challenge because we are often ignorant about our basic assumptions. Assumptions are the mental maps that we tend to follow uncritically. We all have different and often conflicting assumptions, and certainly when we come from different cultures. Equally difficult is the suspension of judgment because we are strongly attached to our opinions and assessments and prefer them to uncertainties.

Dialogue also requires the capacity to listen and be silent. Learning the language of listening is very hard in societies that are increasingly influenced by visual cultures, whereas listening demands an ear-centered culture. The mass media offer talk shows, no listen shows. Moreover, as Krishnamurti said "we listen really to our own noise, our own sound, not to what is being said"—we listen defensively most of the time and not receptively! "We listen to discover what will help us—we listen to anticipate possible danger" (Ellinor & Gerard, 1998, p. 103). The dialogue can only take place where silence is respected. This borders on the impossible in modern societies, where talking never seems to stop and where every void needs to be filled.

The good thing about all this is that the capacity for the dialogue is a problem for all stakeholders. No group or country is more privileged than others. This is something we all need to learn.

Dialogue is an essential approach to the intensification of conflicts around the world between people of different origin, religious values, cultural practices, and languages. Such encounters all too often end in deadly conflict. In the desperate search to solve or rather prevent such conflicts, the question has come up as to whether those who cannot live in peace should be separated from each other by erecting walls between them. However, if one concludes, that neither deadly conflicts nor walls of separation offer sustainable solutions, the only alternative is the effort to engage in dialogue. It needs to be realized though, even if well-intended individuals master the art of the dialogue and are strongly motivated to participate in cross-cultural and cross-religious encounters, the groups they belong to may not want this. We need to seriously count with the historical possibility that the liberal dream about peaceful multiethnic, multireligious societies is a dream indeed (Dahrendorf, 2002). If groups have a long history of serious rivalry, they may not be open to dialogue. It should also be realized that social groups relate to each other from different positions of power. It is questionable whether dialogue among unequal parties is a serious option. The more communication that takes place among unequal parties, the more the risk of greater dependency and powerlessness for the weaker party increases. This tells us that we have to be careful not to adopt the dialogical form of communication as the ultimate panacea for all the world's pressing issues. I would like to think that the dialogue is more promising than the mere transfer of information and knowledge in enabling people to participate in the governance of their own lives. Yet just like expectations about information and knowledge need to be qualified, the same holds true for the communication society.

THE HUMAN RIGHT TO COMMUNICATE

In whatever ways informational developments affect societies, we are likely to see different patterns for the traffic of information among people. Following a proposal by Bordewijk and Van Kaam (1982), four patterns can be distinguished: (a) the dissemination of messages (Bordewijk & Van Kaam called this *allocution*); (b) the consultation of information (like in libraries or on the Web); (c) the registration of data (for public or private purposes); and (d) the exchange of information among people: the modality of conversation. A survey of the existing human rights standards that are relevant to informational developments shows that they cover mainly the dissemination of information, the consultation of information, and the registration of information:

> Human rights for dissemination address the issues of freedom of speech and its limits.
>
> Human rights for consultation address the issues of access and confidentiality.
>
> Human rights for registration address the issues of privacy and security.

The following table provides the overview.

HUMAN RIGHTS PROVISIONS

	Dissemination	Freedom of Expression
Patterns	Consultation	Access to Information
	Registration	Protection of Privacy

A striking omission in international human rights law is that provisions for the fourth pattern—conversation, or communication in the proper sense of that word—are missing. Practically all human rights provisions refer to communication as the *transfer of messages*. This reflects an interpretation of communication that has become rather common since Shannon and Weaver (1949) introduced their mathematical theory of communication. Their model described communication as a linear, one-way process. However, this is a limited and somewhat misleading conception of communication, which ignores that in essence *communicare* refers to a process of sharing, making common, or creating a community. Communication is used for the dissemination of messages (such as in the case of the mass media), consultation of information sources (like searches in libraries or on the World Wide Web), registration of information (as happens in databases), and conversations in which people participate.

The discussion on a right to communicate focuses on this last conception of communication, and its proponents argue that communication in the sense of conversation or dialogue needs special protective and enabling provisions.

Existing human rights law through Article 19 of the UDHR and Article 19 of the ICCPR covers the fundamental right to freedom of opinion and expression. This is undoubtedly an essential basis for processes of dialogue among people, but does not in itself constitute two-way traffic. It is the freedom of the speaker at Hydepark Corner to whom no one has to listen and who may not communicate with anyone in his audience. The Articles also refer to the freedom to hold opinions: This refers to opinions inside your heart that may serve as the communication with yourself, but bear not necessarily any relation to communication with others. It mentions the right to seek information and ideas: This provides for processes of consultation (e.g., gathering the news), which is different from communicating. There is also the right to receive information and ideas: This is in principle also a one-way traffic process; the fact that I can receive whatever information and ideas I want does not imply I am involved in a communication process. Finally, there is the right to impart information and ideas: This refers to the dissemination that goes beyond the freedom of expression, but in the same way does not imply dialogue. In summary, the provisions of Article 19 only address one-way processes of transport, reception, consultation, and allocution, but not the two-way process of conversation. A crucial question for Human Rights in the Information Society is obviously how this omission can be remedied.

What is basically needed is to extend the available human rights provisions with the right to participate in interactive processes. The significance of human rights provisions is that they recognize basic entitlements that human beings can claim for both the protection and enabling of lives in dignity. In this line of thought, it is essential to recognize the conversational pattern of communication as elementary to human dignity. This mode of communication also needs protection plus enabling. The right to communicate puts communication as conversation (both public and private) on the public agenda. It is important that the right to communicate also refers to the private dimension of communication. The provisions of free speech (such as articulated in Article 19 of the UDHR) focus on ideas and information in public space. Their effect in the public sphere also justifies the limitations imposed on free speech. However, speech also needs protection in the private sphere.

The right to communicate necessarily implies a collective dimension. Human rights are often perceived too narrowly as individual rights only. This ignores that people communicate both as individual persons and members of communities. The problem obviously is that the recognition of collective claims could collide with individual claims. However, there is no inherent necessity that claims of communities should be to the detriment of individual claims and could not complement and strengthen these. Communities have common resources, such as knowledge and cultural expressions, and they have communal perspectives on reality. The public dialogue is not merely the conversation among individuals, but also between groups. It is absolutely essential to address the issue of intergroup dialogue because so many lethal conflicts are precisely intergroup rivalries. To focus on individuals only ignores the reality that if groups do not learn to dialogue, individuals' mental openness and conversational skills amount to no positive effect.

RIGHT TO COMMUNICATE: ITS HISTORY

In 1969, Jean D'Arcy introduced the right to communicate by writing, "the time will come when the Universal Declaration of Human Rights will have to encompass a more extensive right than man's right to information. . . . This is the right of men to communicate." D'Arcy proposed to see communication as an interactive process. As Desmond Fisher (1983) commented, "The earlier statements of communications freedoms . . . implied that freedom of information was a one way right from a higher to a lower plane" (p. 9). Fisher saw an increasing need for participation and suggested that "more and more people can read, write and use broadcasting equipment and can no longer, therefore, be denied access to and participation in media processes for lack of communication and handling skills" (p. 9).

From the early debates onward, the right to communicate has been perceived by protagonists as more fundamental than the information rights as accorded by current international law. The essence of the right would be based on the observation that communication is a fundamental social process, a basic human need, and the foundation of all social organization. Since 1974, the notion has been included in UNESCO's program. At the 18th session of the UNESCO General Conference, a resolution was adopted (Resolution 4.121) that affirmed "that all individuals should have equal opportunities to participate actively in the means of communication and to benefit from such means while preserving the right to protection against their abuses."

The resolution authorized the Director General "to study ways and means by which active participation in the communication process may become possible and analyse the right to communicate." In May 1978, a first UNESCO expert seminar on the right to communicate took place at Stockholm (in cooperation with the Swedish National UNESCO Commission). Participants identified different components of the concept of the right to communicate. These included the right to participate, the right to access to communication resources, and information rights. The meeting agreed "that social groups ought to have the rights of access and participation in the communication process. It was also stressed that special attention with regard to the right to communicate should be paid to various minorities-national, ethnic, religious and linguistic" (Fisher, 1982, p. 43). In summary, the Stockholm meeting concluded that

> the right to communicate concept poses "big and messy" problems that require an outlook larger than that provided by any single cultural background, any single professional discipline, or any particular body of professional experience. And although some of the aspects of the concept were felt to be uncomfortable by some participants and observers, these same participants and observers also generally found the concept hopeful and encouraging. (Fisher, 1982, p. 45)

Whereas the Stockholm meeting provided largely an analysis of the right to communicate on the individual and community levels, a second expert seminar focused on the international dimension of the right to communicate. This was the Meeting of Experts on the Right to Communicate at Manila. The meeting was organized in cooperation with the Philippine UNESCO National Commission and took place October 15-19, 1979. The participants proposed that the right to communicate is both an individual and a social right. As a fundamental human right, it should be incorporated in the Universal Declaration of Human Rights. It has validity nationally and internationally. It encompasses duties and responsibilities for individuals, groups, and nations. It requires the allocation of appropriate resources.

In its final report, the UNESCO-appointed MacBride Commission concluded that the recognition of this new right "promises to advance the democratization of communication" (International Commission, 1980, p. 173). The Commission stated, "Communication needs in a democratic society should be met by the extension of specific rights such as the right to be informed, the right to inform, the right to privacy, the right to participate in public communication-all elements of a new concept, the right to communicate. In developing what might be called a new era of social rights, we suggest all the implications of the right to communicate be further explored" (International Commission, 1980, p. 265).

The Commission also observed that "Freedom of speech, of the press, of information and of assembly are vital for the realization of human rights. Extension of these communication freedoms to a broader individual and collective right to communicate is an evolving principle in the democratization process" (International Commission, 1980, p. 265). According to the Commission, "The concept of the right to communicate has yet to receive its final form and its full content . . . it is still at the stage of being thought through in all its implications and gradually enriched" (International Commission, 1980, p. 173). The 1980 UNESCO General Conference in Belgrade confirmed the concept of a right to communicate in terms of "respect for the right of the public, of ethnic and social groups and of individuals to have access to information sources and to participate actively in the communication process" (Resolution 4/19, 14(xi)).

The UNESCO General Conference in Paris of 1983 adopted a resolution on the right to communicate, stating, "Recalling that the aim is not to substitute the notion of the right to communicate for any rights already recognized by the international community, but to increase their scope with regard to individuals and the groups they form, particularly in view of the new possibilities of active communication and dialogue between cultures that are opened up by advances in the media . . . " (Resolution 3.2). The 23rd UNESCO General Conference in 1985 at Sofia requested the Director General to develop activities for the realization of the right to communicate. In the early 1990s, the right to communicate had practically disappeared from UNESCO's agenda. In the Medium-Term Plan for 1990 to 1995, it is no longer a crucial concept. The right to communicate was mentioned, but not translated into operational action.

In 1992, Pekka Tarjanne, Secretary General of the International Telecommunication Union, took up the issue of the right to communicate and stated, "I have suggested to my colleagues that the Universal Declaration of Human Rights should be amended to recognize the right to communicate as a fundamental human right" (p. 45).

During the preparations for the UN World Summit on the Information Society (2003 in Geneva and 2005 in Tunis), the discussion on the right to communicate has been revitalized. This was particularly due to the activities of the

Communication Rights in the Information Society (CRIS) campaign during the preparatory committee meetings (in July 2002 and February 2003). It is especially significant that the UN Secretary General in his public message on World Telecommunication Day (May 17, 2003) reminded the international community "that millions of people in the poorest countries are still excluded from the 'right to communicate,' increasingly seen as a fundamental human right." On June 23, 2003, the International Telecommunication Union published a full-page announcement in *Business Week* that states, "Everyone has the right to communicate." The announcement explains that communication has always been "a human need" and adds to this, "We believe it is also a human right."

In its evolution, the right to communicate has not been without its critics. Fisher (1982) wrote, "The right to communicate embraces a much wider spectrum of communication freedoms than earlier formulations which failed to win general support because of uncertainty about their practical consequences. Inevitably, the new formulation will encounter even greater opposition" (p. 34).

Throughout the debate, the objection was repeatedly raised that "communication is so integral a part of the human condition that it is philosophically unnecessary and perhaps wrong to describe it as a human right" (Fisher, 1982, p. 41). Another objection pointed to the possible use of the concept by powerful groups in society.

> The concept has to be interpreted, and this will be done by groups in power, not by the weak or oppressed. Limits will be fixed within which the right to communicate may be exercised. These borders will be defined on a political basis and will favour present power relationships in the world. The right to communicate is not a concept leading toward change; it is an attempt to give groups working for liberation a feeling of being taken seriously, while in practice the right to communicate will be used to preserve the present order in the world and to stabilize it even further. (Hedebro, 1982, p. 68)

Opposition to the right to communicate has come from different ideological standpoints.

> The concept of the right to communicate is distrusted by the "western" nations which see it as part of the proposals relating to new world information and communication orders, about which they are highly suspicious. . . . In some socialist and Third World countries, opposition to the right derives from the fact that it could be used to justify the continuation of the existing massive imbalance in information flows and the unrestricted importation of western technology and information and, consequently western values. (Fisher, 1982, p. 34)

The U.S. government opposed the right to communicate in earlier debates and denounced the concept as a communist ploy. In the American rejection, the key feature was the link between the right to communicate and the notion of people's rights. Although the reference to people and to people's rights is common in American political history, in the context of UNESCO, this was seen as a defense of state rights and a threat to individual rights.

An important issue in the discussion on a human right to communicate is the question of whether expanding the human rights regime with a new right might endanger the existing provisions. International law is a living process; it still expands, and also the catalogue of human rights has considerably grown over past years to include new rights and freedoms without endangering the basic standards as formulated in the Universal Declaration of Human Rights (UDHR). Indeed there should be no reason that adding the right to communicate would be a problem as long as one leaves the existing framework as is. The last thing anyone should try to do is break open the articles of the UDHR and amend them. That would be a very dangerous route to go because the international community today would certainly not adopt a document so far sighted as the 1948-UDHR.

Another important point raised in current discussion on the right to communicate is whether such a new right lends itself to abuse by governments. All provisions of international law can be abused by governments. Even the UN Charter can be interpreted by UN Member States in abusive ways. Adopting an international standard on communication is in many ways more of a problem for antidemocratic governments than the right to freedom of expression. Allowing people to speak freely in Hyde Park Corner poses less of a threat to governments than allowing citizens to freely communicate with each other. The right to the freedom to communicate goes to the heart of the democratic process and is much more radical than the right to freedom of expression. The right to communicate addresses the urgent need to render deliberative democracy a concrete social-political process. This runs counter to the preference of many governments to limit the role of citizens in public decision making. The current political processes in the European region provide a telling illustration. They tend to reinforce a development in which people are cast in the role of subjects who accept choices made for them by those who govern, rather than being seen as citizens who decide by whom they want to be governed. The European political process seems to be inspired by a great deal of anxiety about European citizens and does not open up for broad and public democratic deliberation. In this climate, the attempt to have a right to communicate adopted by the international community is therefore likely to meet with a great deal of resistance. This is further reinforced by the fundamental egalitarian dimension of the conversational mode of communication. Social inequality and freedom of expression may go together; the right to dialogue requires equality and thus fundamentally challenges social relations of power, both publicly and privately. The dialogue does not work in nonegalitarian structures.

ROAD MAPS

For the protagonists of the right to communicate, there are various possible road maps. First, there is the formal international law trajectory in case the expectation is that the end result should be the incorporation of the right to communicate into the corpus of existing hard or soft international human rights law. This route implies the preparation of a formulation (in the form of a resolution or declaration) that would be adopted by an intergovernmental conference (such as the WSIS) or by the General Conference of a UN agency like UNESCO. Eventually this approach could lead to a special UN conference to draft an international convention.

Second, there is the trajectory whereby representatives of civil movements adopt a statement on the right to communicate as an inspirational document, educational tool, or guidance for social action. They do not seek the consent of other stakeholders such as governments or business. Third, there is the option to expand the community of adopters by using the example of the Declaration of the Hague on the Future of Refugee and Migration Policy. This declaration emerged from a meeting convened by the Society for International Development (November 2002), and the signatories were individuals from civil society, government, and business. Such a statement functions to remind the international community of relevant standards, and it suggests possible future action.

At the end of 2003 and again in 2005, the UN-convened World Summit on the Information Society will address some of the most important issues and concerns in the field of information and communication. The Summit is inspired by the aspiration to find a common vision on the informational developments that currently affect most societies and are conveniently bundled under the heading of the *information society*.

As UN Secretary General Kofi Anan stated in his World Telecommunication Day (May 17, 2003) message, the primary goal of the WSIS is "helping all of the world's people to communicate." If indeed all the world's people should be assisted in participating in the public and private conversations that affect their lives, the international community will have to secure the conditions under which such processes can take place. Conversational communication among individuals and groups—whether in public and private—should be protected against undue interference by third parties; needs confidentiality, space, and time; requires learning the art of conversation; and demands resources for multilingual conversations and the inclusion of disabled people. All of this requires the commitment from a multi-stakeholder community of governments, intergovernmental organizations, civil society, and business.

CONCLUDING NOTE

If all the laudable aspirations that the international human rights movement cherishes were executed, the world would be a different place. The critical question, however, is why over the past 50 years these rights that the international community established were not implemented. Is it realistic to expect that the international community is willing and/or capable to remove the impediments to the realization of human rights? The signs today are not very encouraging. Rather it seems as if human rights around the world are increasingly on the defense and face a tough battle against such interests as national security and law enforcement. Can professionals in media practice, policy, and studies make a difference?

Human rights are a concern for all people. In the human rights framework, all people matter and all people have the obligation to promote and defend human rights. The professionals working with the media as practitioners, researchers, and policymakers have a special responsibility in this. Through the media, knowledge about the existence and meaning of human rights has to be disseminated, violations of human rights have to be exposed, and common ground for the cross-cultural interpretation of human rights has to be found.

Through this book, I have tried to invite professional communicators to take up their special responsibility. The basic motive was not to make them human rights idealists or human rights utopists. I would much rather plead for a human rights realism. Human history is not a linear process as suggested by the writings of thinkers such as Joachim di Fiori, Lessing, Hegel, and Comte. History does not proceed in progressive steps that lead us through Enlightenment and the development of science and technology to moral progress. History is circular and is locked into recurrent waves of both gross immoral conduct and refined moral reflection. Inhumanity is part of the human condition. Gross violations of human rights belong to the choices human beings make. It is tempting to ignore this and to opt—as neoconservatives do—for a schism between the forces of good and evil. In this interpretation of reality, evil—which is represented by the *others*—can be definitely eradicated and can—by force—be replaced by a superior order. This is dangerous missionary thinking that refuses to see that the inhuman inhabits all people whatever their moral pretense. We have to be realistic about the possibility of overcoming our failure as species and be prepared for recurrent immorality. To fight against this with utopian beliefs makes matters only worse. The attempt to realize utopia usually demands much suffering and misery. Therefore, communicators are called on to highlight our human shortcomings as well as to inform their audiences and—most important—to dialogue with their audiences about the prospects for the dignity of life on our common planet. The core of a permanent international and intercultural dialogue about human rights will have to focus—

realistically—on the major obstacles that stand in the way of the realization of human rights. First, there is the human rights requirement that all people are included and no one is excluded from the claim to human dignity. This is difficult because it seems more likely that human beings want to make exceptions. Due process of law for everybody, but we would like to exclude the perpetrators of extreme atrocities. Second, there is the human rights requirement to grant all people the freedom to speak and say things others do not want to hear. However, it would seem to be more in line with human psychology to silence the expressions we do not want to hear. Third, there is the requirement of global solidarity. This goes against a strong human tendency to hate the others—the outsiders, foreigners, migrants. Global solidarity demands that people overcome their almost natural sentiments of nationalism and patriotism.

When we overcome these obstacles, human rights become the *mental maps* that guide people in their efforts to develop decent societies. For these efforts to be effective, communication in the information society is essential: a challenging perspective for communicators.

SUGGESTIONS FOR DISCUSSION

Discuss how a communication society would be different from an information society.

Discuss how realistic the proposal is to establish a parliamentary assembly for matters of global governance.

Discuss the usefulness of an international instrument on the right to communicate.

Discuss the major provisions of such an instrument.

Discuss how it could it be implemented.

Discuss ways in which media professionals can contribute to developing the art of the dialogue.

Discuss your expectations about the future of human rights.

Discuss what your own contribution can be toward the realization of human rights in the 21st century.

Essential Reading on Human Rights

Alfredsson, G., & Eide, A. (Eds.). (1999). *The universal declaration of human rights*. The Hague: Kluwer.
Alston, P. (Ed.). (1992). *The United Nations and human rights. A critical appraisal*. Oxford: Clarendon.
An-Na'im, A. A. (1992). *Human rights in cross-cultural perspectives: A quest for consensus*. Philadelphia: University of Pennsylvania.
Baehr, P. R. (1999). *Human rights: Universality in practice*. Basingstoke: Macmillan.
Bassiouni, Ch. (1992). *Crimes against humanity in international criminal law*. Dordrecht: M. Nijhoff.
Buergenthal, T. (Ed.). (1977). *Human rights, international law and the Helsinki accords*. New York: Allanbeld/Osmun.
Campbell, T., Goldberg, D., McLean, S., & Mullen, T. (Eds.). (1986). *Human rights. From rhetoric to reality*. Oxford: Basil Blackwell.
Cassese, A. (1990). *Human rights in a changing world*. Cambridge: Polity.
Donnelly, J. (1993). *International human rights*. Boulder: Westview.
Eide, A., Alfredsson, G., Melander, G., Rehof, L. A., & Rosas, A. (Eds.) (1992). *The universal declaration of human rights: A commentary*. Oxford: Oxford University Press.
Evans, T. (2001). *The politics of human rights*. London: Pluto.
Humphrey, J. (1989). *No distant millennium. The international law of human rights*. Paris: UNESCO.
Meron, T. (1984). *Human rights in international law*. Oxford: Clarendon.
Nickel, J. W. (1987). *Making sense of human rights*. Berkeley: University of California Press.
Nino, C. S. (1993). *The ethics of human rights*. Oxford: Clarendon.
Renteln, A. D. (1990). *International human rights, universalism versus relativism*. London: Sage.

Roht-Arriaza, N. (Ed.). (1995). *Impunity and human rights in international law and practice*. Oxford: Oxford University Press.

Vincent, R. (1987). *Human rights and international relations*. Cambridge: Cambridge University Press.

Weston, B. H., & Marks, St. P. (Eds.). (1999). *The future of international human rights*. New York: Transnational.

1

Appendix

INTERNATIONAL HUMAN RIGHTS INSTRUMENTS

- Universal Declaration of Human Rights (1948).
- Convention on the Prevention and Punishment of the Crime of Genocide (1948).
- ILO Convention no. 87: Freedom of Association and Protection of the Right to Organize Convention (1948).
- ILO Convention no. 98: Rights to Organize and Collective Bargaining Convention (1949).
- Geneva Convention relative to the Treatment of Prisoners of War (1949).
- Geneva Convention relative to the Protection of Civilian Persons in Time of War (1949).
- Convention for the Suppression of the Traffic in Persons and of the Exploitation of the Prostitution of Others (1950).
- ILO Convention no. 100 concerning Equal Remuneration for Men and Women Workers for Work of Equal Value (1951).
- Convention relating to the Status of Refugees (1951).
- Convention on the International Right of Correction (1952).
- Convention on the Political Rights of Women (1953).
- Convention relating to the Status of Stateless Persons (1954).
- Convention on the Nationality of Married Women (1957).

- ILO Convention no. 105: Abolition of Forced Labor Convention (1957).
- ILO Convention no. 111 concerning Discrimination in Respect of Employment and Occupation (1958).
- UNESCO Convention against Discrimination in Education (1960).
- International Covenant on Economic, Social and Cultural Rights (1966).
- International Covenant on Civil and Political Rights (1966).
- Optional Protocol to the International Covenant on Civil and Political Rights (1966).
- International Convention on the Elimination of All Forms of Racial Discrimination (1966).
- International Convention on the Suppression and Punishment of the Crime of Apartheid (1976).
- Additional Protocol to the Geneva Conventions of August 12, 1949, relating to the Protection of Victims of International Armed Conflicts. Protocol I (1977).
- Additional Protocol to the Geneva Conventions of August 12, 1949, relating to the Protection of Victims of Non-International Armed Conflicts. Protocol II (1977).
- Convention on the Elimination of All Forms of Discrimination Against Women (1979).
- Convention Against Torture and other Cruel, Inhuman or Degrading Treatment or Punishment (1984).
- International Convention against Apartheid in Sports (1985).
- Convention on the Rights of the Child (1989).
- International Convention on the Protection of the Rights of all Migrant Workers and Members of their Families (1990).

REGIONAL HUMAN RIGHTS INSTRUMENTS

Europe

- European Convention for the Protection of Human Rights and Fundamental Freedoms (1950).
- European Social Charter (1961).
- Convention for the Protection of Individuals with regard to Automatic Processing of Personal Data (1981).
- European Convention on the Non-Applicability of Statutory Limitations to Crimes against Humanity and War Crimes (1974).

- European Convention for the Prevention of Torture and Inhuman or Degrading Treatment or Punishment (1987).
- European Agreement on Transfer of Responsibility for Refugees (1980).
- Convention on the Participation of Foreigners in Public Life at Local Level (1992).
- European Convention on the Legal Status of Migrant Workers (1977).
- European Charter for Regional or Minority Languages (1992).

Africa

- African Charter on Human and People's Rights (1981).
- OAU Convention Governing the Specific Aspects of Refugee Problems in Africa (1969).
- African Charter on the Rights and Welfare of the Child (1990).

The Americas

- American Convention on Human Rights (1969).
- Inter-American Convention to Prevent and Punish Torture (1985).
- OAS Convention on Diplomatic Asylum (1954).
- OAS Convention on Territorial Asylum (1954).
- Inter–American Convention on the Granting of Political Rights to Women (1948).
- Inter–American Convention on the Granting of Civil Rights to Women (1948).

Asia

- Declaration of the Basic Duties of ASEAN Peoples and Governments (1983).

Islam

- Universal Islamic Declaration of Human Rights (1981).

2

Appendix

TEXTS OF ESSENTIAL HUMAN RIGHTS INSTRUMENTS

- The Universal Declaration of Human Rights
- The UN International Covenant on Civil and Political Rights
- The UN International Covenant on Economic, Social and Cultural Rights
- The European Convention on Human Rights
- The Declaration on Fundamental Principles Concerning the Contribution of International Understanding, to the Promotion of Human Rights and to Countering Racialism, Apartheid and Incitement to War
- The Convention on the Elimination of All Forms of Discrimination Against Women
- The Convention on the Rights of the Child

TEXT OF THE UNIVERSAL DECLARATION OF HUMAN RIGHTS

(As adopted by the General Assembly on 10 December 1948)

Preamble

Whereas recognition of the inherent dignity and of the equal and inalienable rights of all members of the human family is the foundation of freedom, justice and peace in the world,

Whereas disregard and contempt for human rights have resulted in barbarous acts which have outraged the conscience of mankind, and the advent of a world in which human beings shall enjoy freedom of speech and belief and freedom from fear and want has been proclaimed as the highest aspiration of the common people,

Whereas it is essential, if man is not to be compelled to have recourse, as a last resort, to rebellion against tyranny and oppression, that human rights should be protected by the rule of law,

Whereas it is essential to promote the development of friendly relations between nations,

Whereas the peoples of the United Nations have in the Charter reaffirmed their faith in fundamental human rights, in the dignity and worth of the human person and in the equal rights of men and women and have determined to promote social progress and better standards of life in larger freedom,

Whereas Member States have pledged themselves to achieve, in co-operation with the United Nations, the promotion of universal respect for and observance of human rights and fundamental freedoms,

Whereas a common understanding of these rights and freedoms is of the greatest importance for the full realization of this pledge,

Now, therefore,

The General Assembly

Proclaims this Universal Declaration of Human Rights as a common standard of achievement for all peoples and all nations, to the end that every individual and every organ of society, keeping this Declaration constantly in mind, shall strive by teaching and education to promote respect for these rights and freedoms and by progressive measures, national and international, to secure their universal and effective recognition and observance, both among the peoples of Member States themselves and among the peoples of territories under their jurisdiction.

Article 1

All human beings are born free and equal in dignity and rights. They are endowed with reason and conscience and should act towards one another in a spirit of brotherhood.

Article 2

Everyone is entitled to all the rights and freedoms set forth in this Declaration, without distinction of any kind, such as race, colour, sex, language, religion, political or other opinion, national or social origin, property, birth or other status.

Furthermore, no distinction shall be made on the basis of the political, jurisdictional or international status of the country or territory to which a person belongs, whether it be independent, trust, non-self-governing or under any other limitation of sovereignty.

Article 3

Everyone has the right to life, liberty and the security of person.

Article 4

No one shall be held in slavery or servitude; slavery and the slave trade shall be prohibited in all their forms.

Article 5

No one shall be subjected to torture or to cruel, inhuman or degrading treatment or punishment.

Article 6

Everyone has the right to recognition everywhere as a person before the law.

Article 7

All are equal before the law and are entitled without any discrimination to equal protection of the law. All are entitled to equal protection against any discrimination in violation of this Declaration and against any incitement to such discrimination.

Article 8

Everyone has the right to an effective remedy by the competent national tribunals for acts violating the fundamental rights granted him by the constitution or by law.

Article 9

No one shall be subjected to arbitrary arrest, detention or exile.

Article 10

Everyone is entitled in full equality to a fair and public hearing by an independent and impartial tribunal, in the determination of his rights and obligations and of any criminal charge against him.

Article 11

1. Everyone charged with a penal offense has the right to be presumed innocent until proved guilty according to law in a public trial at which he has had all the guarantees necessary for his defense.
2. No one shall be held guilty of any penal offense on account of any act or omission which did not constitute a penal offense, under national or international law, at the time when it was committed. Nor shall a heavier penalty be imposed than the one that was applicable at the time the penal offense was committed.

Article 12

No one shall be subjected to arbitrary interference with his privacy, family, home or correspondence, nor to attacks upon his honour and reputation. Everyone has the right to the protection of the law against such interference or attacks.

Article 13

1. Everyone has the right to freedom of movement and residence within the borders of each State.
2. Everyone has the right to leave any country, including his own, and to return to his country.

Article 14

1. Everyone has the right to seek and to enjoy in other countries asylum from persecution.
2. This right may not be invoked in the case of prosecutions genuinely arising from non-political crimes or from acts contrary to the purposes and principles of the United Nations.

Article 15

1. Everyone has the right to a nationality.
2. No one shall be arbitrarily deprived of his nationality nor denied the right to change his nationality.

Article 16

1. Men and women of full age, without any limitation due to race, nationality or religion, have the right to marry and to found a family. They are entitled to equal rights as to marriage, during marriage and at its dissolution.

2. Marriage shall be entered into only with the free and full consent of the intending spouses.
3. The family is the natural and fundamental group unit of society and is entitled to protection by society and the State.

Article 17

1. Everyone has the right to own property alone as well as in association with others.
2. No one shall be arbitrarily deprived of his property.

Article 18

Everyone has the right to freedom of thought, conscience and religion; this right includes freedom to change his religion or belief, and freedom, either alone or in community with others and in public or private, to manifest his religion or belief in teaching, practice, worship and observance.

Article 19

Everyone has the right to freedom of opinion and expression; this right includes freedom to hold opinions without interference and to seek, receive and impart information and ideas through any media and regardless of frontiers.

Article 20

1. Everyone has the right to freedom of peaceful assembly and association.
2. No one may be compelled to belong to an association.

Article 21

1. Everyone has the right to take part in the government of his country, directly or through freely chosen representatives.
2. Everyone has the right to equal access to public service in his country.
3. The will of the people shall be the basis of the authority of government; this will shall be expressed in periodic and genuine elections which shall be by universal and equal suffrage and shall be held by secret vote or by equivalent free voting procedures.

Article 22

Everyone, as a member of society, has the right to social security and is entitled to realization, through national effort and international co-operation and in accordance with the organization and resources of each State, of the economic, social and cultural rights indispensable for his dignity and the free development of his personality.

Article 23

1. Everyone has the right to work, to free choice of employment, to just and favourable conditions of work and to protection against unemployment.

2. Everyone, without any discrimination, has the right to equal pay for equal work.
3. Everyone who works has the right to just and favourable remuneration ensuring for himself and his family an existence worthy of human dignity, and supplemented, if necessary, by other means of social protection.
4. Everyone has the right to form and to join trade unions for the protection of his interests.

Article 24

Everyone has the right to rest and leisure, including reasonable limitation of working hours and periodic holidays with pay.

Article 25

1. Everyone has the right to a standard of living adequate for the health and well-being of himself and of his family, including food, clothing, housing, and medical care and necessary social services, and the right to security in the event of unemployment, sickness, disability, widowhood, old age or other lack of livelihood in circumstances beyond his control.
2. Motherhood and childhood are entitled to special care and assistance. All children, whether born in or out of wedlock, shall enjoy the same social protection.

Article 26

1. Everyone has the right to education. Education shall be free, at least in the elementary and fundamental stage. Elementary education shall be compulsory. Technical and professional education shall be made generally available and higher education shall be equally accessible to all on the basis of merit.
2. Education shall be directed to the full development of the human personality and to the strengthening of respect for human rights and fundamental freedoms. It shall promote understanding, tolerance and friendship among all nations, racial or religious groups, and shall further the activities of the United Nations for the maintenance of peace.
3. Parents have a prior right to choose the kind of education that shall be given to their children.

Article 27

1. Everyone has the right freely to participate in the cultural life of the community, to enjoy the arts and to share in scientific advancement and its benefits.
2. Everyone has the right to the protection of the moral and material interests resulting from any scientific, literary or artistic production of which he is the author.

Article 28

Everyone is entitled to a social and international order in which the rights and freedoms set forth in this Declaration can be fully realized.

Article 29

1. Everyone has duties to the community in which alone the free and full development of his personality is possible.
2. In the exercise of his rights and freedoms, everyone shall be subject only to such limitations as are determined by law solely for the purpose of securing due recognition and respect for the rights and freedoms of others and of meeting the just requirements of morality, public order and the general welfare in a democratic society.
3. These rights and freedoms may in no case be exercised contrary to the purpose and principles of the United Nations.

Article 30

Nothing in this Declaration may be interpreted as implying for any State, group or person any right to engage in any activity or to perform any act aimed at the destruction of any of the rights and freedoms set forth herein.

INTERNATIONAL COVENANT ON CIVIL AND POLITICAL RIGHTS

Adopted and opened for signature, ratification and accession by General Assembly resolution 2200 A (XXI) of 16 December 1966

Entry into force: 23 March 1976 in accordance with Article 49.

Preamble

The States Parties to the present Covenant,

Considering that, in accordance with the principles proclaimed in the Charter of the United Nations, recognition of the inherent dignity and of the equal and inalienable rights of all members of the human family is the foundation of freedom, justice and peace in the world.

Recognizing that these rights derive from the inherent dignity of the human person,

Recognizing that, in accordance with the Universal Declaration of Human Rights, the ideal of free human beings enjoying civil and political freedom and freedom from fear and want can only be achieved if conditions are created whereby everyone may enjoy his civil and political rights, as well as his economic, social and cultural rights,

Considering the obligation of States under the Charter of the United Nations to promote universal respect for, and observance of, human rights and freedoms,

Realizing that the individual, having duties to other individuals and to the community to which he belongs, is under a responsibility to strive for the promotion and observance of the rights recognized in the present Covenant,

Agree upon the following articles:

Part I

Article 1

1. All peoples have the right of self-determination. By virtue of that right they freely determine their political status and freely pursue their economic, social and cultural development.
2. All peoples may, for their own ends, freely dispose of their natural wealth and resources without prejudice to any obligations arising out of international economic cooperation, based upon the principle of mutual benefit, and

international law. In no case may a people be deprived of its own means of subsistence.

3. The States Parties to the present Covenant, including those having responsibility for the administration of Non-Self-Governing and Trust Territories, shall promote the realization of the right of self-determination, and shall respect that right, in conformity with the provisions of the Charter of the United Nations.

Part II

Article 2

1. Each State Party to the present Covenant undertakes to respect and to ensure to all individuals within its territory and subject to its jurisdiction the rights recognized in the present Covenant, without distinction of any kind, such as race, colour, sex, language, religion, political or other opinion, national or social origin, property, birth or other status.
2. Where not already provided for by existing legislative or other measures, each State Party to the present Covenant undertakes to take the necessary steps, in accordance with its constitutional processes and with the provisions of the present Covenant, to adopt such legislative or other measures as may be necessary to give effect to the rights recognized in the present Covenant.
3. Each State Party to the present Covenant undertakes:
   (a) To ensure that any person whose rights or freedoms as herein recognized are violated shall have an effective remedy, notwithstanding that the violation has been committed by persons acting in an official capacity;
   (b) To ensure that any person claiming such a remedy shall have his right there to determined by competent judicial, administrative or legislative authorities, or by any other competent authority provided for by the legal system of the State, and to develop the possibilities of judicial remedy;
   (c) To ensure that the competent authorities shall enforce such remedies when granted.

Article 3

The States Parties to the present Covenant undertake to ensure the equal right of men and women to the enjoyment of all civil and political rights set forth in the present Covenant.

Article 4

1. In time of public emergency which threatens the life of the nation and the existence of which is officially proclaimed, the States Parties to the present Covenant may take measures derogating from their obligations under the

present Covenant to the extent strictly required by the exigencies of the situation, provided that such measures are not inconsistent with their other obligations under international law and do not involve discrimination solely on the ground of race, colour, sex, language, religion or social origin.

2. No derogation from Articles 6, 7, 8 (Paragraphs 1 and 2), 11, 15, 16 and 18 may be made under this provision.
3. Any State party to the present Covenant availing itself of the right of derogation shall immediately inform the other States Parties to the present Covenant, through the intermediary of the Secretary-General of the United Nations, of the provisions from which it has derogated and of the reasons by which it was actuated. A further communication shall be made, through the same intermediary, on the date on which it terminates such derogation.

Article 5

1. Nothing in the present Covenant may be interpreted as implying for any State, group or person any right to engage in any activity or perform any act aimed at the destruction of any of the rights and freedoms recognized herein or at their limitation to a greater extent than is provided for in the present Covenant.
2. There shall be no restriction upon or derogation from any of the fundamental human rights recognized or existing in any State Party to the present Covenant pursuant to law, conventions, regulations or custom on the pretext that the present Covenant does not recognize such rights or that it recognizes them to a lesser extent.

Part III

Article 6

1. Every human being has the inherent right to life. This right shall be protected by law. No one shall be arbitrarily deprived of his life.
2. In countries which have not abolished the death penalty, sentence of death may be imposed only for the most serious crimes in accordance with the law in force at the time of the commission of the crime and not contrary to the provisions of the present Covenant and to the Convention on the Prevention and Punishment of the Crime of Genocide. This penalty can only be carried out pursuant to a final judgement rendered by a competent court.
3. When deprivation of life constitutes the crime of genocide, it is understood that nothing in this article shall authorize any State Party to the present Covenant to derogate in any way from any obligation assumed under the provisions of the Convention on the Prevention and Punishment of the Crime of Genocide.
4. Anyone sentenced to death shall have the right to seek pardon or commutation of the sentence. Amnesty, pardon or commutation of the sentence of death may be granted in all cases.

5. Sentence of death shall not be imposed for crimes committed by persons below eighteen years of age and shall not be carried out on pregnant women.
6. Nothing in this article shall be invoked to delay or to prevent the abolition of capital punishment by any State Party to the present Covenant.

Article 7

No one shall be subjected to torture or to cruel, inhuman or degrading treatment or punishment. In particular, no one shall be subjected without his free consent to medical or scientific experimentation.

Article 8

1. No one shall be held in slavery; slavery and the slave trade in all their forms shall be prohibited.
2. No one shall be held in servitude.
3.
   (a) No one shall be required to perform forced or compulsory labour;
   (b) Paragraph 3 (a) shall not be held to preclude, in countries where imprisonment with hard labour may be imposed as a punishment for a crime, the performance of hard labour in pursuance of a sentence to such punishment by a competent court;
   (c) For the purpose of this paragraph the term "forced or compulsory labour" shall not include:
      (i) Any work or service, not referred to in sub-paragraph *(b)*, normally required of a person who is under detention in consequence of a lawful order of a court, or of a person during conditional release from such detention;
      (ii) Any service of a military character and, in countries where conscientious objection is recognized, any national service required by law of conscientious objectors;
      (iii) Any service exacted in cases of emergency or calamity threatening the life or wellbeing of the community;
      (iv) Any work or service which forms part of normal civil obligations.

Article 9

1. Everyone has the right to liberty and security of person. No one shall be subjected to arbitrary arrest or detention. No one shall be deprived of his liberty except on such grounds and in accordance with such procedure as are established by law.
2. Anyone who is arrested shall be informed, at the time of arrest, of the reasons for his arrest and shall be promptly informed of any charges against him.

3. Anyone arrested or detained on a criminal charge shall be brought promptly before a judge or other officer authorized by law to exercise judicial power and shall be entitled to trial within a reasonable time or to release. It shall not be the general rule that persons awaiting trial shall be detained in custody, but release may be subject to guarantees to appear for trial, at any other stage of the judicial proceedings, and, should occasion arise, for execution of the judgement.
4. Anyone who is deprived of his liberty by arrest or detention shall be entitled to take proceedings before a court, in order that that court may decide without delay on the lawfulness of his detention and order his release if the detention is not lawful.
5. Anyone who has been victim of unlawful arrest or detention shall have an enforceable right to compensation.

Article 10

1. All persons deprived of their liberty shall be treated with humanity and with respect for the inherent dignity of the human person.
2.
   (a) Accused persons shall, save in exceptional circumstances, be segregated from convicted persons and shall be subject to separate treatment appropriate to their status as unconvicted persons;
   (b) Accused juvenile persons shall be separated from adults and brought as speedily as possible for adjudication.
3. The penitentiary system shall comprise treatment of prisoners the essential aim of which shall be their reformation and social rehabilitation. Juvenile offenders shall be segregated from adults and be accorded treatment appropriate to their age and legal status.

Article 11

No one shall be imprisoned merely on the ground of inability to fulfill a contractual obligation.

Article 12

1. Everyone lawfully within the territory of a State shall, within that territory, have the right to liberty of movement and freedom to choose his residence.
2. Everyone shall be free to leave any country, including his own.
3. The above mentioned rights shall not be subject to any restrictions except those which are provided by law, are necessary to protect national security, public order *(ordre public),* public health or morals or the rights and freedoms of others, and are consistent with the other rights recognized in the present Covenant.
4. No one shall be arbitrarily deprived of the right to enter his own country.

Article 13

An alien lawfully in the territory of a State Party to the present Covenant may be expelled therefrom only in pursuance of a decision reached in accordance with law and shall, except where compelling reasons of national security otherwise require, be allowed to submit the reasons against his expulsion and to have his case reviewed by, and represented for the purpose before, the competent authority or a person or persons especially designated by the competent authority.

Article 14

1. All persons shall be equal before the courts and tribunals. In the determination of any criminal charge against him, or of his rights and obligations in a suit at law, everyone shall be entitled to a fair and public hearing by a competent, independent and impartial tribunal established by law. The Press and the public may be excluded from all or part of a trial for reasons of morals, public order *(ordre public)* or national security in a democratic society, or when the interest of the private lives of the parties so requires, or to the extent strictly necessary in the opinion of the court in special circumstances where publicity would prejudice the interests of justice; but any judgement rendered in a criminal case or in a suit at law shall be made public except where the interest of juvenile persons otherwise requires or the proceedings concern matrimonial disputes of the guardianship of children.
2. Everyone charged with a criminal offense shall have the right to be presumed innocent until proved guilty according to law.
3. In the determination of any criminal charge against him, everyone shall be entitled to the following minimum guarantees, in full equality:
   (a) To be informed promptly and in detail in a language which he understands of the nature and cause of the charge against him.
   (b) To have adequate time and facilities for the preparation of his defense and to communicate with counsel of his own choosing;
   (c) To be tried without undue delay;
   (d) To be tried in his presence, and to defend himself in person or through legal assistance of his own choosing; to be informed if he does not have legal assistance, of this right; and to have legal assistance assigned to him, in any case where the interests of justice so require, and without payment by him in any such case if he does not have sufficient means to pay for it;
   (e) To examine, or have examined, the witnesses against him and to obtain the attendance and examination of witnesses on his behalf under the same conditions as witnesses against him;
   (f) To have the free assistance of an interpreter if he cannot understand or speak the language used in court;
   (g) Not to be compelled to testify against himself or to confess guilt.

4. In the case of juvenile persons, the procedure shall be such as will take account of their age and the desirability of promoting their rehabilitation.
5. Everyone convicted of a crime shall have the right to his conviction and sentence being reviewed by a higher tribunal according to law.
6. When a person has by a final decision been convicted of a criminal offense and when subsequently his conviction has been reversed or he has been pardoned on the ground that a new or newly discovered fact shows conclusively that there has been a miscarriage of justice, the person who has suffered punishment as a result of such conviction shall be compensated according to law, unless it is proved that the non-disclosure of the unknown fact in time is wholly or partly attributable to him.
7. No one shall be liable to be tried or punished again for an offense for which he has already been finally convicted or acquitted in accordance with the law and penal procedure of each country.

Article 15

1. No one shall be held guilty of any criminal offense on account of any act or omission which did not constitute a criminal offense, under national or international law, at the time when it was committed. Nor shall a heavier penalty be imposed than the one that was applicable at the time when the criminal offense was committed. If, subsequent to the commission of the offense, provision is made by law for the imposition of the lighter penalty, the offender shall benefit thereby.
2. Nothing in this article shall prejudice the trial and punishment of any person for any act or omission which, at the time when it was committed, was criminal according to the general principles of law recognized by the community of nations.

Article 16

Everyone shall have the right to recognition everywhere as a person before the law.

Article 17

1. No one shall be subjected to arbitrary or unlawful interference with his privacy, family, home or correspondence, nor to unlawful attacks on his honour and reputation.
2. Everyone has the right to the protection of the law against such interference or attacks.

Article 18

1. Everyone shall have the right to freedom of thought, conscience and religion. This right shall include freedom to have or to adopt a religion or belief of his choice, and freedom, either individually or in community with others

and in public or private, to manifest his religion or belief in worship, observance, practice and teaching.
2. No one shall be subject to coercion which would impair his freedom to have or to adopt a religion or belief of his choice.
3. Freedom to manifest one's religion or beliefs may be subject only to such limitations as are prescribed by law and are necessary to protect public safety, order, health, or morals or the fundamental rights and freedoms of others.
4. The States Parties to the present Covenant undertake to have respect for the liberty of parents and, when applicable, legal guardians to ensure the religious and moral education of their children in conformity with their own convictions.

Article 19

1. Everyone shall have the right to hold opinions without interference.
2. Everyone shall have the right to freedom of expression; this right shall include freedom to seek, receive and impart information and ideas of all kinds regardless of frontiers, either orally, in writing or in print, in the form of art, or through any other media of his choice.
3. The exercise of the rights provided for in Paragraph 2 of this article carries with it special duties and responsibilities. It may therefore be subject to certain restrictions, but these shall only be such as are provided by law and are necessary:
   (a) For respect of the rights or reputations of others;
   (b) For the protection of national security or of public order (*ordre public*), or of public health or morals.

Article 20

1. Any propaganda for war shall be prohibited by law.
2. Any advocacy of national, racial or religious hatred that constitutes incitement to discrimination, hostility or violence shall be prohibited by law.

Article 21

The right of peaceful assembly shall be recognized. No restrictions may be placed on the exercise of this right other than those imposed in conformity with the law and which are necessary in a democratic society in the interests of national security or public safety, public order *(order public),* the protection of public health or morals or the protection of the rights and freedoms of others.

Article 22

1. Everyone shall have the right to freedom of association with others, including the right to form and join trade unions for the protection of his interests.
2. No restrictions may be placed on the exercise of this right other than those which are prescribed by law and which are necessary in a democratic soci-

ety in the interests of national security or public safety, public order *(ordre public),* the protection of public health or morals or the protection of the rights and freedoms of others. This article shall not prevent the imposition of lawful restrictions on members of the armed forces and of the police in their exercise of this right.

3. Nothing in this article shall authorize States Parties to the International Labour Organisation Convention of 1948 concerning Freedom of Association and Protection of the Right to Organize to take legislative measures which would prejudice, or to apply the law in such a manner as to prejudice the guarantees provided for in that Convention.

Article 23

1. The family is the natural and fundamental group unit of society and is entitled to protection by society and the State.
2. The right of men and women of marriageable age to marry and to found a family shall be recognized.
3. No marriage shall be entered into without the free and full consent of the intending spouses.
4. States Parties to the present Covenant shall take appropriate steps to ensure equality of rights and responsibilities of spouses as to marriage, during marriage and at its dissolution. In the case of dissolution, provision shall be made for the necessary protection of any children.

Article 24

1. Every child shall have, without any discrimination as to race, colour, sex, language, religion, national or social origin, property or birth, the right to such measures of protection as are required by his status as a minor, on the part of his family, society and the State.
2. Every child shall be registered immediately after birth and shall have a name.
3. Every child has the right to acquire a nationality.

Article 25

Every citizen shall have the right and the opportunity, without any of the distinctions mentioned in Article 2 and without unreasonable restrictions:

(a) To take part in the conduct of public affairs, directly or through freely chosen representatives;

(b) To vote and to be elected at genuine periodic elections which shall be by universal and equal suffrage and shall be held by secret ballot, guaranteeing the free expression of the will of the electors;

(c) To have access, on general terms of equality, to public service in his country.

Article 26

All persons are equal before the law and are entitled without any discrimination to the equal protection of the law. In this respect, the law shall prohibit any discrimination and guarantee to all persons equal and effective protection against discrimination on any ground such as race, colour, sex, language, religion, political or other opinion, national or social origin, property, birth or other status.

Article 27

In those States in which ethnic, religious or linguistic minorities exist, persons belonging to such minorities shall not be denied the right, in community with the other members of their group, to enjoy their own culture, to profess and practice their own religion or to use their own language.

Part IV

Article 28

1. There shall be established a Human Rights Committee (hereafter referred to in the present Covenant as the Committee). It shall consist of eighteen members and shall carry out the functions hereinafter provided.
2. The Committee shall be composed of nationals of the States Parties to the present Covenant who shall be persons of high moral character and recognized competence in the field of human rights, consideration being given to the usefulness of the participation of some persons having legal experience.
3. The members of the Committee shall be elected and shall serve in their personal capacity.

Article 29

1. The members of the Committee shall be elected by secret ballot from a list of persons possessing the qualifications prescribed in Article 28 and nominated for the purpose by the States Parties to the present Covenant.
2. Each State Party to the present Covenant may nominate not more than two persons. These persons shall be nationals of the nominating State.
3. A person shall be eligible for renomination.

Article 30

1. The initial election shall be held no later than six months after the date of the entry into force of the present Covenant.
2. At least four months before the date of each election to the Committee, other than an election to fill a vacancy declared in accordance with Article 34, the Secretary-General of the United Nations shall address a written invitation to the States Parties to the present Covenant to submit their nominations for membership of the Committee within three months.

3. The Secretary-General of the United Nations shall prepare a list in alphabetical order of all the persons thus nominated, with an indication of the States Parties which have nominated them, and shall submit it to the States Parties to the present Covenant no later than one month before the date of each election.
4. Elections of the members of the Committee shall be held at a meeting of the States Parties to the present Covenant convened by the Secretary-General of the United Nations at the Headquarters of the United Nations. At that meeting, for which two thirds of the States Parties to the present Covenant shall constitute a quorum, the persons elected to the Committee shall be those nominees who obtain the largest number of votes and an absolute majority of the votes of the representatives of States Parties present and voting.

Article 31

1. The Committee may not include more than one national of the same State.
2. In the election of the Committee, consideration shall be given to equitable geographical distribution of membership and to the representation of the different forms of civilization and of the principal legal systems.

Article 32

1. The members of the Committee shall be elected for a term of four years. They shall be eligible for reelection if renominated. However, the terms of nine of the members elected at the first election shall expire at the end of two years; immediately after the first election, the names of these nine members shall be chosen by lot by the Chairman of the meeting referred to in Article 30, Paragraph 4.
2. Elections at the expiry of office shall be held in accordance with the preceding articles of this part of the present Covenant.

Article 33

1. If, in the unanimous opinion of the other members, a member of the Committee has ceased to carry out his functions for any cause other than absence of a temporary character, the Chairman of the Committee shall notify the Secretary-General of the United Nations, who shall then declare the seat of that member to be vacant.
2. In the event of the death or the resignation of a member of the Committee, the Chairman shall immediately notify the Secretar-General of the United Nations, who shall declare the seat vacant from the date of death or the date on which the resignation takes effect.

Article 34

1. When a vacancy is declared in accordance with Article 33 and if the term of office of the member to be replaced does not expire within six months of the

declaration of the vacancy, the Secretary-General of the United Nations shall notify each of the States Parties to the present Covenant, which may within two months submit nominations in accordance with Article 29 for the purpose of filling the vacancy.

2. The Secretary-General of the United Nations shall prepare a list in alphabetical order of the persons thus nominated and shall submit it to the States Parties to the present Covenant. The election to fill the vacancy shall then take place in accordance with the relevant provisions of this part of the present Covenant.
3. A member of the Committee elected to fill a vacancy declared in accordance with Article 33 shall hold office for the remainder of the term of the member who vacated the seat on the Committee under the provisions of that article.

Article 35

The members of the Committee shall, with the approval of the General Assembly of the United Nations, receive emoluments from United Nations resources on such terms and conditions as the General Assembly may decide, having regard to the importance of the Committee's responsibilities.

Article 36

The Secretary-General of the United Nations shall provide the necessary staff and facilities for the effective performance of the functions of the Committee under the present Covenant.

Article 37

1. The Secretary-General of the United Nations shall convene the initial meeting of the Committee at the Headquarters of the United Nations.
2. After its initial meeting, the Committee shall meet at such times as shall be provided in its rules of procedure.
3. The Committee shall normally meet at the Headquarters of the United Nations or at the United Nations office at Geneva.

Article 38

Every member of the Committee shall, before taking up his duties, make a solemn declaration in open committee that he will perform his functions impartially and conscientiously.

Article 39

1. The Committee shall elect its officers for a term of two years. They may be re-elected.
2. The Committee shall establish its own rules of procedure, but these rules shall provide, *inter alia,* that:
   (a) Twelve members shall constitute a quorum;

(b) Decisions of the Committee shall be made by a majority vote of the members present.

Article 40

1. The States Parties to the present Covenant undertake to submit reports on the measures they have adopted which give effect to the rights recognized herein and on the progress made in the enjoyment of those rights:
   (a) Within one year of the entry into force of the present Covenant for the States Parties concerned;
   (b) Thereafter whenever the Committee so requests.
2. All reports shall be submitted to the Secretary-General of the United Nations, who shall transmit them to the Committee for consideration. Reports shall indicate the factors and difficulties, if any, affecting the implementation of the present Covenant.
3. The Secretary-General of the United Nations may, after consultation with the Committee, transmit to the specialized agencies concerned copies of such parts of the reports as may fill within their field of competence.
4. The Committee shall study the reports submitted by the States Parties to the present Covenant. It shall transmit its reports, and such general comments as it may consider appropriate, to the States Parties. The Committee may also transmit to the Economic and Social Council these comments along with the copies of the reports it has received from States Parties to the present Covenant.
5. The States Parties to the present Covenant may submit to the Committee observations on any comments that may be made in accordance with Paragraph 4 of this article.

Article 41

1. A State Party to the present Covenant may at any time declare under this article that it recognizes the competence of the Committee to receive and consider communications to the effect that a State Party claims that another State Party is not fulfilling its obligations under the present Covenant. Communications under this article may be received and considered only if submitted by a State Party which has made a declaration recognizing in regard to itself the competence of the Committee. No communication shall be received by the Committee if it concerns a State Party which has not made such a declaration. Communications received under this article shall be dealt with in accordance with the following procedure:
   (a) If a State Party to the present Covenant considers that another State Party is not giving effect to the provisions of the present Covenant, it may, by written communication, bring the matter to the attention of that State Party. Within three months after the receipt of the communication the receiving State shall afford the State which sent the commu-

nication an explanation, or any other statement in writing clarifying the matter which should include, to the extent possible and pertinent, reference to domestic procedures and remedies taken, pending, or available in the matter.

(b) If the matter is not adjusted to the satisfaction of both States Parties concerned within six months after the receipt by the receiving State of the initial communication, either State shall have the right to refer the matter to the Committee, by notice given to the Committee and to the other State.

(c) The Committee shall deal with a matter referred to it only after it has ascertained that all available domestic remedies have been invoked and exhausted in the matter, in conformity with the generally recognized principles of international law. This shall not be the rule where the application of the remedies is unreasonably prolonged.

(d) The Committee shall hold closed meetings when examining communications under this article.

(e) Subject to the provisions of sub-paragraph *(c)*, the Committee shall make available its good offices to the States Parties concerned with a view to a friendly solution of the matter on the basis of respect for human rights and fundamental freedoms as recognized in the present Covenant.

(f) In any matter referred to it, the Committee may call upon the States Parties concerned, referred to in sub-paragraph *(b)*, to supply any relevant information.

(g) The States Parties concerned, referred to in sub-paragraph *(b)*, shall have the right to be represented when the matter is being considered in the Committee and to make submissions orally and/or in writing.

(h) The Committee shall, within twelve months after the date of receipt of notice under subparagraph *(b)*, submit a report:

(i) If a solution within the terms of sub-paragraph *(e)* is reached, the Committee shall confine its report to a brief statement of the facts and of the solution reached.

(j) If a solution within the terms of sub-paragraph *(e)* is not reached, the Committee shall confine its report to a brief statement of the facts; the written submissions and record of the oral submissions made by the States Parties concerned shall be attached to the report.

In every matter, the report shall be communicated to the States Parties concerned.

2. The provisions of this article shall come into force when ten States Parties to the present Covenant have made declarations under Paragraph 1 of this article. Such declarations shall be deposited by the States Parties with the

Secretary-General of the United Nations, who shall transmit copies thereof to the other States Parties. A declaration may be withdrawn at any time by notification to the Secretary-General. Such a withdrawal shall not prejudice the consideration of any matter which is the subject of a communication already transmitted under this article; no further communication by any State Party shall be received after the notification of withdrawal of the declaration has been received by the Secretary-General, unless the State Party concerned has made a new declaration.

Article 42

1. *(a)* If a matter referred to the Committee in accordance with Article 41 is not resolved to the satisfaction of the States Parties concerned, the Committee may, with the prior consent of the States Parties concerned, appoint an *ad hoc* Conciliation Commission (hereinafter referred to as the Commission). The good offices of the Commission shall be made available to the States Parties concerned with a view to an amicable solution of the matter on the basis of respect for the present Covenant;
   (b) The Commission shall consist of five persons acceptable to the States Parties concerned. If the States Parties concerned fail to reach agreement within three months on all or part of the composition of the Commission, the members of the Commission concerning whom no agreement has been reached shall be elected by secret ballot by a two-thirds majority vote of the Committee from among its members.
2. The members of the Commission shall serve in their personal capacity. They shall not be nationals of the States Parties concerned, or of a State not party to the present Covenant, or of a State Party which has not made a declaration under Article 41.
3. The Commission shall elect its own Chairman and adopt its own rules of procedure.
4. The meetings of the Commission shall normally be held at the Headquarters of the United Nations or at the United Nations Office at Geneva. However, they may be held at such other convenient places as the Commission may determine in consultation with the Secretary-General of the United Nations and the States Parties concerned.
5. The secretariat provided in accordance with Article 36 shall also service the commissions appointed under this article.
6. The information received and collated by the Committee shall be made available to the Commission and the Commission may call upon the States Parties concerned to supply any other relevant information.
7. When the Commission has fully considered the matter, but in any event not later than twelve months after having been seized of the matter, it shall sub mit to the Chairman of the Committee a report for communication to the States Parties concerned:

(*a*) If the Commission is unable to complete its consideration of the matter within twelve months, it shall confine its report to a brief statement of the status of its consideration of the matter;

(*b*) If an amicable solution to the matter on the basis of respect for human rights as recognized in the present Covenant is reached, the Commission shall confine its report to a brief statement of the facts and of the solution reached;

(*c*) If a solution within the terms of sub-paragraph (*b*) is not reached, the Commission's report shall embody its findings on all questions of fact relevant to the issues between the States Parties concerned, and its views on the possibilities of an amicable solution of the matter. This report shall also contain the written submissions and a record of the oral submissions made by the States Parties concerned;

(*d*) If the Commission's report is submitted under sub-paragraph (*c*), the States Parties concerned shall, within three months of the receipt of the report, notify the Chairman of the Committee whether or not they accept the contents of the report of the Commission.

8. The provisions of this article are without prejudice to the responsibilities of the Committee under Article 41.
9. The States Parties concerned shall share equally all the expenses of the members of the Commission in accordance with estimates to be provided by the SecretaryGeneral of the United Nations.
10. The Secretary-General of the United Nations shall be empowered to pay the expenses of the members of the Commission, if necessary, before reimbursement by the States Parties concerned, in accordance with Paragraph 9 of this article.

Article 43

The members of the Committee, and of the ad hoc conciliation commissions which may be appointed under Article 42, shall be entitled to the facilities, privileges and immunities of experts on mission for the United Nations as laid down in the relevant sections of the Convention on the Privileges and Immunities of the United Nations.

Article 44

The provisions for the implementation of the present Covenant shall apply without prejudice to the procedures prescribed in the field of human rights by or under the constituent instruments and the conventions of the United Nations and of the specialized agencies and shall not prevent the States Parties to the present Covenant from having recourse to other procedures for settling a dispute in accordance with general or special international agreements in force between them.

Article 45

The Committee shall submit to the General Assembly of the United Nations, through the Economic and Social Council, an annual report on its activities.

Part V

Article 46

Nothing in the present Covenant shall be interpreted as impairing the provisions of the Charter of the United Nations and of the constitutions of the specialized agencies which define the respective responsibilities of the various organs of the United Nations and of the specialized agencies in regard to the matters dealt with in the present Covenant.

Article 47

Nothing in the present Covenant shall be interpreted as impairing the inherent right of all peoples to enjoy and utilize fully and freely their natural wealth and resources.

Part VI

Article 48

1. The present Covenant is open for signature by any State Member of the United Nations or member of any of its specialized agencies, by any State Party to the Statute of the International Court of Justice, and by any other State which has been invited by the General Assembly of the United Nations to become a party to the present Covenant.
2. The present Covenant is subject to ratification. Instruments of ratification shall be deposited with the SecretaryGeneral of the United Nations.
3. The present Covenant shall be open to accession by any State referred to in Paragraph 1 of this article.
4. Accession shall be effected by the deposit of an instrument of accession with the Secretary-General of the United Nations.
5. The Secretary-General of the United Nations shall inform all States which have signed this Covenant or acceded to it of the deposit of each instrument of ratification or accession.

Article 49

1. The present Covenant shall enter into force three months after the date of the deposit with the Secretary-General of the United Nations of the thirty-fifth instrument of ratification or instrument of accession.
2. For each State ratifying the present Covenant or acceding to it after the deposit of the thirty-fifth instrument of ratification or instrument of acces-

sion, the present Covenant shall enter into force three months after the date of the deposit of its own instrument of ratification or instrument of accession.

Article 50

The provisions of the present Covenant shall extend to all parts of federal States without any limitations or exceptions.

Article 51

1. Any State Party to the present Covenant may propose an amendment and file it with the Secretary-General of the United Nations. The Secretary-General of the United Nations shall thereupon communicate any proposed amendments to the States Parties to the present Covenant with a request that they notify him whether they favour a conference of States Parties for the purpose of considering and voting upon the proposals. In the event that at least one third of the States Parties favours such a conference, the Secretary-General shall convene the conference under the auspices of the United Nations. Any amendment adopted by a majority of the States Parties present and voting at the conference shall be submitted to the General Assembly of the United Nations for approval.
2. Amendments shall come into force when they have been approved by the General Assembly of the United Nations and accepted by a two-thirds majority of the States Parties to the present Covenant in accordance with their respective constitutional processes.
3. When amendments come into force, they shall be binding on those States Parties which have accepted them, other States Parties still being bound by the provisions of the present Covenant and any earlier amendment which they have accepted.

Article 52

Irrespective of the notifications made under Article 48, Paragraph 5, the Secretary-General of the United Nations shall inform all States referred to in Paragraph 1 of the same article of the following particulars:

- *(a)* Signatures, ratifications and accessions under Article 48;
- *(b)* The date of the entry into force of the present Covenant under Article 49 and the date of the entry into force of any amendments under Article 51.

Article 53

1. The present Covenant, of which the Chinese, English, French, Russian and Spanish texts are equally authentic, shall be deposited in the archives of the United Nations.
2. The Secretary-General of the United Nations shall transmit certified copies of the present Covenant to all States referred to in Article 48.

OPTIONAL PROTOCOL TO THE INTERNATIONAL COVENANT ON CIVIL AND POLITICAL RIGHTS

Adopted and opened for signature, ratification and accession by General Assembly resolution 2200 A (XXI) of 16 December 1966

ENTRY INTO FORCE: 23 March 1976, in accordance with Article 9.

The States Parties to the present Protocol,

Considering that in order further to achieve the purposes of the Covenant on Civil and Political Rights (hereinafter referred to as the Covenant) and the implementation of its provisions it would be appropriate to enable the Human Rights Committee set up in part IV of the Covenant (hereinafter referred to as the Committee) to receive and consider, as provided in the present Protocol, communications from individuals claiming to be victims of violations of any of the rights set forth in the Covenant.

Have agreed as follows:

Article 1

A State Party to the Covenant that becomes a party to the present Protocol recognizes the competence of the Committee to receive and consider communications from individuals subject to its jurisdiction who claim to be victims of a violation by that State Party of any of the rights set forth in the Covenant. No communication shall be received by the Committee if it concerns a State Party to the Covenant which is not a party to the present Protocol.

Article 2

Subject to the provisions of Article 1, individuals who claim that any of their rights enumerated in the Covenant have been violated and who have exhausted all available domestic remedies may submit a written communication to the Committee for consideration.

Article 3

The Committee shall consider inadmissible any communication under the present Protocol which is anonymous, or which it considers to be an abuse of the right of submission of such communications or to be incompatible with the provisions of the Covenant.

Article 4

1. Subject to the provisions of Article 3, the Committee shall bring any communications submitted to it under the present Protocol to the attention of the

State Party to the present Protocol alleged to be violating any provision of the Covenant.

2. Within six months, the receiving State shall submit to the Committee written explanations or statements clarifying the matter and the remedy, if any, that may have been taken by that State.

Article 5

1. The Committee shall consider communications received under the present Protocol in the light of all written information made available to it by the individual and by the State Party concerned.
2. The Committee shall not consider any communication from an individual unless it has ascertained that:
   (a) The same matter is not being examined under another procedure of international investigation or settlement:
   (b) The individual has exhausted all available domestic remedies. This shall not be the rule where the application of the remedies is unreasonably prolonged.
3. The Committee shall hold closed meetings when examining communications under the present Protocol.
4. The Committee shall forward its views to the State Party concerned and to the individual.

Article 6

The Committee shall include in its annual report under Article 45 of the Covenant a summary of its activities under the present Protocol.

Article 7

Pending the achievement of the objectives of resolution 1514 (XV) adopted by the General Assembly of the United Nations on 14 December 1960 concerning the Declaration on the Granting of Independence to Colonial Countries and Peoples, the provisions of the present Protocol shall in no way limit the right of petition granted to these peoples by the Charter of the United Nations and other international conventions and instruments under the United Nations and its specialized agencies.

Article 8

1. The present Protocol is open for signature by any State which has signed the Covenant.
2. The present Protocol is subject to ratification by any State which has ratified or acceded to the Covenant. Instruments of ratification shall be deposited with the Secretary-General of the United Nations.
3. The present Protocol shall be open to accession by any State which has ratified or acceded to the Covenant.

4. Accession shall be effected by the deposit of an instrument of accession with the Secretary-General of the United Nations.
5. The Secretary-General of the United Nations shall inform all States which have signed the present Protocol or acceded to it of the deposit of each instrument of ratification or accession.

Article 9

1. Subject to the entry into force of the Covenant, the present Protocol shall enter into force three months after the date of the deposit with the Secretary-General of the United Nations of the tenth instrument of ratification or instrument of accession.
2. For each State ratifying the present Protocol or acceding to it after the deposit of the tenth instrument of ratification or instrument of accession, the present Protocol shall enter into force three months after the date of the deposit of its own instrument of ratification or instrument of accession.

Article 10

The provisions of the present Protocol shall extend to all parts of federal States without any limitations or exceptions.

Article 11

1. Any State Party to the present Protocol may propose an amendment and file it with the Secretary-General of the United Nations. The Secretary-General shall thereupon communicate any proposed amendments to the States Parties to the present Protocol with a request that they notify him whether they favour a conference of States Parties for the purpose of considering and voting upon the proposal. In the event that at least one third of the States Parties favours such a conference, the Secretary-General shall convene the conference under the auspices of the United Nations. Any amendment adopted by a majority of the States Parties present and voting at the conference shall be submitted to the General Assembly of the United Nations for approval.
2. Amendments shall come into force when they have been approved by the General Assembly of the United Nations and accepted by a two-thirds majority of the States Parties to the present Protocol in accordance with their respective constitutional processes.
3. When amendments come into force, they shall be binding on those States Parties which have accepted them, other States Parties still being bound by the provisions of the present Protocol and any earlier amendment which they have accepted.

Article 12

1. Any State Party may denounce the present Protocol at any time by written notification addressed to the Secretary-General of the United Nations.

Denunciation shall take effect three months after the date of receipt of the notification by the Secretary-General.

2. Denunciation shall be without prejudice to the continued application of the provisions of the present Protocol to any communication submitted under Article 2 before the effective date of denunciation.

Article 13

Irrespective of the notifications made under Article 8, Paragraph 5, of the present Protocol, the Secretary-General of thc United Nations shall inform all States referred to in Article 48, Paragraph 1, of the Covenant of the following particulars:

(a) Signatures, ratifications and accessions under Article 8;
(b) The date of the entry into force of the present Protocol under Article 9 and the date of the entry into force of any amendments under Article 11;
(c) Denunciations under Article 12.

Article 14

1. The present Protocol, of which the Chinese, English, French, Russian and Spanish texts are equally authentic, shall be deposited in the archives of the United Nations.
2. The Secretary-General of the United Nations shall transmit certified copies of the present Protocol to all States referred to in Article 48 of the Covenant.

INTERNATIONAL COVENANT ON ECONOMIC, SOCIAL AND CULTURAL RIGHTS

Adopted and opened for signature, ratification and accession by General Assembly resolution 2200 A (XXI) of 16 December 1966

Entry into force: 3 January 1976, in accordance with Article 27.

Preamble

The States Parties to the present Covenant,

Considering that, in accordance with the principles proclaimed in the Charter of the United Nations, recognition of the inherent dignity and of the equal and inalienable rights of all members of the human family is the foundation of freedom, justice and peace in the world.

Recognizing that these rights derive from the inherent dignity of the human person,

Recognizing that, in accordance with the Universal Declaration of Human Rights, the ideal of free human beings enjoying freedom from fear and want can only be achieved if conditions are created whereby everyone may enjoy his economic, social and cultural rights, as well as his civil and political rights,

Considering the obligation of States under the Charter of the United Nations to promote universal respect for, and observance of, human rights and freedoms,

Realizing that the individual, having duties to other individuals and to the community to which he belongs, is under a responsibility to strive for the promotion and observance of the rights recognized in the present Covenant.

Agree upon the following articles:

Part I

Article 1

1. All peoples have the right of self-determination. By virtue of that right they freely determine their political status and freely pursue their economic, social and cultural development.
2. All peoples may, for their own ends, freely dispose of their natural wealth and resources without prejudice to any obligations arising out of international economic cooperation, based upon the principle of mutual benefit, and international law. In no case may a people be deprived of its own means of subsistence.

3. The States Parties to the present Covenant, including those having responsibility for the administration of Non-Self-Governing and Trust Territories, shall promote the realization of the right of self-determination, and shall respect that right, in conformity with the provisions of the Charter of the United Nations.

Part II

Article 2

1. Each State Party to the present Covenant undertakes to take steps, individually and through international assistance and cooperation, especially economic and technical, to the maximum of its available resources, with a view to achieving progressively the full realization of the rights recognized in the present Covenant by all appropriate means, including particularly the adoption of legislative measures.
2. The States Parties to the present Covenant undertake to guarantee that the rights enunciated in the present Covenant will be exercised without discrimination of any kind as to race, colour, sex, language, religion, political or other opinion, national or social origin property, birth or other status.
3. Developing countries, with due regard to human rights and their national economy, may determine to what extent they would guarantee the economic rights recognized in the present Covenant to nonnationals.

Article 3

The States Parties to the present Covenant undertake to ensure the equal right of men and women to the enjoyment of all economic, social and cultural rights set forth in the present Covenant.

Article 4

The States Parties to the present Covenant recognize that, in the enjoyment of those rights provided by the State in conformity with the present Covenant, the State may subject such rights only to such limitations as are determined by law only in so far as this may be compatible with the nature of these rights and solely for the purpose of promoting the general welfare in a democratic society.

Article 5

1. Nothing in the present Covenant may be interpreted as implying for any State, group or person any right to engage in any activity or to perform any act aimed at the destruction of any of the rights or freedoms recognized herein, or at their limitation to a greater extent than is provided for in the present Covenant.
2. No restriction upon or derogation from any of the fundamental human rights recognized or existing in any country in virtue of law, conventions, regulations or custom shall be admitted on the pretext that the present Covenant does not recognize such rights or that it recognizes them to a lesser extent.

Part III

Article 6

1. The States Parties to the present Covenant recognize the right to work, which includes the right of everyone to the opportunity to gain his living by work which he freely chooses or accepts, and will take appropriate steps to safeguard this right.
2. The steps to be taken by a State Party to the present Covenant to achieve the full realization of this right shall include technical and vocational guidance and training programmes, policies and techniques to achieve steady economic, social and cultural development and full and productive employment under conditions safeguarding fundamental political and economic freedoms to the individual.

Article 7

The States Parties to the present Covenant recognize the right of everyone to the enjoyment of just and favourable conditions of work which ensure, in particular:

(a) Remuneration which provides all workers, as minimum, with:
  - (i) Fair wages and equal remuneration for work of equal value without distinction of any kind, in particular women being guaranteed conditions of work not inferior to those enjoyed by men, with equal pay for equal work;
  - (ii) A decent living for themselves and their families in accordance with the provisions of the present covenant;

(b) Safe and healthy working conditions;

(c) Equal opportunity for everyone to be promoted in his employment to an appropriate higher level, subject to no considerations other than those of seniority and competence;

(d) Rest, leisure and reasonable limitation of working hours and periodic holidays with pay, as well as remuneration for public holidays.

Article 8

1. The States Parties to the present Covenant undertake to ensure:

   (a) The right of everyone to form trade unions and join the trade union of his choice, subject only to the rules of the organization concerned, for the promotion and protection of his economic and social interests. No restrictions may be placed on the exercise of this right other than those prescribed by law and which are necessary in a democratic society in the interests of national security or public order or for the protection of the rights and freedoms of others;

   (b) The right of trade unions to establish national federations or confederations and the right of the latter to form or join international trade-union organizations;

(c) The right of trade unions to function freely subject to no limitations other than those prescribed by law and which are necessary in a democratic society in the interests of national security or public order or for the protection of the rights and freedoms of others;
(d) The right to strike, provided that it is exercised in conformity with the laws of the particular country.

2. This article shall not prevent the imposition of lawful restrictions on the exercise of these rights by members of the armed forces or of the police or of the administration of the State.
3. Nothing in this article shall authorize States Parties to the International Labour Organisation Convention of 1948 concerning Freedom of Association and Protection of the Right to Organize to take legislative measures which would prejudice, or apply the law in such a manner as would prejudice, the guarantees provided for in that Convention.

Article 9

The States Parties to the present Covenant recognize the right of everyone to social security, including social insurance.

Article 10

The States Parties to the present Covenant recognize that:

1. The widest possible protection and assistance should be accorded to the family, which is the natural and fundamental group unit of society, particularly for its establishment and while it is responsible for the care and education of dependent children. Marriage must be entered into with the free consent of the intending spouses.
2. Special protection should be accorded to mothers during a reasonable period before and after childbirth. During such period working mothers should be accorded paid leave or leave with adequate social security benefits.
3. Special measures of protection and assistance should be taken on behalf of all children and young persons without any discrimination for reasons of parentage or other conditions. Children and young persons should be protected from economic and social exploitation. Their employment in work harmful to their morals or health or dangerous to life or likely to hamper their normal development should be punishable by law. States should also set age limits below which the paid employment of child labour should be prohibited and punishable by law.

Article 11

1. The States Parties to the present Covenant recognize the right of everyone to an adequate standard of living for himself and his family, including adequate food, clothing and housing, and to the continuous improvement of living conditions. The States Parties will take appropriate steps to ensure the

realization of this right recognizing to this effect the essential importance of international cooperation based on free consent.

2. The States Parties to the present Covenant, recognizing the fundamental right of everyone to be free from hunger, shall take, individually and through international co-operation, the measures, including specific programmes, which are needed.
   (a) To improve methods of production, conservation and distribution of food by making full use of technical and scientific knowledge, by disseminating knowledge of thc principles of nutrition and by developing or reforming agrarian systems in such a way as to achieve the most efficient development and utilization of natural resources;
   (b) Taking into account the problems of both food-importing and food-exporting countries, to ensure an equitable distribution of world food supplies in relation to need.

<u>*Article 12*</u>

1. The States Parties to the present Covenant recognize the right of everyone to the enjoyment of the highest attainable standard of physical and mental health.
2. The steps to be taken by the States Parties to the present Covenant to achieve the full realization of this right shall include those necessary for:
   (a) The provision for the reduction of the stillbirth-rate and of infant mortality and for the healthy development of the child;
   (b) The improvement of all aspects of environmental and industrial hygiene;
   (c) The prevention, treatment and control of epidemic, endemic, occupational and other diseases;
   (d) The creation of conditions which would assure to all medical service and medical attention in the event of sickness.

<u>*Article 13*</u>

1. The States Parties to the present Covenant recognize the right of everyone to education. They agree that education shall be directed to the full development of the human personality and the sense of its dignity, and shall strengthen the respect for human rights and fundamental freedoms. They further agree that education shall enable all persons to participate effectively in a free society, promote understanding, tolerance and friendship among all nations and all racial, ethnic or religious groups, and further the activities of the United Nations for the maintenance of peace.
2. The States Parties to the present Covenant recognize that, with a view to achieving the full realization of this right:
   (a) Primary education shall be compulsory and available free to all;
   (b) Secondary education in its different forms, including technical and

vocational secondary education, shall be made generally available and accessible to all by every appropriate means, and in particular by the progressive introduction of free education;

(c) Higher education shall be made equally accessible to all, on the basis of capacity, by every appropriate means, and in particular by the progressive introduction of free education;

(d) Fundamental education shall be encouraged or intensified as far as possible for those persons who have not received or completed the whole period of their primary education;

(e) The development of a system of schools at all levels shall be actively pursued, an adequate fellowship system shall be established, and the material conditions of teaching staff shall be continuously improved.

3. The States Parties to the present Covenant undertake to have respect for the liberty of parents and, when applicable, legal guardians to choose for their children schools, other than those established by the public authorities, which conform to such minimum educational standards as may be laid down or approved by the State and to ensure the religious and moral education of their children in conformity with their own convictions.

4. No part of this article shall be construed so as to interfere with the liberty of individuals and bodies to establish and direct educational institutions, subject always to the observance of the principles set forth in paragraph I of this article and to the requirement that the education given in such institutions shall conform to such minimum standards as may be laid down by the State.

Article 14

Each State Party to the present Covenant which, at the time of becoming a Party, has not been able to secure in its metropolitan territory or other territories under its jurisdiction compulsory primary education, free of charge, undertakes, within two years, to work out and adopt a detailed plan of action for the progressive implementation, within a reasonable number of years, to be fixed in the plan, of the principle of compulsory education free of charge for all.

Article 15

1. The States Parties to the present Covenant recognize the right of everyone:
   (a) To take part in cultural life;
   (b) To enjoy the benefits of scientific progress and its applications;
   (c) To benefit from the protection of the moral and material interests resulting from any scientific, literary or artistic production of which he is the author.
2. The steps to be taken by the States Parties to the present Covenant to achieve the full realization of this right shall include those necessary for the conservation, the development and the diffusion of science and culture.
3. The States Parties to the present Covenant undertake to respect the freedom indispensable for scientific research and creative activity.

4. The States Parties to the present Covenant recognize the benefits to be derived from the encouragement and development of international contacts and cooperation in the scientific and cultural fields.

Part IV

Article 16

1. The States Parties to the present Covenant undertake to submit in conformity with this part of the Covenant reports on the measures which they have adopted and the progress made in achieving the observance of the rights recognized herein.
2.
   (a) All reports shall be submitted to the Secretary-General of the United Nations, who shall transmit copies to the Economic and Social Council for consideration in accordance with the provisions of the present Covenant;
   (b) The Secretary-General of the United Nations shall also transmit to the specialized agencies copies of the reports, or any relevant parts therefrom, from States Parties to the present Covenant which are also members of these specialized agencies in so far as these reports, or parts therefrom, relate to any matters which fall within the responsibilities of the said agencies in accordance with their constitutional instruments.

Article 17

1. The States Parties to the present Covenant shall furnish their reports in stages, in accordance with a programme to be established by the Economic and Social Council within one year of the entry into force of the present Covenant after consultation with the States Parties and the specialized agencies concerned.
2. Reports may indicate factors and difficulties affecting the degree of fulfillment of obligations under the present Covenant.
3. Where relevant information has previously been furnished to the United Nations or to any specialized agency by any State Party to the present Covenant, it will not be necessary to reproduce that information, but a precise reference to the information so furnished will suffice.

Article 18

Pursuant to its responsibilities under the Charter of the United Nations in the field of human rights and fundamental freedoms, the Economic and Social Council may make arrangements with the specialized agencies in respect of their reporting to it on the progress made in achieving the observance of the provisions of the present Covenant falling within the scope of their activities. These reports may include particulars of decisions and recommendations on such implementation adopted by their competent organs.

Article 19

The Economic and Social Council may transmit to the Commission on Human Rights for study and general recommendation or, as appropriate, for information the reports concerning human rights submitted by States in accordance with Articles 16 and 17, and those concerning human rights submitted by the specialized agencies in accordance with Article 18.

Article 20

The States Parties to the present Covenant and the specialized agencies concerned may submit comments to the Economic and Social Council on any general recommendation under Article 19 or reference to such general recommendation in any report of the Commission on Human Rights or any documentation referred to therein.

Article 21

The Economic and Social Council may submit from time to time to the General Assembly reports with recommendations of a general nature and a summary of the information received from the States Parties to the present Covenant and the specialized agencies on the measures taken and the progress made in achieving general observance of the rights recognized in the present Covenant.

Article 22

The Economic and Social Council may bring to the attention of other organs of the United Nations, their subsidiary organs and specialized agencies concerned with furnishing technical assistance any matters arising out of the reports referred to in this part of the present Covenant which may assist such bodies in deciding, each within its field of competence, on the advisability of international measures likely to contribute to the effective progressive implementation of the present Covenant.

Article 23

The States Parties to the present Covenant agree that international action for the achievement of the rights recognized in the present Covenant includes such methods as the conclusion of conventions, the adoption of recommendations, the furnishing of technical assistance and the holding of regional meetings and technical meetings for the purpose of consultation and study organized in conjunction with the Governments concerned.

Article 24

Nothing in the present Covenant shall be interpreted as impairing the provisions of the Charter of the United Nations and of the constitutions of the specialized agencies which define the respective responsibilities of the various organs of the United Nations and of the specialized agencies in regard to the matters dealt with in the present Covenant.

Article 25

Nothing in the present Covenant shall be interpreted as impairing the inherent right of all peoples to enjoy and utilize fully and freely their natural wealth and resources.

Part V

Article 26

1. The present Covenant is open for signature by any State Member of the United Nations or member of any of its specialized agencies, by any State Party to the Statute of the International Court of Justice, and by any other State which has been invited by the General Assembly of the United Nations to become a party to the present Covenant.
2. The present Covenant is subject to ratification. Instruments of ratification shall be deposited with the Secretary-General of the United Nations.
3. The present Covenant shall be open to accession by any State referred to in Paragraph 1 of this article.
4. Accession shall be effected by the deposit of an instrument of accession with the Secretary-General of the United Nations.
5. The Secretary-General of the United Nations shall inform all States which have signed the present Covenant or acceded to it of the deposit of each instrument of ratification or accession.

Article 27

1. The present Covenant shall enter into force three months after the date of the deposit with the Secretary-General of the United Nations of the thirty-fifth instrument of ratification or instrument of accession.
2. For each State ratifying the present Covenant or acceding to it after the deposit of the thirty-fifth instrument of ratification or instrument of accession, the present Covenant shall enter into force three months after the date of the deposit of its own instrument of ratification or instrument of accession.

Article 28

The provisions of the present Covenant shall extend to all parts of federal States without any limitations or exceptions.

Article 29

1. Any State Party to the present Covenant may propose an amendment and file it with the Secretary- General of the United Nations. The Secretary-General shall thereupon communicate any proposed amendments to the States Parties to the present Covenant with a request that they notify him whether they favour a conference of States Parties for the purpose of considering and voting upon the proposals. In the event that at least one third of

the States Parties favours such a conference, the Secretary-General shall convene the conference under the auspices of the United Nations. Any amendment adopted by a majority of the States Parties present and voting at the conference shall be submitted to the General Assembly of the United Nations for approval.

2. Amendments shall come into force when they have been approved by the General Assembly of the United Nations and accepted by a two-thirds majority of the States Parties to the present Covenant in accordance with their respective constitutional processes.
3. When amendments come into force they shall be binding on those States Parties which have accepted them, other States Parties still being bound by the provisions of the present Covenant and any earlier amendment which they have accepted.

Article 30

Irrespective of the notifications made under Article 26, Paragraph 5, the Secretary-General of the United Nations shall inform all States referred to in Paragraph 1 of the same article of the following particulars:

(a) Signatures, ratifications and accessions under Article 26;

(b) The date of the entry into force of the present Covenant under Article 27 and the date of the entry into force of any amendments under Article 29.

Article 31

1. The present Covenant, of which the Chinese, English, French, Russian and Spanish texts are equally authentic, shall be deposited in the archives of the United Nations.
2. The Secretary-General of the United Nations shall transmit certified copies of the present Covenant to all States referred to in Article 26.

THE EUROPEAN CONVENTION FOR THE PROTECTION OF HUMAN RIGHTS AND FUNDAMENTAL FREEDOMS

The European Convention on Human Rights

The Governments signatory hereto, being Members of the Council of Europe,

Considering the Universal Declaration of Human Rights proclaimed by the

General Assembly of the United Nations on 10 December 1948;

Considering that this Declaration aims at securing the universal and effective recognition and observance of the Rights therein declared;

Considering that the aim of the Council of Europe is the achievement of greater unity between its Members and that one of the methods by which the aim is to be pursued is the maintenance and further realization of Human Rights and Fundamental Freedoms;

Reaffirming their profound belief in those Fundamental Freedoms which are the foundation of justice and peace in the world and are best maintained on the one hand by an effective political democracy and on the other by a common understanding and observance of the Human Rights upon which they depend;

Being resolved, as the Governments of European countries which are like-minded and have a common heritage of political traditions, ideals, freedom and the rule of law to take the first steps for the collective enforcement of certain of the Rights stated in the Universal Declaration;

Have agreed as follows:

Article 1

The High Contracting Parties shall secure to everyone within their jurisdiction the rights and freedoms defined in Section I of this Convention.

SECTION I

Article 2

Everyone's right to life shall be protected by law. No one shall be deprived of his life intentionally save in the execution of a sentence of a court following his conviction of a crime for which this penalty is provided by law.

Deprivation of life shall not be regarded as inflicted in contravention of this article when it results from the use of force which is no more than absolutely necessary:

(a) in defense of any person from unlawful violence;
(b) in order to effect a lawful arrest or to prevent escape of a person lawfully detained;
(c) in action lawfully taken for the purpose of quelling a riot or insurrection.

Article 3

No one shall be subjected to torture or to inhuman or degrading treatment or punishment.

Article 4

No one shall be held in slavery or servitude.
No one shall be required to perform forced or compulsory labour.
For the purpose of this article the term forced or compulsory labour' shall not include:

(a) any work required to be done in the ordinary course of detention imposed according to the provisions of Article 5 of this Convention or during conditional release from such detention;
(b) any service of a military character or, in case of conscientious objectors in countries where they are recognized, service exacted instead of compulsory military service;
(c) any service exacted in case of an emergency or calamity threatening the life or well-being of the community;
(d) any work or service which forms part of normal civic obligations.

Article 5

Everyone has the right to liberty and security of person.
No one shall be deprived of his liberty save in the following cases and in accordance with a procedure prescribed by law:

(a) the lawful detention of a person after conviction by a competent court;
(b) the lawful arrest or detention of a person for non-compliance with the lawful order of a court or in order to secure the fulfilment of any obligation prescribed by law;
(c) the lawful arrest or detention of a person effected for the purpose of bringing him before the competent legal authority of reasonable suspicion of having committed and offense or when it is reasonably considered necessary to prevent his committing an offense or fleeing after having done so;
(d) the detention of a minor by lawful order for the purpose of educational supervision or his lawful detention for the purpose of bringing him before the competent legal authority;
(e) the lawful detention of persons for the prevention of the spreading of infectious diseases, of persons of unsound mind, alcoholics or drug addicts, or vagrants;

(f) the lawful arrest or detention of a person to prevent his effecting an unauthorized entry into the country or of a person against whom action is being taken with a view to deportation or extradition.

Everyone who is arrested shall be informed promptly, in a language which he understands, of the reasons for his arrest and the charge against him.

Everyone arrested or detained in accordance with the provisions of Paragraph 1(c) of this article shall be brought promptly before a judge or other officer authorized by law to exercise judicial power and shall be entitled to trial within a reasonable time or to release pending trial. Release may be conditioned by guarantees to appear for trial.

Everyone who is deprived of his liberty by arrest or detention shall be entitled to take proceedings by which the lawfulness of his detention shall be decided speedily by a court and his release ordered if the detention is not lawful.

Everyone who has been the victim of arrest or detention in contravention of the provisions of this article shall have an enforceable right to compensation.

Article 6

In the determination of his civil rights and obligations or of any criminal charge against him, everyone is entitled to a fair and public hearing within a reasonable time by an independent and impartial tribunal established by law. Judgement shall be pronounced publicly by the press and public may be excluded from all or part of the trial in the interest of morals, public order or national security in a democratic society, where the interests of juveniles or the protection of the private life of the parties so require, or the extent strictly necessary in the opinion of the court in special circumstances where publicity would prejudice the interests of justice.

Everyone charged with a criminal offense shall be presumed innocent until proved guilty according to law.

Everyone charged with a criminal offense has the following minimum rights:

(a) to be informed promptly, in a language which he understands and in detail, of the nature and cause of the accusation against him;

(b) to have adequate time and the facilities for the preparation of his defense;

(c) to defend himself in person or through legal assistance of his own choosing or, if he has not sufficient means to pay for legal assistance, to be given it free when the interests of justice so require;

(d) to examine or have examined witnesses against him and to obtain the attendance and examination of witnesses on his behalf under the same conditions as witnesses against him;

(e) to have the free assistance of an interpreter if he cannot understand or speak the language used in court.

Article 7

No one shall be held guilty of any criminal offense on account of any act or omission which did not constitute a criminal offense under national or international law at the time when it was committed. Nor shall a heavier penalty be imposed than the one that was applicable at the time the criminal offense was committed.

This article shall not prejudice the trial and punishment of any person for any act or omission which, at the time when it was committed, was criminal according the general principles of law recognized by civilized nations.

Article 8

Everyone has the right to respect for his private and family life, his home and his correspondence.

There shall be no interference by a public authority with the exercise of this right except such as is in accordance with the law and is necessary in a democratic society in the interests of national security, public safety or the economic well-being of the country, for the prevention of disorder or crime, for the protection of health or morals, or for the protection of the rights and freedoms of others.

Article 9

Everyone has the right to freedom of thought, conscience and religion; this right includes freedom to change his religion or belief, and freedom, either alone or in community with others and in public or private, to manifest his religion or belief, in worship, teaching, practice and observance.

Freedom to manifest one's religion or beliefs shall be subject only to such limitations as are prescribed by law and are necessary in a democratic society in the interests of public safety, for the protection of public order, health or morals, or the protection of the rights and freedoms of others.

Article 10

Everyone has the right to freedom of expression. This right shall include freedom to hold opinions and to receive and impart information and ideas without interference by public authority and regardless of frontiers. This article shall not prevent States from requiring the licensing of broadcasting, television or cinema enterprises.

The exercise of these freedoms, since it carries with it duties and responsibilities, may be subject to such formalities, conditions, restrictions or penalties as are prescribed by law and are necessary in a democratic society, in the interests of national security, territorial integrity or public safety, for the prevention of disorder or crime, for the protection of health or morals, for the protection of the reputation or the rights of others, for preventing the disclosure of information received in confidence, or for maintaining the authority and impartiality of the judiciary.

Article 11

Everyone has the right to freedom of peaceful assembly and to freedom of association with others, including the right to form and to join trade unions for the protection of his interests.

No restrictions shall be placed on the exercise of these rights other than such as are prescribed by law and are necessary in a democratic society in the interests of national security or public safety, for the prevention of disorder or crime, for the protection of health or morals or for the protection of the rights and freedoms of others. This article shall not prevent the imposition of lawful restrictions on the exercise of these rights by members of the armed forces, of the police or of the administration of the State.

Article 12

Men and women of marriageable age have the right to marry and to found a family, according to the national laws governing the exercise of this right.

Article 13

Everyone whose rights and freedoms as set forth in this Convention are violated shall have an effective remedy before a national authority notwithstanding that the violation has been committed by persons acting in an official capacity.

Article 14

The enjoyment of the rights and freedoms set forth in this Convention shall be secured without discrimination on any ground such as sex, race, colour, language, religion, political or other opinion, national or social origin, association with a national minority, property, birth or other status.

Article 15

In time of war or other public emergency threatening the life of the nation any High Contracting Party may take measures derogating from its obligations under this Convention to the extent strictly required by the exigencies of the situation, provided that such measures are not inconsistent with its other obligations under international law.

No derogation from Article 2, except in respect of deaths resulting from lawful acts of war, or from Articles 3, 4 (Paragraph 1) and 7 shall be made under this provision.

Any High Contracting Party availing itself of this right of derogation shall keep the Secretary-General of the Council of Europe fully informed of the measures which it has taken and the reasons therefore. It shall also inform the Secretary-General of the Council of Europe when such measures have ceased to operate and the provisions of the Convention are again being fully executed.

Article 16

Nothing in Articles 10, 11, and 14 shall be regarded as preventing the High Contracting Parties from imposing restrictions on the political activity of aliens.

Article 17

Nothing in this Convention may be interpreted as implying for any State, group or person any right to engage in any activity or perform any act aimed at the destruction on any of the rights and freedoms set forth herein or at their limitation to a greater extent than is provided for in the Convention.

Article 18

The restrictions permitted under this Convention to the said rights and freedoms shall not be applied for any purpose other than those for which they have been prescribed.

SECTION II

Article 19

To ensure the observance of the engagements undertaken by the High Contracting Parties in the present Convention, there shall be set up: A European Commission of Human Rights hereinafter referred to as 'the Commission'; A European Court of Human Rights, hereinafter referred to as 'the Court'.

SECTION III

Article 20

The Commission shall consist of a number of members equal to that of the High Contracting Parties. No two members of the Commission may be nationals of the same state.

Article 21

The members of the Commission shall be elected by the Committee of Ministers by an absolute majority of votes, from a list of names drawn up by the Bureau of the Consultative Assembly; each group of the Representatives of the High Contracting Parties in the Consultative Assembly shall put forward three candidates, of whom two at least shall be its nationals. As far as applicable, the same procedure shall be followed to complete the Commission in the event of other States subsequently becoming Parties to this Convention, and in filing casual vacancies.

Article 22

The members of the Commission shall be elected for a period of six years. They may be re-elected. However, of the members elected at the first election, the terms of seven members shall expire at the end of three years. The members whose terms are to expire at the end of the initial period of three years shall be chosen by lot by the Secretary-General of the Council of Europe immediately after the first election has been completed. A member of the Commission elected to replace a member whose term of office has not expired shall hold office for the remainder of his predecessor's term. The members of the Commission shall hold office until replaced. After having been replaced, they shall continue to deal with such cases as they already have under consideration.

Article 23

The members of the Commission shall sit on the Commission in their individual capacity.

Article 24

Any High Contracting Party may refer to the Commission, through the Secretary-General of the Council of Europe, any alleged breach of the provisions of the Convention by another High Contracting Party.

Article 25

The Commission may receive petitions addressed to the Secretary-General of the Council of Europe from any person, non-governmental organization or group of individuals claiming to the victim of a violation by one of the High Contracting Parties of the rights set forth in this Convention, provided that the High Contracting Party against which the complaint has been lodged has declared that it recognizes the competence of the Commission to receive such petitions. Those of the High Contracting Parties who have made such a declaration undertake not to hinder in any way the effective exercise of this right. Such declarations may be made for a specific period. The declarations shall be deposited with the Secretary-General of the Council of Europe who shall transmit copies thereof to the High Contracting Parties and publish them. The Commission shall only exercise the powers provided for in this article when at least six High Contracting Parties are bound by declarations made in accordance with the preceding paragraphs.

Article 26

The Commission may only deal with the matter after all domestic remedies have been exhausted, according to the generally recognized rules of international law, and within a period of six months from the date on which the final decision was taken.

Article 27

The Commission shall not deal with any petition submitted under Article 25 which

(a) is anonymous, or

(b) is substantially the same as a matter which has already been examined by the Commission or has already been submitted to another procedure or international investigation or settlement and if it contains no relevant new information.

The Commission shall consider inadmissible any petition submitted under Article 25 which it considers incompatible with the provisions of the present Convention, manifestly ill-founded, or an abuse of the right of petition. The Commission shall reject any petition referred to it which it considers inadmissible under Article 26.

Article 28

In the event of the Commission accepting a petition referred to it:

(a) it shall, with a view to ascertaining the facts undertake together with the representatives of the parties and examination of the petition and, if need be, an investigation, for the effective conduct of which the States concerned shall furnish all necessary facilities, after an exchange of views with the Commission;

(b) it shall place itself at the disposal of the parties concerned with a view to securing a friendly settlement of the matter on the basis of respect for Human Rights as defined in this Convention.

Article 29

The Commission shall perform the functions set out in Article 28 by means of a Sub-Commission consisting of seven members of the Commission. Each of the parties concerned may appoint as members of this Sub-Commission a person of its choice. The remaining members shall be chosen by lot in accordance with arrangements prescribed in the Rules of Procedure of the Commission.

Article 30

If the Sub-Commission succeeds in effecting a friendly settlement in accordance with Article 28, it shall draw up a Report which shall be sent to the States concerned, to the Committee of Ministers and to the Secretary-General of the Council of Europe for publication. This Report shall be confined to a brief statement of the facts and of the solution reached.

Article 31

If a solution is not reached, the Commission shall draw up a Report on the facts and state its opinion as to whether the facts found disclose a breach by the State concerned of its obligations under the Convention. The opinions of all the members of the Commission on this point may be stated in the Report. The Report shall be transmitted to the Committee of Ministers. It shall also be transmitted to the States concerned, who shall not be at liberty to publish it. In transmitting the Report to the Committee of Ministers the Commission may make such proposals as it thinks fit.

Article 32

If the question is not referred to the Court in accordance with Article 48 of this Convention within a period of three months from the date of the transmission of the Report to the Committee of Ministers, the Committee of Ministers shall decide by a majority of two-thirds of the members entitled to sit on the Committee whether there has been a violation of the Convention. In the affirmative case the Committee of Ministers shall prescribe a period during which the Contracting Party concerned must take the measures required by the decision of the Committee of Ministers. If the High Contracting Party concerned has not taken satisfactory measures within the prescribed period, the Committee of Ministers shall decide by the majority provided for in Paragraph 1 above what effect shall be given to its original decision and shall publish the Report. The High Contracting Parties undertake to regard as binding on them any decision which the Committee of Ministers may take in application of the preceding paragraphs.

Article 33

The Commission shall meet 'in camera'.

Article 34

The Commission shall take its decision by a majority of the Members present and voting; the Sub-Commission shall take its decisions by a majority of its members.

Article 35

The Commission shall meet as the circumstances require. The meetings shall be convened by the Secretary-General of the Council of Europe.

Article 36

The Commission shall draw up its own rules of procedure.

Article 37

The secretariat of The Commission shall be provided by the Secretary-General of the Council of Europe.

SECTION IV

Article 38

The European Court of Human Rights shall consist of a number of judges equal to that of the Members of the Council of Europe. No two judges may be nationals of the State.

Article 39

The members of the Court shall be elected by the Consultative Assembly by a majority of the votes cast from a list of persons nominated by Members of the Council of Europe; each Member shall nominate three candidates, of whom two at least shall be its nationals. As far as applicable, the same procedure shall be followed to complete the Court in the event of the admission of new members of the Council of Europe, and in filling casual vacancies. The candidates shall be of high moral character and must either possess the qualifications required for appointment to high judicial office or be jurisconsults of recognized competence.

Article 40

The members of the Court shall be elected for a period of nine years. They may be re-elected. However, of the members elected at the first election the terms of four members shall expire at the end of three years, and the terms of four more members shall expire at the end of six years. The members whose terms are to expire at the end of the initial periods of three and six years shall be chosen by lot by the Secretary-General immediately after the first election has been completed. A member of the Court elected to replace a member whose term of office has not expired shall hold office for the remainder of his predecessor's term. The members of the Court shall hold office until replaced. After having been replaced, they shall continue to deal with such cases as they already have under consideration.

Article 41

The Court shall elect the President and Vice-President for a period of three years. They may be re-elected.

Article 42

The members of the Court shall receive for each day of duty a compensation to be determined by the Committee of Ministers.

Article 43

For the consideration of each case brought before it the Court shall consist of a Chamber composed of seven judges. There shall sit as an 'ex officio' member of the Chamber the judge who is a national of any State party concerned, or, if there is none, a person of its choice who shall sit in the capacity of judge; the names of the other judges shall be chosen by lot by the President before the opening of the case.

Article 44

Only the High Contracting Parties and the Commission shall have the right to bring a case before the Court.

Article 45

The jurisdiction of the Court shall extend to all cases concerning the interpretation and application of the present Convention which the High Contracting Parties or the Commission shall refer to it in accordance with Article 48.

Article 46

Any of the High Contracting Parties may at any time declare that it recognizes as compulsory 'ipso facto' and without special agreement the jurisdiction of the Court in all matters concerning the interpretation and application of the present Convention. The declarations referred to above may be made unconditionally or on condition of reciprocity on the part of several or certain other High Contracting Parties or for a specified period. These declarations shall be deposited with the Secretary-General of the Council of Europe who shall transmit copies thereof to the High Contracting Parties.

Article 47

The Court may only deal with a case after the Commission has acknowledged the failure of efforts for a friendly settlement and within the period of three months provided for in Article 32.

Article 48

The following may bring a case before the Court, provided that the High Contracting Party concerned, if there is only one, or the High Contracting Parties concerned, if there is more than one, are subject to the compulsory jurisdiction of the Court, or failing that, with the consent of the High Contracting Party concerned, if there is only one, or of the High Contracting Parties concerned if there is more than one:

(a) the Commission;
(b) a High Contracting Party whose national is alleged to be a victim;
(c) a High Contracting Party which referred the case to the Commission;
(d) a High Contracting Party against which the complaint has been lodged.

Article 49

In the event of dispute as to whether the Court has the jurisdiction, the matter shall be settled by the decision of the Court.

Article 50

If the Court finds that a decision or a measure taken by a legal authority or any other authority of a High Contracting Party, is completely or partially in conflict with the obligations arising from the present convention, and if the internal law of the said Party allows only partial reparation to be made for the consequences of this decision or measure, the decision of the Court shall, if necessary, afford just satisfaction to the injured party.

Article 51

Reasons shall be given for the judgement of the Court. If the judgement does not represent in whole or in part the unanimous opinion of the judges, any judges shall be entitled to deliver a separate opinion.

Article 52

The judgement of the Court shall be final.

Article 53

The High Contracting Parties undertake to abide by the decision of the Court in any case to which they are parties.

Article 54

The judgement of the Court shall be transmitted to the Committee of Ministers which shall supervise its execution.

Article 55

The Court shall draw up its own rules and shall determine its own procedure.

Article 56

The first election of the members of the Court shall take place after the declarations by the High Contracting Parties mentioned in Article 46 have reached a total of eight. No case can be brought before the Court before this election.

SECTION V

Article 57

On receipt of a request from the Secretary-General of the Council of Europe any High Contracting Party shall furnish an explanation of the manner in which its internal law ensures the effective implementation of any of the provisions of this Convention.

Article 58

The expenses of the Commission and the Court shall be borne by the Council of Europe.

Article 59

The members of the Commission and of the Court shall be entitled, during the discharge of their functions, to the privileges and immunities provided for in Article 40 of the Statute of the Council of Europe and in the agreements made thereunder.

Article 60

Nothing in this Convention shall be construed as limiting or derogating from any of the human rights and fundamental freedoms which may be ensured under the laws of any High Contracting Party or under any other agreement to which it is a Party.

Article 61

Nothing in this Convention shall prejudice the powers conferred on the Committee of Ministers by the Statute of the Council of Europe.

Article 62

The High Contracting Parties agree that, except by special agreement, they will not avail themselves of treaties, conventions or declarations in force between them for the purpose of submitting, by way of petition, a dispute arising out of the interpretation or application of this Convention to a means of settlement other than those provided for in this Convention.

Article 63

Any State may at the time of its ratification or at any time thereafter declare by notification addressed to the Secretary-General of the Council of Europe that the present Convention shall extend to all or any of the territories for whose international relations it is responsible. The Convention shall extend to the territory or territories named in the notification as from the thirtieth day after the receipt of this notification by the Secretary-General of the Council of Europe. The provisions of this Convention shall be applied in such territories with due regard, however, to local requirements. Any State which has made a declaration in accordance with Paragraph 1 of this article may at any time thereafter declare on behalf of one or more of the territories to which the declaration relates that it accepts the competence of the Commission to receive petitions from individuals, non-governmental organizations or groups of individuals in accordance with Article 25 of the present Convention.

Article 64

Any State may, when signing this Convention or when depositing its instrument of ratification, make a reservation in respect of any particular provision of the Convention to the extent that any law then in force in its territory is not in con formity with the provision. Reservations of a general character shall not be permitted under this article. Any reservation made under this article shall contain a brief statement of the law concerned.

Article 65

A High Contracting Party may denounce the present Convention only after the expiry of five years from the date of which it became a Party to it and after six months' notice contained in a notification addressed to the Secretary-General of the Council of Europe, who shall inform the other High Contracting Parties. Such a denunciation shall not have the effect of releasing the High Contracting Party concerned from its obligations under this Convention in respect of any act which, being capable of constituting a violation of such obligations, may have been performed by it before the date at which the denunciation became effective. Any High Contracting Party which shall cease to be a Member of the Council of Europe shall cease to be a Party to this Convention under the same conditions. The Convention may be denounced in accordance with the provisions of the preceding paragraphs in respect of any territory to which it has been declared to extend under the terms of Article 63.

Article 66

This Convention shall be open to the signature of the Members of the Council of Europe. It shall be ratified. Ratifications shall be deposited with the Secretary-General of the Council of Europe. The present Convention shall come into force after the deposit of ten instruments of ratification. As regards any signatory ratifying subsequently, the Convention shall come into force at the date of the deposit of its instrument of ratification. The Secretary-General of the Council of Europe shall notify all the Members of the Council of Europe of the entry into force of the Convention, the names of the High Contracting Parties who have ratified it, and the deposit of all instruments of ratification which may be effected subsequently.

Done at Rome this 4th day of November, 1950, in English and French, both text being equally authentic, in a single copy which shall remain deposited in the archives of the Council of Europe. The Secretary-General shall transmit certified copies to each of the signatories

DECLARATION ON FUNDAMENTAL PRINCIPLES CONCERNING THE CONTRIBUTION OF INTERNATIONAL UNDERSTANDING, TO THE PROMOTION OF HUMAN RIGHTS AND TO COUNTERING RACIALISM, APARTHEID AND INCITEMENT TO WAR

Proclaimed by the General Conference of the United Nations Educational Scientific and Cultural Organization at its twentieth session,

on 28 November 1978

Preamble

The General Conference,

Recalling that by virtue of its Constitution the purpose of UNESCO is to "contribute to peace and security by promoting collaboration among the nations through education, science and culture in order to further universal respect for justice, for the rule of law and for the human rights and fundamental freedoms" (Art. I, 1), and that to realize this purpose the Organization will strive "to promote the free flow of ideas by word and image" (Art. I, 2).

Further recalling that under the Constitution the Member States of UNESCO, "believing in full and equal opportunities for education for all, in the unrestricted pursuit of objective truth, and in the free exchange of ideas and knowledge, are agreed and determined to develop and to increase the means of communication between their peoples and to employ these means for the purposes of mutual understanding and a truer and more perfect knowledge of each other's lives" (sixth preambular paragraph),

Recalling the purposes and principles of the United Nations, as specified in its Charter,

Recalling the Universal Declaration of Human Rights, adopted by the General Assembly of the United Nations in 1948 and particularly Article 19 thereof, which provides that "everyone has the right to freedom of opinion and expression; this right includes freedom to hold opinions without interference and to seek, receive and impart information and ideas through any media and regardless of frontiers"; and the International Covenant on Civil and Political Rights, adopted by the General Assembly of the United Nations in 1966, Article 19 of which proclaims the same principles and Article 20 of which condemns incitement to war, the advocacy of national, racial or religious hatred and any form of discrimination, hostility or violence,

Recalling Article 4 of the International Convention on the Elimination of all Forms of Racial Discrimination, adopted by the General Assembly of the United Nations in 1965, and the International Convention on the Suppression and Punishment of the Crime of *Apartheid*, adopted by the General Assembly of the United Nations in 1973, whereby the States acceding to these Conventions undertook to adopt immediate and positive measures designed to eradicate all incitement to, or acts of, racial discrimination, and agreed to prevent any encouragement of the crime of *Apartheid* and similar segregationist policies of their own manifestations.

Recalling the Declaration on the Promotion among Youth of the Ideals of Peace, Mutual Respect and Understanding between Peoples, adopted by the General Assembly of the United Nations in 1965,

Recalling the declarations and resolutions adopted by the various organs of the United Nations concerning the establishment of a new international economic order and the role UNESCO is called upon to play in this respect,

Recalling the Declaration of the Principles of International Cultural Co-operation, adopted by the General Conference of UNESCO in 1966,

Recalling Resolution 59 (I) of the General Assembly of the United Nations, adopted in 1946 and declaring:

"Freedom of information in a fundamental human right and is the touchstone of all the freedoms to which the United Nations is consecrated;

"Freedom of information requires as an indispensable element the willingness and capacity to employ its privileges without abuse. It requires as a basic discipline the moral obligation to seek the facts without prejudice and to spread knowledge without malicious intent,

"*Recalling* Resolution 110 (II) of the General Assembly of the United Nations, adopted in 1947, condemning all forms of propaganda which are designed or likely to provoke or encourage any threat to the peace, breach of the peace, or act or aggression,

Recalling Resolution 127 (II), also adopted by the General Assembly in 1947, which invites Member States to take measures, within the limits of constitutional procedures, to combat the diffusion of false or distorted reports likely to injure friendly relations between States, as well as the other resolutions of the General Assembly concerning the mass media and their contribution to strengthening peace, trust and friendly relations among States,

Recalling Resolution 9.12 adopted by the General Conference of UNESCO in 1968, reiterating UNESCO's objective to help to eradicate colonialism and racialism, and Resolution 12.1 adopted by the General Conference in 1976, which proclaims that colonialism, neo-colonialism and racialism in all its forms and manifestations are incompatible with the fundamental aims of UNESCO,

Recalling Resolution 4.301 adopted in 1970 by the General Conference of UNESCO on the contribution of the information media to furthering international understanding and co-operation in the interests of peace and human welfare, and to countering propaganda on behalf of war, racialism, *Apartheid* and hatred among nations and aware of the fundamental contribution that mass media can make to the realizations of these objectives,

Recalling the Declaration on Race and Racial Prejudice adopted by the General Conference of UNESCO at its twentieth session,

Conscious of the complexity of the problems of information in modern society, of the diversity of solutions which have been offered to them, as evidenced in particular by the consideration given to them within UNESCO, and of the legitimate desire of all parties concerned that their aspirations, points of view and cultural identity be taken into due consideration,

Conscious of the aspirations of the developing countries for the establishment of a new, more just and more effective world information and communication order,

Proclaims on this twenty-eighth day of November 1978 this Declaration on Fundamental Principles concerning the Contribution of the Mass Media to Strengthening Peace and International Understanding, to the Promotion of Human Rights and to Countering Racialism, *Apartheid* and Incitement to War.

Article I

The strengthening of peace and international understanding, the promotion of human rights and the countering of racialism, *Apartheid* and incitement to war demand a free flow and a wider and better balanced dissemination of information. To this end, the mass media have a leading contribution to make. This contribution will be more effective to the extent that the information reflects the different aspects of the subject dealt with.

Article II

1. The exercise of freedom of opinion, expression and information, recognized as an integral part of human rights and fundamental freedoms, is a vital factor in the strengthening of peace and international understanding.
2. Access by the public to information should be guaranteed by the diversity of the sources and means of information available to it, thus enabling each individual to check to accuracy of facts and to appraise events objectively. To this end, journalists must have freedom to report and the fullest possible facilities of access to information. Similarly, it is important that the mass

media be responsive to concerns of peoples and individuals, thus promoting the participation of the public in the elaboration of information.

3. With a view to the strengthening of peace and international understanding, to promoting human rights and to countering racialism, *Apartheid* and incitement to war, the mass media throughout the world, by reason of their role, contribute to promoting human rights, in particular by giving expression to oppressed peoples who struggle against colonialism, neo-colonialism, foreign occupation and all forms of racial discrimination and oppression and who are unable to make their voices heard within their own territories.
4. If the mass media are to be in a position to promote the principles of this Declaration in their activities, it is essential that journalists and other agents of the mass media, in their own country or abroad, be assured of protection guaranteeing them the best conditions for the exercise of their profession.

Article III

1. The mass media have an important contribution to make to the strengthening of peace and international understanding and in countering racialism, *Apartheid* and incitement to war.
2. In countering aggressive war, racialism, apartheid and other violations of human rights which are *inter alia* spawned by prejudice and ignorance, the mass media, by disseminating information on the aims, aspirations, cultures and needs of all peoples, contribute to eliminate ignorance and misunderstanding between peoples, to make nationals of a country sensitive to the needs and desires of others, to ensure the respect of the rights and dignity of all nations, all peoples and all individuals without distinction of race, sex, language, religion or nationality and to draw attention to the great evils which afflict humanity, such as poverty, malnutrition and diseases, thereby promoting the formulation by states of the policies best able to promote the reduction of international tension and the peaceful and equitable settlement of international disputes.

Article IV

The mass media have an essential part to play in the education of young people in a spirit of peace, justice, freedom, mutual respect and understanding, in order to promote human rights, equality of rights as between all human beings and all nations, and economic and social progress. Equally, they have an important role to play in making known the views and aspirations of the younger generation.

Article V

In order to respect freedom of opinion, expression and information and in order that information may reflect all points of view, it is important that the points of view presented by those who consider that the information published or disseminated about them has seriously prejudiced their effort to strengthen peace and international understanding, to promote human rights or to counter racialism, *Apartheid* and incitement to war be disseminated.

Article VI

For the establishment of a new equilibrium and greater reciprocity in the flow of information, which will be conducive to the institution of a just and lasting peace and to the economic and political independence of the developing countries, it is necessary to correct the inequalities in the flow of information to and from developing countries, and between those countries. To this end, it is essential that their mass media should have conditions and resources enabling them to gain strength and expand, and to cooperate both among themselves and with the mass media in developed countries.

Article VII

By disseminating more widely all of the information concerning the universally accepted objectives and principles which are the bases of the resolutions adopted by the different organs of the United Nations, the mass media contribute effectively to the strengthening of peace and international understanding, to the promotion of human rights, and to the establishment of a more just and equitable international economic order.

Article VIII

Professional organization, and people who participate in the professional training of journalists and other agents of the mass media and who assist them in performing their functions in a responsible manner should attach special importance to the principles of this Declaration when drawing up and ensuring application of their codes of ethics.

Article IX

In the spirit of this Declaration, it is for the international community to contribute to the creation of the conditions for a free flow and wider and more balanced dissemination of information, and of the conditions for the protection, in the exercise of their functions, of journalists and other agents of the mass media. UNESCO is well placed to make a valuable contribution in this respect.

Article X

1. With due respect for constitutional provisions designed to guarantee freedom of information and for the applicable international instruments and agreements, it is indispensable to create and maintain throughout the world the conditions which make it possible for the organizations and persons professionally involved in the dissemination of information to achieve the objectives of this Declaration.

2. It is important that a free flow and wider and better balanced dissemination of information be encouraged.
3. To this end, it is necessary that States facilitate the procurement by the mass media in the developing countries of adequate conditions and resources enabling them to gain strength and expand, and that they support co-operation by the latter both among themselves and with the mass media in developed countries.
4. Similarly, on a basis of equality of rights, mutual advantage and respect for the diversity of the cultures which go to make up the common heritage of mankind, it is essential that bilateral and multilateral exchanges of information among all States, and in particular between those which have different economic and social systems, be encouraged and developed.

Article XI

For this declaration to be fully effective it is necessary, with due respect for the legislative and administrative provisions and the other obligations of Member States, to guarantee the existence of favourable conditions for the operation of the mass media, in conformity with the provisions of the Universal Declaration of Human Rights and with the corresponding principles proclaimed in the International Covenant on Civil and Political Rights adopted by the General Assembly of the United Nations in 1966.

CONVENTION ON THE ELIMINATION OF ALL FORMS OF DISCRIMINATION AGAINST WOMEN

"...the full and complete development of a country, the welfare of the world and the cause of peace require the maximum participation of women on equal terms with men in all fields."

CONTENTS

The States Parties to the present Convention,

Noting that the Charter of the United Nations reaffirms faith in fundamental human rights, in the dignity and worth of the human person and in the equal rights of man and women,

Noting that the Universal Declaration of Human Rights affirms the principle of the inadmissibility of discrimination and proclaims that all human beings are born free and equal in dignity and rights and that everyone is entitled to all the rights and freedoms set forth therein, without distinction of any kind, including distinction based on sex,

Noting that the States Parties to the International Covenants on Human Rights have the obligation to ensure the equal right of men and women to enjoy all economic, social, cultural, civil and political rights,

Considering the international conventions concluded under the auspices of the United Nations and the specialized agencies promoting equality of rights of men and women,

Noting also the resolutions, declarations and recommendations adopted by the United Nations and the specialized agencies promoting equality of rights of men and women,

Concerned, however, that despite these various instruments extensive discrimination against women continues to exist,

Recalling that discrimination against women violates the principles of equality of rights and respect for human dignity, is an obstacle to the participation of women, on equal terms with men, in the political, social,economic and cultural life of their countries, hampers the growth of the prosperity of society and the family and makes more difficult the full development of the potentialities of women in the service of their countries and of humanity,

Concerned that in situations of poverty women have the least access to food, health, education, training and opportunities for employment and other needs,

Convinced that the establishment of the new international economic order based on equity and justice will contribute significantly towards the promotion of equality between men and women,

Emphasizing that the eradication of apartheid, of all forms of racism, racial discrimination, colonialism, neo-colonialism, aggression, foreign occupation and domination and interference in the internal affairs of States is essential to the full enjoyment of the rights of men and women,

Affirming that the strengthening of international peace and security, relaxation of international tension, mutual co-operation among all States irrespective of their social and economic systems, general and complete disarmament, and in particular nuclear disarmament under strict and effective international control, the affirmation of the principles of justice, equality and mutual benefit in relations among countries and the realization of the right of peoples under alien and colonial domination and foreign occupation to self-determination and independence, as well as respect for national sovereignty and territorial integrity, will promote social progress and development and as a consequence will contribute to the attainment of full equality between men and women,

Convinced that the full and complete development of a country, the welfare of the world and the cause of peace require the maximum participation of women on equal terms with men in all fields,

Bearing in mind the great contribution of women to the welfare of the family and to the development of society, so far not fully recognized, the social significance of maternity and the role of both parents in the family and in the upbringing of children, and aware that the role of women in procreation should not be a basis for discrimination but that the upbringing of children requires a sharing of responsibility between men and women and society as a whole,

Aware that a change in the traditional role of men as well as the role of women in society and in the family is needed to achieve full equality between men and women,

Determined to implement the principles set forth in the Declaration on the Elimination of Discrimination against Women and, for that purpose, to adopt the measures required for the elimination of such discrimination in all its forms and manifestations,

Have agreed on the following:

PART I

ARTICLE 1. For the purposes of the present Convention, the term "discrimination against women" shall mean any distinction, exclusion or restriction made on the basis of sex which has the effect or purpose of impairing or nullifying the recognition, enjoyment or exercise by women irrespective of their marital status, on a basis of equality of men and women, of human rights and fundamental freedoms in the political, economic, social, cultural, civil or any other field.

ARTICLE 2. States Parties condemn discrimination against women in all its forms, agree to pursue by all appropriate means and without delay a policy of eliminating discrimination against women and, to this end, undertake:

(*a*) To embody the principle of the equality of men and women in their national constitutions or other appropriate legislation if not yet incorporated therein and to ensure, through law and other appropriate means, the practical realization of this principle;

(*b*) To adopt appropriate legislative and other measures, including sanctions where appropriate, prohibiting all discrimination against women;

(*c*) To establish legal protection of the rights of women on an equal basis with men and to ensure through competent national tribunals and other public institutions the effective protection of women against any act of discrimination;

(*d*) To refrain from engaging in any act or practice of discrimination against women and to ensure that public authorities and institutions shall act in conformity with this obligation;

(*e*) To take all appropriate measures to eliminate discrimination against women by any person, organization or enterprise;

(*f*) To take all appropriate measures, including legislation, to modify or abolish existing laws, regulations, customs and practices which constitute discrimination against women;

(g) To repeal all national penal provisions which constitute discrimination against women.

ARTICLE 3. States Parties shall take in all fields, in particular in the political, social, economic and cultural fields, all appropriate measures, including legislation, to ensure the full development and advancement of women, for the purpose of guaranteeing them the exercise and enjoyment of human rights and fundamental freedoms on a basis of equality with men.

ARTICLE 4.1. Adoption by States Parties of temporary special measures aimed at accelerating de facto equality between men and women shall not be considered discrimination as defined in the present Convention, but shall in no way entail as a consequence the maintenance of unequal or separate standards; these measures shall be discontinued when the objectives of equality of opportunity and treatment have been achieved.

2. Adoption by States Parties of special measures, including those measures contained in the present Convention, aimed at protecting maternity shall not be considered discriminatory.

Article 5. States Parties shall take all appropriate measures:

(a) To modify the social and cultural patterns of conduct of men and women, with a view to achieving the elimination of prejudices and customary and all other practices which are based on the idea of the inferiority or the superiority of either of the sexes or on stereotyped roles for men and women;

(b) To ensure that family education includes a proper understanding of maternity as a social function and the recognition of the common responsibility of men and women in the upbringing and development of their children, it being understood that the interest of the children is the primordial consideration in all cases.

ARTICLE 6. States Parties shall take all appropriate measures, including legislation, to suppress all forms of traffic in women and exploitation of prostitution of women.

PART II

ARTICLE 7. States Parties shall take all appropriate measures to eliminate discrimination against women in the political and public life of the country and, in particular, shall ensure to women, on equal terms with men, the right:

(a) To vote in all elections and public referenda and to be eligible for election to all publicly elected bodies;

(b) To participate in the formulation of government policy and the implementation thereof and to hold public office and perform all public functions at all levels of government;

(c) To participate in non-governmental organizations and associations concerned with the public and political life of the country.

ARTICLE 8. States Parties shall take all appropriate measures to ensure to women, on equal terms with men and without any discrimination, the opportunity to represent their.

Governments at the international level and to participate in the work of international organizations.

ARTICLE 9.1. States Parties shall grant women equal rights with men to acquire, change or retain their nationality. They shall ensure in particular that neither marriage to an alien nor change of nationality by the husband during marriage shall automatically change the nationality of the wife, render her stateless or force upon her the nationality of the husband.

2. States Parties shall grant women equal rights with men with respect to the nationality of their children.

PART III

ARTICLE 10. States Parties shall take all appropriate measures to eliminate discrimination against women in order to ensure to them equal rights with men in the field of education and in particular to ensure, on a basis of equality of men and women:

- (a) The same conditions for career and vocational guidance, for access to studies and for the achievement of diplomas in educational establishments of all categories in rural as well as in urban areas; this equality shall be ensured in preschool, general, technical, professional and higher technical education, as well as in all types of vocational training;
- (b) Access to the same curricula, the same examinations, teaching staff with qualifications of the same standard and school premises and equipment of the same quality;
- (c) The elimination of any stereotyped concept of the roles of men and women at all levels and in all forms of education by encouraging coeducation and other types of education which will help to achieve this aim and, in particular, by the revision of textbooks and school programmes and the adaptation of teaching methods;
- (d) The same opportunities to benefit from scholarships and other study grants;
- (e) The same opportunities for access to programmes of continuing education including adult and functional literacy programmes, particularly those aimed at reducing, at the earliest possible time, any gap in education existing between men and women;
- (f) The reduction of female student drop-out rates and the organization of programmes for girls and women who have left school prematurely;
- (g) The same opportunities to participate actively in sports and physical education;
- (h) Access to specific educational information to help to ensure the health and well-being of families, including information and advice on family planning.

ARTICLE 11. 1. States Parties shall take all appropriate measures to eliminate discrimination against women in the field of employment in order to ensure, on a basis of equality of men and women, the same rights, in particular:

- (a) The right to work as an inalienable right of all human beings;
- (b) The right to the same employment opportunities, including the application of the same criteria for selection in matters of employment;

(c) The right to free choice of profession and employment, the right to promotion, job security and all benefits and conditions of service and the right to receive vocational training and retraining, including apprenticeships, advanced vocational training and recurrent training;
(d) The right to equal remuneration, including benefits, and to equal treatment in respect of work of equal value, as well as equality of treatment in the evaluation of the quality of work;
(e) The right to social security, particularly in cases of retirement, unemployment, sickness, invalidity and old age and other incapacity to work, as well as the right to paid leave;
(f) The right to protection of health and to safety in working conditions, including the safeguarding of the function of reproduction.

2. In order to prevent discrimination against women on the grounds of marriage or maternity and to ensure their effective right to work, States Parties shall take appropriate measures:
(a) To prohibit, subject to the imposition of sanctions, dismissal on the grounds of pregnancy or of maternity leave and discrimination in dismissals on the basis of marital status;
(b) To introduce maternity leave with pay or with comparable social benefits without loss of former employment, seniority or social allowances;
(c) To encourage the provision of the necessary supporting social services to enable parents to combine family obligations with work responsibilities and participation in public life, in particular through promoting the establishment and development of a network of child-care facilities;
(d) To provide special protection to women during pregnancy in types of work proved to be harmful to them.

3. Protective legislation relating to matters covered in this article shall be reviewed periodically in the light of scientific and technological knowledge and shall be revised, repealed or extended as necessary.

ARTICLE 12.1. States Parties shall take all appropriate measures to eliminate discrimination against women in the field of health care in order to ensure, on a basis of equality of men and women, access to health care services, including those related to family planning.

2. Notwithstanding the provisions of Paragraph 1 of this article, States Parties shall ensure to women appropriate services in connexion with pregnancy, confinement and the post-natal period, granting free services where necessary, as well as adequate nutrition during pregnancy and lactation.

ARTICLE 13. States Parties shall take all appropriate measures to eliminate discrimination against women in other areas of economic and social life in order to ensure, on a basis of equality of men and women, the same rights, in particular:
(a) The right to family benefits;
(b) The right to bank loans, mortgages and other forms of financial credit;
(c) The right to participate in recreational activities, sports and all aspects of cultural life.

ARTICLE 14.1. States Parties shall take into account the particular problems faced by rural women and the significant roles which rural women play in the economic survival of their families, including their work in the non-monetized sectors of the economy, and shall take all appropriate measures to ensure the application of the provisions of this Convention to women in rural areas.

2. States Parties shall take all appropriate measures to eliminate discrimination against women in rural areas in order to ensure, on a basis of equality of men and women, that they participate in and benefit from rural development and, in particular, shall ensure to such women the right:

(a) To participate in the elaboration and implementation of development planning at all levels;
(b) To have access to adequate health care facilities, including information, counselling and services in family planning;
(c) To benefit directly from social security programmes;
(d) To obtain all types of training and education, formal and non-formal, including that relating to functional literacy, as well as, inter alia, the benefit of all community and extension services, in order to increase their technical proficiency;
(e) To organize self-help groups and co-operatives in order to obtain equal access to economic opportunities through employment or self-employment;
(f) To participate in all community activities;
(g) To have access to agricultural credit and loans, marketing facilities, appropriate technology and equal treatment in land and agrarian reform as well as in land resettlement schemes;
(h) To enjoy adequate living conditions, particularly in relation to housing, sanitation, electricity and water supply, transport and communications.

PART IV

ARTICLE 15. 1. States Parties shall accord to women equality with men before the law.

2. States Parties shall accord to women, in civil matters, a legal capacity identical to that of men and the same opportunities to exercise that capacity. In particular, they shall give women equal rights to conclude contracts and to administer property and shall treat them equally in all stages of procedure in courts and tribunals.

3. States Parties agree that all contracts and all other private instruments of any kind with a legal effect which is directed at restricting the legal capacity of women shall be deemed null and void.

4. States Parties shall accord to men and women the same rights with regard to the law relating to the movement of persons and the freedom to choose their residence and domicile.

ARTICLE 16. 1. States Parties shall take all appropriate measures to eliminate discrimination against women in all matters relating to marriage and family relations and in particular shall ensure, on a basis of equality of men and women:

(a) The same right to enter into marriage;
(b) The same right freely to choose a spouse and to enter into marriage only with their free and full consent;

6

(c) The same rights and responsibilities during marriage and at its dissolution;
(d) The same rights and responsibilities as parents, irrespective of their marital status, in matters relating to their children; in all cases the interests of the children shall be paramount;
(e) The same rights to decide freely and responsibly on the number and spacing of their children and to have access to the information, education and means to enable them to exercise these rights;
(f) The same rights and responsibilities with regard to guardianship, wardship, trusteeship and adoption of children, or similar institutions where these concepts exist in national legislation; in all cases the interests of the children shall be paramount;
(g) The same personal rights as husband and wife, including the right to choose a family name, a profession and an occupation;
(h) The same rights for both spouses in respect of the ownership, acquisition, management, administration, enjoyment and disposition of property, whether free of charge or for a valuable consideration.

2. The betrothal and the marriage of a child shall have no legal effect, and all necessary action, including legislation, shall be taken to specify a minimum age for marriage and to make the registration of marriages in an official registry compulsory.

PART V

ARTICLE 17.1. For the purpose of considering the progress made in the implementation of the present Convention, there shall be established a Committee on the Elimination of Discrimination against Women (hereinafter referred to as the Committee) consisting, at the time of entry into force of the Convention, of eighteen and, after ratification of or accession to the Convention by the thirty-fifth State Party, of twenty-three experts of high moral standing and competence in the field covered by the Convention. The experts shall be elected by States Parties from among their nationals and shall serve in their personal capacity, consideration being given to equitable geographical distribution and to the representation of the different forms of civilization as well as the principal legal systems.

2. The members of the Committee shall be elected by secret ballot from a list of persons nominated by States Parties. Each State Party may nominate one person from among its own nationals.

3. The initial election shall be held six months after the date of the entry into force of the present Convention. At least three months before the date of each election the Secretary-General of the United Nations shall address a letter to the States Parties inviting them to submit their nominations within two months. The Secretary-General shall prepare a list in alphabetical order of all persons thus nominated, indicating the States Parties which have nominated them, and shall submit it to the States Parties.

4. Elections of the members of the Committee shall be held at a meeting of States Parties convened by the Secretary-General at United Nations Headquarters. At that meeting, for which two-thirds of the States Parties shall constitute a quorum, the persons elected to the Committee shall be those nominees who obtain the largest

number of votes and an absolute majority of the votes of the representatives of States Parties present and voting.

5. The members of the Committee shall be elected for a term of four years. However, the terms of nine of the members elected at the first election shall expire at the end of two years; immediately after the first election the names of these nine members shall be chosen by lot by the Chairman of the Committee.

6. The election of the five additional members of the Committee shall be held in accordance with the provisions of Paragraphs 2, 3 and 4 of this article, following the thirty-fifth ratification or accession. The terms of two of the additional members elected on this occasion shall expire at the end of two years, the names of these two members having been chosen by lot by the Chairman of the Committee.

7. For the filling of casual vacancies, the State Party whose expert has ceased to function as a member of the Committee shall appoint another expert from among its nationals, subject to the approval of the Committee.

8. The members of the Committee shall, with the approval of the General Assembly, receive emoluments from United Nations resources on such terms and conditions as the Assembly may decide, having regard to the importance of the Committee's responsibilities.

9. The Secretary-General of the United Nations shall provide the necessary staff and facilities for the effective performance of the functions of the Committee under the present Convention.

ARTICLE 18.1. States Parties undertake to submit to the Secretary-General of the United Nations, for consideration by the Committee, a report on the legislative, judicial, administrative or other measures which they have adopted to give effect to the provisions of the present Convention and on the progress made in this respect:

(a) Within one year after the entry into force for the State concerned;

and

(b) Thereafter at least every four years and further whenever the Committee so requests.

2. Reports may indicate factors and difficulties affecting the degree of fulfillment of obligations under the present Convention.

ARTICLE 19.1. The Committee shall adopt its own rules of procedure.

2. The Committee shall elect its officers for a term of two years.

ARTICLE 20.1. The Committee shall normally meet for a period of not more than two weeks annually in order to consider the reports submitted in accordance with Article 18 of the present Convention.

2. The meetings of the Committee shall normally be held at United Nations Headquarters or at any other convenient place as determined by the Committee.

ARTICLE 21.1. The Committee shall, through the Economic and Social Council, report annually to the General Assembly of the United Nations on its activities and may make suggestions and general recommendations based on the examination of reports and information received from the States Parties. Such suggestions and general recommendations shall be included in the report of the Committee together with comments, if any, from States Parties.

2. The Secretary-General shall transmit the reports of the Committee to the Commission on the Status of Women for its information.

ARTICLE 22. The specialized agencies shall be entitled to be represented at the consideration of the implementation of such provisions of the present Convention as fall within the scope of their activities. The Committee may invite the specialized agencies to submit reports on the implementation of the Convention in areas falling within the scope of their activities.

PART VI

ARTICLE 23. Nothing in this Convention shall affect any provisions that are more conducive to the achievement of equality between men and women which may be contained:

(a) In the legislation of a State Party; or
(b) In any other international convention, treaty or agreement in force for that State.

ARTICLE 24. States Parties undertake to adopt all necessary measures at the national level aimed at achieving the full realization of the rights recognized in the present Convention.

ARTICLE 25.1. The present Convention shall be open for signature by all States.

2. The Secretary-General of the United Nations is designated as the depositary of the present Convention.

3. The present Convention is subject to ratification. Instruments of ratification shall be deposited with the Secretary-General of the United Nations.

4. The present Convention shall be open to accession by all States. Accession shall be effected by the deposit of an instrument of accession with the Secretary-General of the United Nations.

ARTICLE 26.1. A request for the revision of the present Convention may be made at any time by any State Party by means of a notification in writing addressed to the Secretary-General of the United Nations.

2. The General Assembly of the United Nations shall decide upon the steps, if any, to be taken in respect of such a request.

ARTICLE 27.1. The present Convention shall enter into force on the thirtieth day after the date of deposit with the Secretary-General of the United Nations of the twentieth instrument of ratification or accession.

2. For each State ratifying the present Convention or acceding to it after the deposit of the twentieth instrument of ratification or accession, the Convention shall enter into force on the thirtieth day after the date of the deposit of its own instrument of ratification or accession.

ARTICLE 28.1. The Secretary-General of the United Nations shall receive and circulate to all States the text of reservations made by States at the time of ratification or accession.

2. A reservation incompatible with the object and purpose of the present Convention shall not be permitted.

3. Reservations may be withdrawn at any time by notification to this effect addressed to the Secretary-General of the United Nations, who shall then inform all States thereof. Such notification shall take effect on the date on which it is received.

ARTICLE 29. 1. Any dispute between two or more States Parties concerning the interpretation or application of the present Convention which is not settled by negotiation shall, at the request of one of them, be submitted to arbitration. If within six months from the date of the request for arbitration the parties are unable to agree on the organization of the arbitration, any one of those parties may refer the dispute to the International Court of Justice by request in conformity with the Statute of the Court.

2. Each State Party may at the time of signature or ratification of this Convention or accession thereto declare that it does not consider itself bound by Paragraph 1 of this article. The other States Parties shall not be bound by that paragraph with respect to any State Party which has made such a reservation.

3. Any State Party which has made a reservation in accordance with Paragraph 2 of this article may at any time withdraw that reservation by notification to the Secretary-General of the United Nations.

ARTICLE 30. The present Convention, the Arabic, Chinese, English, French, Russian and Spanish texts of which are equally authentic, shall be deposited with the Secretary-General of the United Nations.

IN WITNESS WHEREOF the undersigned, duly authorized, have signed the present Convention.

CONVENTION ON THE RIGHTS OF THE CHILD

(Adopted by the United Nations General Assembly on 20 November 1989)

Preamble

The States Parties to the present Convention,

Considering that, in accordance with the principles proclaimed in the Charter of the United Nations, recognition of the inherent dignity and of the equal and inalienable rights of all members of the human family is the foundation of freedom, justice and peace in the world,

Bearing in mind that the peoples of the United Nations have, in the Charter, reaffirmed their faith in fundamental human rights and in the dignity and worth of the human person, and have determined to promote social progress and better standards of life in larger freedom,

Recognizing that the United Nations has, in the Universal Declaration of Human Rights and in the International Covenants on Human Rights, proclaimed and agreed that everyone is entitled to all the rights and freedoms set forth therein, without distinction of any kind, such as race, colour, sex, language, religion, political or other opinion, national or social origin, property, birth or other status,

Recalling that, in the Universal Declaration of Human Rights, the United Nations has proclaimed that childhood is entitled to special care and assistance,

Convinced that the family, as the fundamental group of society and the natural environment for the growth and well-being of all its members and particularly children, should be afforded the necessary protection and assistance so that it can fully assume its responsibilities within the community,

Recognizing that the child, for the full and harmonious development of his or her personality, should grow up in a family environment, in an atmosphere of happiness, love and understanding,

Considering that the child should be fully prepared to live an individual life in society, and brought up in the spirit of the ideals proclaimed in the Charter of the United Nations, and in particular in the spirit of peace, dignity, tolerance, freedom, equality and solidarity,

Bearing in mind that the need to extend particular care to the child has been stated in the Geneva Declaration of the Rights of the Child of 1924 and in the Declaration of the Rights of the Child adopted by the General Assembly on 20 November 1959 and recognized in the Universal Declaration of Human Rights, in the International Covenant on Civil and Political Rights (in particular in Articles 23 and 24), in the International Covenant on Economic, Social and

Cultural Rights (in particular in Article 10) and in the statutes and relevant instruments of specialized agencies and international organizations concerned with the welfare of children,

Bearing in mind that, as indicated in the Declaration of the Rights of the Child, "the child, by reason of his physical and mental immaturity, needs special safeguards and care, including appropriate legal protection, before as well as after birth",

Recalling the provisions of the Declaration on Social and Legal Principles relating to the Protection and Welfare of Children, with Special Reference to Foster Placement and Adoption Nationally and Internationally: the United Nations Standard Minimum Rules for the Administration of Juvenile Justice (The Beijing Rules); and the Declaration on the Protection of Women and Children in Emergency and Armed Conflict,

Recognizing that, in all countries in the world, there are children living in exceptionally difficult conditions, and that such children need special consideration,

Taking due account of the importance of the traditions and cultural values of each people for the protection and harmonious development of the child,

Recognizing the importance of international co-operation for improving the living conditions of children in every country, in particular in the developing countries,

Have agreed as follows:

Part I

Article 1

For the purposes of the present Convention, a child means every human being below the age of eighteen years unless, under the law applicable to the child, majority is attained earlier.

Article 2

1. States Parties shall respect and ensure the rights set forth in the present Convention to each child within their jurisdiction without discrimination of any kind, irrespective of the child's or his or her parent's or legal guardian's race, colour, sex, language, religion, political or other opinion, national, ethnic or social origin, property, disability, birth or other status.
2. States Parties shall take all appropriate measures to ensure that the child is protected against all forms of discrimination or punishment on the basis of the status, activities, expressed opinions, or beliefs of the child's parents, legal guardians, or family members.

Article 3

1. In all actions concerning children, whether undertaken by public or private social welfare institutions, courts of law, administrative authorities or legislative bodies, the best interests of the child shall be a primary consideration.
2. States Parties undertake to ensure the child such protection and care as is necessary for his or her well-being, taking into account the rights and duties of his or her parents, legal guardians, or other individuals legally responsible for him or her, and, to this end, shall take all appropriate legislative and administrative measures.
3. States Parties shall ensure that the institutions, services and facilities responsible for the care or protection of children shall conform with the standards established by competent authorities, particularly in the areas of safety, health, in the number and suitability of their staff, as well as competent supervision.

Article 4

States Parties shall undertake all appropriate legislative, administrative, and other measures for the implementation of the rights recognized in the present Convention. With regard to economic, social and cultural rights, States Parties shall undertake such measures to the maximum extent of their available resources and, where needed, within the framework of international co-operation.

Article 5

States Parties shall respect the responsibilities, rights and duties of parents or, where applicable, the members of the extended family or community as provided for by local custom, legal guardians or other persons legally responsible for the child, to provide, in a manner consistent with the evolving capacities of the child, appropriate direction and guidance in the exercise by the child of the rights recognized in the present Convention.

Article 6

1. States Parties recognize that every child has the inherent right to life.
2. States Parties shall ensure to the maximum extent possible the survival and development of the child.

Article 7

1. The child shall be registered immediately after birth and shall have the right from birth to a name, the right to acquire a nationality and, as far as possible, the right to know and be cared for by his or her parents.
2. States Parties shall ensure the implementation of these rights in accordance with their national law and their obligations under the relevant international instruments in this field, in particular where the child would otherwise be stateless.

Article 8

1. States Parties undertake to respect the right of the child to preserve his or her identity, including nationality, name and family relations as recognized by law without unlawful interference.
2. Where a child is illegally deprived of some or all of the elements of his or her identity, States Parties shall provide appropriate assistance and protection, with a view to speedily re-establishing his or her identity.

Article 9

1. States Parties shall ensure that a child shall not be separated from his or her parents against their will, except when competent authorities subject to judicial review determine, in accordance with applicable law and procedures, that such separation is necessary for the best interests of the child. Such determination may be necessary in a particular case such as one involving abuse or neglect of the child by the parents, or one where the parents are living separately and a decision must be made as to the child's place of residence.
2. In any proceedings pursuant to Paragraph 1 of the present article, all interested parties shall be given an opportunity to participate in the proceedings and make their views known.
3. States Parties shall respect the right of the child who is separated from one or both parents to maintain personal relations and direct contact with both parents on a regular basis, except if it is contrary to the child's best interests.
4. Where such separation results from any action initiated by a State Party, such as the detention, imprisonment, exile, deportation or death (including death arising from any cause while the person is in the custody of the State) of one or both parents or of the child, that State Party shall, upon request, provide the parents, the child or, if appropriate, another member of the family with the essential information concerning the whereabouts of the absent member(s) of the family unless the provision of the information would be detrimental to the well-being of the child. States Parties shall further ensure that the submission of such a request shall of itself entail no adverse consequences for the person(s) concerned.

Article 10

1. In accordance with the obligation of States Parties under Article 9, Paragraph 1, applications by a child or his or her parents to enter or leave a State Party for the purpose of family reunification shall be dealt with by States Parties in a positive, humane and expeditious manner. States Parties shall further ensure that the submission of such a request shall entail no adverse consequences for the applicants and for the members of their family.
2. A child whose parents reside in different States shall have the right to maintain on a regular basis, save in exceptional circumstances, personal relations and direct contacts with both parents. Towards that end and in accordance

with the obligation of States Parties under Article 9, Paragraph 1, States Parties shall respect the right of the child and his or her parents to leave any country, including their own, and to enter their own country. The right to leave any country shall be subject only to such restrictions as are prescribed by law and which are necessary to protect the national security, public order *(ordre public),* public health or morals or the rights and freedoms of others and are consistent with the other rights recognized in the present Convention.

Article 11

1. States Parties shall take measures to combat the illicit transfer and non-return of children abroad.
2. To this end, States Parties shall promote the conclusion of bilateral or multilateral agreements or accession to existing agreements.

Article 12

1. States Parties shall assure to the child who is capable of forming his or her own views the right to express those views freely in all manners affecting the child, the views of the child being given due weight in accordance with the age and maturity of the child.
2. For this purpose, the child shall in particular be provided the opportunity to be heard in any judicial and administrative proceedings affecting the child, either directly, or through a representative or an appropriate body, in a manner consistent with the procedural rules of national law.

Article 13

1. The child shall have the right to freedom of expression; this right shall include freedom to seek, receive and impart information and ideas of all kinds, regardless of frontiers, either orally, in writing or in print, in the form of art, or through any other media of the child's choice.
2. The exercise of this right may be subject to certain restrictions, but these shall only be such as are provided by law and are necessary:
   (a) For respect of the rights or reputations of others; or
   (b) For the protection of national security or of public order *(ordre public)*, or of public health or morals.

Article 14

1. States Parties shall respect the right of the child to freedom of thought, conscience and religion.
2. States Parties shall respect the rights and duties of the parents and, when applicable, legal guardians, to provide direction to the child in the exercise of his or her right in a manner consistent with the evolving capacities of the child.

3. Freedom to manifest one's religion or beliefs may be subject only to such limitations as are prescribed by law and are necessary to protect public safety, order health or morals, or the fundamental rights and freedoms of others.

Article 15

1. States Parties recognize the rights of the child to freedom of association and to freedom of peaceful assembly.
2. No restrictions may be placed on the exercise of these rights other than those imposed in conformity with the law and which are necessary in a democratic society in the interests of national security or public safety, public order *(ordre public)*, the protection of public health or morals or the protection of the rights and freedoms of others.

Article 16

1. No child shall be subjected to arbitrary or unlawful interference with his or her privacy, family, home or correspondence, nor to unlawful attacks on his or her honour and reputation.
2. The child has the right to the protection of the law against such interference or attacks.

Article 17

States Parties recognize the important function performed by the mass media and shall ensure that the child has access to information and material from a diversity of national and international sources, especially those aimed at the promotion of his or her social, spiritual and moral well-being and physical and mental health. To this end, States Parties shall:

- *(a)* Encourage the mass media to disseminate information and material of social and cultural benefit to the child and in accordance with the spirit of Article 29;
- *(b)* Encourage international co-operation in the production, exchange and dissemination of such information and material from a diversity of cultural, national and international sources;
- *(c)* Encourage the production and dissemination of children's books;
- *(d)* Encourage the mass media to have particular regard to the linguistic needs of the child who belongs to a minority group or who is indigenous;
- *(e)* Encourage the development of appropriate guidelines for the protection of the child from information and material injurious to his or her well-being, bearing in mind the provisions of Articles 13 and 18.

Article 18

1. States Parties shall use their best efforts to ensure recognition of the principle that both parents have common responsibilities for the upbringing and

development of the child. Parents or, as the case may be, legal guardians, have the primary responsibility for the upbringing and development of the child. The best interests of the child will be their basic concern.

2. For the purpose of guaranteeing and promoting the rights set forth in the present Convention, States Parties shall render appropriate assistance to parents and legal guardians in the performance of their child-rearing responsibilities and shall ensure the development of institutions, facilities and services for the care of children.
3. States Parties shall take all appropriate measures to ensure that children of working parents have the right to benefit from child-care services and facilities for which they are eligible.

Article 19

1. States Parties shall take all appropriate legislative, administrative, social and educational measures to protect the child from all forms of physical or mental violence, injury or abuse, neglect or negligent treatment, maltreatment or exploitation, including sexual abuse, while in the care of parent(s), legal guardian(s) or any other person who has the care of the child.
2. Such protective measures should, as appropriate, include effective procedures for the establishment of social programmes to provide necessary support for the child and for those who have the care of the child, as well as for other forms of prevention and for identification, reporting, referral, investigation treatment and follow-up of instances of child maltreatment described heretofore, and, as appropriate, for judicial involvement.

Article 20

1. A child temporarily or permanently deprived of his or her family environment, or in whose own best interests cannot be allowed to remain in that environment, shall be entitled to special protection and assistance provided by the State.
2. States Parties shall in accordance with their national laws ensure alternative care for such a child.
3. Such care could include. *inter alia,* foster placement, *kafalah* of Islamic law, adoption or if necessary placement in suitable institutions for the care of children. When considering solutions, due regard shall be paid to the desirability of continuity in a child's upbringing and to the child's ethnic, religious, cultural and linguistic background.

Article 21

States Parties that recognize and/or permit the system of adoption shall ensure that the best interests of the child shall be the paramount consideration and they shall:

(a) Ensure that the adoption of a child is authorized only by competent authorities who determine, in accordance with applicable law and procedures and on the basis of all pertinent and reliable information, that the adoption is permissible in view of the child's status concerning parents, relatives and legal guardians and that, if required, the persons concerned have given their informed consent to the adoption on the basis of such counselling as may be necessary;

(b) Recognize that inter-country adoption may be considered as an alternative means of child's care, if the child cannot be placed in a foster or an adoptive family or cannot in any suitable manner be cared for in the child's country of origin;

(c) Ensure that the child concerned by inter-country adoption enjoys safeguards and standards equivalent to those existing in the case of national adoption;

(d) Take all appropriate measures to ensure that, in inter-country adoption, the placement does not result in improper financial gain for those involved in it;

(e) Promote, where appropriate, the objectives of the present article by concluding bilateral or multilateral arrangements or agreements, and endeavour, within this framework, to ensure that the placement of the child in another country is carried out by competent authorities or organs.

Article 22

1. States Parties shall take appropriate measures to ensure that a child who is seeking refugee status or who is considered a refugee in accordance with applicable international or domestic law and procedures shall, whether unaccompanied or accompanied by his or her parents or by any other person, receive appropriate protection and humanitarian assistance in the enjoyment of applicable rights set forth in the present Convention and in other international human rights or humanitarian instruments to which the said States are Parties.
2. For this purpose, States Parties shall provide, as they consider appropriate, co-operation in any efforts by the United Nations and other competent intergovernmental organizations or non-governmental organizations co-operating with the United Nations to protect and assist such a child and to trace the parents or other members of the family of any refugee child in order to obtain information necessary for reunification with his or her family. In cases where no parents or other members of the family can be found, the child shall be accorded the same protection as any other child permanently or temporarily deprived of his or her family environment for any reason, as set forth in the present Convention.

Article 23

1. States Parties recognize that a mentally or physically disabled child should enjoy a full and decent life, in conditions which ensure dignity, promote self-reliance and facilitate the child's active participation in the community.
2. States Parties recognize the right of the disabled child to special care and shall encourage and ensure the extension, subject to available resources, to the eligible child and those responsible for his or her care, of assistance for which application is made and which is appropriate to the child's condition and to the circumstances of the parents or others caring for the child.
3. Recognizing the special needs of a disabled child, assistance extended in accordance with Paragraph 2 of the present article shall be provided free of charge, whenever possible, taking into account the financial resources of the parents or others caring for the child, and shall be designed to ensure that the disabled child has effective access to and receives education, training, health care services, rehabilitation services, preparation for employment and recreation opportunities in a manner conducive to the child's achieving the fullest possible social integration and individual development, including his or her cultural and spiritual development.
4. States Parties shall promote, in the spirit of international co-operation, the exchange of appropriate information in the field of preventive health care and of medical, psychological and functional treatment of disabled children, including dissemination of and access to information concerning methods of rehabilitation, education and vocational services, with the aim of enabling States Parties to improve their capabilities and skills and to widen their experience in these areas. In this regard, particular account shall be taken of the needs of developing countries.

Article 24

1. States Parties recognize the right of the child to the enjoyment of the highest attainable standard of health and to facilities for the treatment of illness and rehabilitation of health. States Parties shall strive to ensure that no child is deprived of his or her right of access to such health care services.
2. States Parties shall pursue full implementation of this right and, in particular, shall take appropriate measures:
   (a) To diminish infant and child mortality;
   (b) To ensure the provision of necessary medical assistance and health care to all children with emphasis on the development of primary health care;
   (c) To combat disease and malnutrition, including within the framework of primary health care, through, *inter alia,* the application of readily available technology and through the provision of adequate nutritious foods and clean drinking-water, taking into consideration the dangers and risks of environmental pollution;

(d) To ensure appropriate pre-natal and post-natal health care for mothers;
(e) To ensure that all segments of society, in particular parents and children, are informed, have access to education and are supported in the use of basic knowledge of child health and nutrition, the advantages of breast-feeding, hygiene and environmental sanitation and the prevention of accidents;
(f) To develop preventive health care, guidance for parents and family planning education and services.

3. States Parties shall take all effective and appropriate measures with a view to abolishing traditional practices prejudicial to the health of children.
4. States Parties undertake to promote and encourage international cooperation with a view to achieving progressively the full realization of the right recognized in the present article. In this regard, particular account shall be taken of the needs of developing countries.

Article 25

States Parties recognize the right of a child who has been placed by the competent authorities for the purposes of care, protection or treatment of his or her physical or mental health, to a periodic review of the treatment provided to the child and all other circumstances relevant to his or her placement.

Article 26

1. States Parties shall recognize for every child the right to benefit from social security, including social insurance, and shall take the necessary measures to achieve the full realization of this right in accordance with their national law.
2. The benefits should, where appropriate, be granted, taking into account the resources and the circumstances of the child and persons having responsibility for the maintenance of the child, as well as any other consideration relevant to an application for benefits made by or on behalf of the child.

Article 27

1. States Parties recognize the right of every child to a standard of living adequate for the child's physical, mental, spiritual, moral and social development.
2. The parent(s) or others responsible for the child have the primary responsibility to secure, within their abilities and financial capacities, the conditions of living necessary for the child's development.
3. States Parties, in accordance with national conditions and within their means, shall take appropriate measures to assist parents and others responsible for the child to implement this right and shall in case of need provide material assistance and support programmes, particularly with regard to nutrition, clothing and housing.

4. States Parties shall take all appropriate measures to secure the recovery of maintenance for the child from the parents or other persons having financial responsibility for the child, both within the State Party and from abroad. In particular, where the person having financial responsibility for the child lives in a State different from that of the child, States Parties shall promote the accession to international agreements or the conclusion of such agreements, as well as the making of other appropriate arrangements.

Article 28

1. States Parties recognize the right of the child to education, and with a view to achieving this right progressively and on the basis of equal opportunity, they shall, in particular:
   (a) Make primary education compulsory and available free to all;
   (b) Encourage the development of different forms of secondary education, including general and vocational education, make them available and accessible to every child, and take appropriate measures such as the introduction of free education and offering financial assistance in case of need;
   (c) Make higher education accessible to all on the basis of capacity by every appropriate means;
   (d) Make educational and vocational information and guidance available and accessible to all children;
   (e) Take measures to encourage regular attendance at schools and the reduction of drop-out rates.
2. States Parties shall take all appropriate measures to ensure that school discipline is administered in a manner consistent with the child's human dignity and in conformity with the present Convention.
3. States Parties shall promote and encourage international co-operation in matters relating to education, in particular with a view to contributing to the elimination of ignorance and illiteracy throughout the world and facilitating access to scientific and technical knowledge and modern teaching methods. In this regard, particular account shall be taken of the needs of developing countries.

Article 29

1. States Parties agree that the education of the child shall be directed to:
   (a) The development of the child's personality, talents and mental and physical abilities to their fullest potential;
   (b) The development of respect for human rights and fundamental freedoms, and for the principles enshrined in the Charter of the United Nations;
   (c) The development of respect for the child's parents, his or her own cultural identity, language and values, for the national values of the coun-

try in which the child is living, the country from which he or she may originate and for civilizations different from his or her own;

(d) The preparation of the child for responsible life in a free society, in the spirit of understanding, peace, tolerance, equality of sexes, and friendship among all peoples, ethnic, national and religious groups and persons of indigenous origin;

(e) The development of respect for the natural environment.

2. No part of the present article or Article 28 shall be construed so as to interfere with the liberty of individuals and bodies to establish and direct educational institutions, subject always to the observance of the principles set forth in Paragraph 1 of the present article and to the requirements that the education given in such institutions shall conform to such minimum standards as may be laid down by the State.

Article 30

In those States in which ethnic, religious or linguistic minorities or persons of indigenous origin exist, a child belonging to such a minority or who is indigenous shall not be denied the right, in community with other members of his or her group, to enjoy his or her own culture, to profess and practice his or her own religion, or to use his or her own language.

Article 31

1. States Parties recognize the right of the child to rest and leisure, to engage in play and recreational activities appropriate to the age of the child and to participate freely in cultural life and the arts.
2. States Parties shall respect and promote the right of the child to participate fully in cultural and artistic life and shall encourage the provision of appropriate and equal opportunities for cultural, artistic, recreational and leisure activity.

Article 32

1. States Parties recognize the right of the child to be protected from economic exploitation and from performing any work that is likely to be hazardous or to interfere with the child's education, or to be harmful to the child's health or physical, mental, spiritual, moral or social development.
2. States Parties shall take legislative, administrative, social and educational measures to ensure the implementation of the present article. To this end, and having regard to the relevant provisions of other international instruments, States Parties shall in particular:

(a) Provide for a minimum age or minimum ages for admission to employment;

(b) Provide for appropriate regulation of the hours and conditions of employment;

(c) Provide for appropriate penalties or other sanctions to ensure the effective enforcement of the present article.

Article 33

States Parties shall take all appropriate measures, including legislative, administrative, social and educational measures, to protect children from the illicit use of narcotic drugs and psychotropic substances as defined in the relevant international treaties, and to prevent the use of children in the illicit production and trafficking of such substances.

Article 34

States Parties undertake to protect the child from all forms of sexual exploitation and sexual abuse. For these purposes, States Parties shall in particular take all appropriate national, bilateral and multilateral measures to prevent:

(a) The inducement or coercion of a child to engage in any unlawful sexual activity;
(b) The exploitative use of children in prostitution or other unlawful sexual practices;
(c) The exploitative use of children in pornographic performances and materials.

Article 35

States Parties shall take all appropriate national, bilateral and multilateral measures to prevent the abduction of, the sale of or traffic in children for any purpose or in any form.

Article 36

States Parties shall protect the child against all other forms of exploitation prejudicial to any aspects of the child's welfare.

Article 37

States Parties shall ensure that:

(a) No child shall be subjected to torture or other cruel, inhuman or degrading treatment or punishment. Neither capital punishment nor life imprisonment without possibility of release shall be imposed for offenses committed by persons below eighteen years of age;
(b) No child shall be deprived of his or her liberty unlawfully or arbitrarily. The arrest, detention or imprisonment of a child shall be in conformity with the law and shall be used only as a measure of last resort and for the shortest appropriate period of time;

(c) Every child deprived of liberty shall be treated with humanity and respect for the inherent dignity of the human person, and in a manner which takes into account the needs of persons of his or her age. In particular, every child deprived of liberty shall be separated from adults unless it is considered in the child's best interest not to do so and shall have the right to maintain contact with his or her family through correspondence and visits, save in exceptional circumstances;

(d) Every child deprived of his or her liberty shall have the right to prompt access to legal and other appropriate assistance, as well as the right to challenge the legality of the deprivation of his or her liberty before a court or other competent, independent and impartial authority, and to a prompt decision on any such action.

Article 38

1. States Parties undertake to respect and to ensure respect for rules of international humanitarian law applicable to them in armed conflicts which are relevant to the child.
2. States Parties shall take all feasible measures to ensure that persons who have not attained the age of fifteen years do not take a direct part in hostilities.
3. States Parties shall refrain from recruiting any person who has not attained the age of fifteen years into their armed forces. In recruiting among those persons who have attained the age of fifteen years but who have not attained the age of eighteen years, States Parties shall endeavour to give priority to those who are oldest.
4. In accordance with their obligations under international humanitarian law to protect the civilian population in armed conflicts, States Parties shall take all feasible measures to ensure protection and care of children who are affected by armed conflict.

Article 39

States Parties shall take all appropriate measures to promote physical and psychological recovery and social reintegration of a child victim of: any form of neglect, exploitation, or abuse; torture or any other form of cruel, inhuman or degrading treatment or punishment; or armed conflicts. Such recovery and reintegration shall take place in an environment which fosters the health, self-respect and dignity of the child.

Article 40

1. States Parties recognize the right of every child alleged as, accused of, or recognized as having infringed the penal law to be treated in a manner consistent with the promotion of the child's sense of dignity and worth, which reinforces the child's respect for the human rights and fundamental free-

doms of others and which takes into account the child's age and the desirability of promoting the child's reintegration and the child's assuming a constructive role in society.

2. To this end, and having regard to the relevant provisions of international instruments, States Parties shall, in particular, ensure that:
   (a) No child shall be alleged as, be accused of, or recognized as having infringed the penal law by reason of acts or omissions that were not prohibited by national or international law at the time they were committed;
   (b) Every child alleged as or accused of having infringed the penal law has at least the following guarantees:
      (i) To be presumed innocent until proven guilty according to law;
      (ii) To be informed promptly and directly of the charges against him or her, and, if appropriate, through his or her parents or legal guardians, and to have legal or other appropriate assistance in the preparation and presentation of his or her defense;
      (iii) To have the matter determined without delay by a competent, independent and impartial authority or judicial body in a fair hearing according to law, in the presence of legal or other appropriate assistance and, unless it is considered not to be in the best interest of the child, in particular, taking into account his or her age or situation, his or her parents or legal guardians;
      (iv) Not to be compelled to give testimony or to confess guilt; to examine or have examined adverse witnesses and to obtain the participation and examination of witnesses on his or her behalf under conditions of equality;
      (v) If considered to have infringed the penal law, to have this decision and any measures imposed in consequence thereof reviewed by a higher competent, independent and impartial authority or judicial body according to law;
      (vi) To have the free assistance of an interpreter if the child cannot understand or speak the language used;
      (vii) To have his or her privacy fully respected at all stages of the proceedings.

3. States Parties shall seek to promote the establishment of laws, procedures, authorities and institutions specifically applicable to children alleged as, accused of, or recognized as having infringed the penal law, and, in particular:
   (a) The establishment of a minimum age below which children shall be presumed not to have the capacity to infringe the penal law;
   (b) Whenever appropriate and desirable, measures for dealing with such children without resorting to judicial proceedings, providing that human rights and legal safeguards are fully respected.

4. A variety of dispositions, such as care, guidance and supervision orders; counselling; probation; foster care; education and vocational training programmes and other alternatives to institutional care shall be available to ensure that children are dealt with in a manner appropriate to their well-being and proportionate both to their circumstances and the offense.

Article 41

Nothing in the present Convention shall affect any provisions which are more conducive to the realization of the rights of the child and which may be contained in:

(a) The law of a State Party; or
(b) International law in force for that State.

Part II

Article 42

States Parties undertake to make the principles and provisions of the Convention widely known, by appropriate and active means, to adults and children alike.

Article 43

1. For the purpose of examining the progress made by States Parties in achieving the realization of the obligations undertaken in the present Convention, there shall be established a Committee on the Rights of the Child, which shall carry out the functions hereinafter provided.
2. The Committee shall consist of ten experts of high moral standing and recognized competence in the field covered by this Convention. The members of the Committee shall be elected by States Parties from among their nationals and shall serve in their personal capacity, consideration being given to equitable geographical distribution, as well as to the principal legal systems.
3. The members of the Committee shall be elected by secret ballot from a list of persons nominated by States Parties. Each State Party may nominate one person from among its own nationals.
4. The initial election to the Committee shall be held no later than six months after the date of the entry into force of the present convention and thereafter every second year. At least four months before the date of each election, the Secretary-General of the United Nations shall address a letter to States Parties inviting them to submit their nominations within two months. The Secretary-General shall subsequently prepare a list in alphabetical order of all persons thus nominated, indicating States Parties which have nominated them, and shall submit it to the States Parties to the present Convention.

5. The elections shall be held at meetings of States Parties convened by the Secretary-General at United Nations Headquarters. At those meetings, for which two thirds of States Parties shall constitute a quorum, the persons elected to the Committee shall be those who obtain the largest number of votes and an absolute majority of the votes of the representatives of States Parties present and voting.
6. The members of the Committee shall be elected for a term of four years. They shall be eligible for re-election if renominated. The term of five of the members elected at the first election shall expire at the end of two years; immediately after the first election, the names of these five members shall be chosen by lot by the Chairman of the meeting.
7. If a member of the Committee dies or resigns or declares that for any other cause he or she can no longer perform the duties of the Committee, the State Party which nominated the member shall appoint another expert from among its nationals to serve for the remainder of the term, subject to the approval of the Committee.
8. The Committee shall establish its own rules of procedure.
9. The Committee shall elect its officers for a period of two years.
10. The meetings of the Committee shall normally be held at United Nations Headquarters or at any other convenient place as determined by the Committee. The Committee shall normally meet annually. The duration of the meetings of the Committee shall be determined, and reviewed, if necessary, by a meeting of the States Parties to the present Convention, subject to the approval of the General Assembly.
11. The Secretary-General of the United Nations shall provide the necessary staff and facilities for the effective performance of the functions of the Committee under the present Convention.
12. With the approval of the General Assembly, the members of the Committee established under the present Convention shall receive emoluments from United Nations resources on such terms and conditions as the Assembly may decide.

Article 44

1. States Parties undertake to submit to the Committee, through the Secretary-General of the United Nations, reports on the measures they have adopted which give effect to the rights recognized herein and on the progress made on the enjoyment of those rights:
   (a) Within two years of the entry into force of the Convention for the State Party concerned;
   (b) Thereafter every five years.
2. Reports made under the present article shall indicate factors and difficulties, if any, affecting the degree of fulfillment of the obligations under the present Convention. Reports shall also contain sufficient information to provide

the Committee with a comprehensive understanding of the implementation of the Convention in the country concerned.

3. A State Party which has submitted a comprehensive initial report to the Committee need not, in its subsequent reports submitted in accordance with Paragraph 1 *(b)* of the present article, repeat basic information previously provided.
4. The Committee may request from States Parties further information relevant to the implementation of the Convention.
5. The Committee shall submit to the General Assembly, through the Economic and Social Council, every two years, reports on its activities.
6. States Parties shall make their reports widely available to the public in their own countries.

Article 45

In order to foster the effective implementation of the Convention and to encourage international co-operation in the field covered by the Convention:

(a) The specialized agencies, the United Nations Children's Fund, and other United Nations organs shall be entitled to be represented at the consideration of the implementation of such provisions of the present Convention as fall within the scope of their mandate. The Committee may invite the specialized agencies, the United Nations Children's Fund and other competent bodies as it may consider appropriate to provide expert advice on the implementation of the Convention in areas falling within the scope of their respective mandates. The Committee may invite the specialized agencies, the United Nations Children's Fund, and other United Nations organs to submit reports on the implementation of the Convention in areas falling within the scope of their activities;

(b) The Committee shall transmit, as it may consider appropriate, to the specialized agencies, the United Nations Children's Fund and other competent bodies, any reports from States Parties that contain a request, or indicate a need, for technical advice or assistance, along with the Committee's observations and suggestions, if any, on these requests or indications

(c) The Committee may recommend to the General Assembly to request the Secretary-General to undertake on its behalf studies on specific issues relating to the rights of the child.

(d) The Committee may make suggestions and general recommendations based on information received pursuant to Articles 44 and 45 of the present Convention. Such suggestions and general recommendations shall be transmitted to any State Party concerned and reported to the General Assembly, together with comments, if any, from States Parties.

Part III

Article 46

The present Convention shall be open for signature by all States.

Article 47

The present Convention is subject to ratification. Instruments of ratification shall be deposited with the SecretaryGeneral of the United Nations.

Article 48

The present Convention shall remain open for accession by any State. The instruments of accession shall be deposited with the Secretary-General of the United Nations.

Article 49

1. The present Convention shall enter into force on the thirtieth day following the date of deposit with the Secretary-General of the United Nations of the twentieth instrument of ratification or accession.
2. For each State ratifying or acceding to the Convention after the deposit of the twentieth instrument of ratification or accession, the Convention shall enter into force on the thirtieth day after the deposit by such State of its instrument of ratification or accession.

Article 50

1. Any State Party may propose an amendment and file it with the Secretary-General of the United Nations. The Secretary-General shall thereupon communicate the proposed amendment to States Parties, with a request that they indicate whether they favour a conference of States Parties for the purpose of considering and voting upon the proposals. In the event that, within four months from the date of such communication, at least one third of the States Parties favour such a conference, the Secretary-General shall convene the conference under the auspices of the United Nations. Any amendment adopted by a majority of States Parties present and voting at the conference shall be submitted to the General Assembly for approval.
2. An amendment adopted in accordance with Paragraph 1 of the present article shall enter into force when it has been approved by the General Assembly of the United Nations and accepted by a two-thirds majority of States Parties.
3. When an amendment enters into force, it shall be binding on those States Parties which have accepted it, other States Parties still being bound by the provisions of the present Convention and any earlier amendments which they have accepted.

Article 51

1. The Secretary-General of the United Nations shall receive and circulate to all States the text of reservations made by States at the time of ratification or accession.
2. A reservation incompatible with the object and purpose of the present Convention shall not be permitted.
3. Reservations may be withdrawn at any time by notification to that effect addressed to the Secretary-General of the United Nations, who shall then inform all States. Such notification shall take effect on the date on which it is received by the Secretary-General.

Article 52

A State Party may denounce the present Convention by written notification to the Secretary-General of the United Nations. Denunciation becomes effective one year after the date of receipt of the notification by the Secretary-General.

Article 53

The Secretary-General of the United Nations is designated as the depositary of the present Convention.

Article 54

The original of the present Convention, of which the Arabic, Chinese, English, French, Russian and Spanish texts are equally authentic, shall be deposited with the Secretary-General of the United Nations.

In witness thereof the undersigned plenipotentiaries, being duly authorized thereto by their respective Governments, have signed the present Convention.

References

Addo, M. K. (Ed.). (1999). *Human rights standards and the responsibility of transnational corporations*. The Hague: Kluwer Law International.

Addo, M. K. (1999). *The corporation as a victim of human rights violations*. In M. K. Addo (Ed.), *Human rights standards and the responsibility of transnational corporations* (pp. 187–196). The Hague: Kluwer Law International.

Akehurst, M. (1991). *A modern introduction to international law* (6th ed.). London: HarperCollins.

Alderman, E., & Kennedy, C. (1995). *The right to privacy*. New York: Vintage Books.

Alfredsson, G., & Eide, A. (Eds.). (1999). *The universal declaration of human rights*. The Hague: Kluwer.

Alston, P. (Ed.). (1992). *The United Nations and human rights. A critical appraisal*. Oxford: Clarendon.

AMIC. (Ed.). (2000). *Media & human rights in Asia*. Singapore: Author.

An-Na'im, A. A. (1992). *Human rights in cross-cultural perspectives: A quest for consensus*. Philadelphia: University of Pennsylvania.

An-Na'im, A. A., Gort, J. D., Jansen, H., & Vroom, H.M. (Eds.). (1995). *Human rights and religious values*. Amsterdam: Editions Rodopi.

Aronovitch, H. (2002). The harm of hate propaganda. In M. Pendakur & R. Harris (Eds.), *Citizenship and participation in the information age* (pp. 147–163). Aurora: Garamond.

Article XIX. (1996). *Broadcasting genocide*. London: Author.

Baehr, P.R. (1999). *Human rights: Universality in practice*. Basingstoke: Macmillan.

Barendt, E. (1985). *Freedom of speech*. Oxford: Clarendon.

Bassiouni, Ch. (1992). *Crimes against humanity in international criminal law*. Dordrecht: M. Nijhoff.

Bauer, J. R., & Bell, D. A. (Eds.). (1999). *The East Asian challenge for human rights*. Cambridge: Cambridge University Press.

Baxi, U. (1999). Voices of suffering, fragmented universality, and the future of human rights. In B. H. Weston & Marks, S. P. (Eds.), *The future of international human rights* (pp. 101–156). New York: Transnational Publishers.

Beck, U. (1992). *Risk society. Towards a new modernity*. London: Sage.

Becker, J. (2002). *Information und Gesellschaft* [Information and society]. Wien: Springer Verlag.

Berting, J. A. O. (1990). *Human rights in a pluralist world*. Westport: Meckler.

Bettig, R. V. (2003). Copyright and the commodification of culture. *Media Development, 1*, 3–9.

Bordewijk, J.L., & Kaam, B. van (1982). *Allocutie*. Baarn, bosch & Keunig.

Boven, Th. C. van (1982). Distinguishing criteria of human rights. In K. Vasak (Ed.), *The international dimensions of human rights* (pp. 43–59). Paris: Unesco.

Brody, E. B. (1993). *Biomedical technology and human rights*. Paris: UNESCO.

Brownlie, I. (Ed.). (1981). *Basic documents on human rights*. Oxford: Oxford University Press.

Buergenthal, T. (Ed.). (1977). *Human rights, international law and the Helsinki Accords*. New York: Allanbeld/Osmun.

Campbell, T., Goldberg, D., McLean, S., & Mullen, T. (Eds.). (1986). *Human rights. From rhetoric to reality*. Oxford: Basil Blackwell.

Cassese, A. (1990). *Human rights in a changing world*. Cambridge: Polity.

Chan, J. (1999). A Confucian perspective on human rights for contemporary China, In T. R. Bauer & D. A. Bell (Eds.), *The East Asian challenge for human rights* (pp. 212–237). Cambridge: Cambridge University Press.

Chomsky, N., & Herman, E.S. (1979a). *After the cataclysm. Postwar Indochina and the reconstruction of imperial ideology. The political economy of human rights* (Volume II). Montreal: Black Rose Books.

Chomsky, N., & Herman, E.S. (1979b). *The Washington connection and Third World fascism. The political economy of human rights* (Volume I). Montreal: Black Rose Books.

Christians, C. G., Ferré, J. P., & Fackler, P. M. (1993). *Good news. Social ethics & the press*. New York: Oxford University Press.

Colas, A. (2002). *International civil society*. Oxford: Polity Press.

Coliver, S. (Ed.). (1992). *Striking a balance: Hate speech, freedom of expression and nondiscrimination*. London: Article XIX.

Coliver, S. (Ed.). (1993). *Press law and practice. A comparative study of press freedom in European and other democracies*. London, Article XIX.

Collins, O. (Ed.). (1998). *Speeches that changed the world: History in the making*. London: Harper Collins.

Corillon, C. (1989). The role of science and scientists in human rights. *The Annals of the American Academy of Political and Social Science, 506*, 129–140.

Couprie, E., & Olsson, H. (1987). *Freedom of communication under the law*. Manchester: The European Institute for the Media.

D'Arcy, J. (1969). Direct broadcasting satellites and the right to communicate. *EBU Review, 118*, 14–18.

Daes, E. I. A. (1983). *The individual's duties to the community and the limitations on human rights and freedoms under Article 29 of the Universal Declaration of Human Rights*. New York: United Nations.

Dahrendorf, R. (2002, May). Getrennt, aber gleichberechtigt [Separated but equal in rights]. *Der Standard*, p. 39.

David, R., & Brierley, J.E.C. (1985). *Major legal systems in the world today*. London: Stevens.

Diffie, W., & Landau, S. (1999). *Privacy on the line. The politics of wiretapping and encryption*. Cambridge: The MIT Press.

Donnelly, J. (1986). International human rights regimes. *International Organization*, *40*(3), 599–642.

Donnelly, J. (1993). *International human rights*. Boulder: Westview.

Donnelly, J. (1999). Human rights and Asian values: A defense of "Western" universalism. In J.R. Bauer & D.A. Bell, (Eds.), *The East Asian challenge for human rights* (pp. 60–87). Cambridge: Cambridge University Press.

Duncan, J. (Ed.). (1996). *Between speech and silence. Hate speech, pornography and the New South Africa*. Johannesburg: Freedom of Expression Institute.

Dworkin, R. (1977). *Taking rights seriously*. London: Duckhart.

Dworkin, R. (1985). *A matter of principle*. Cambridge, MA: Harvard University Press.

Dworkin, R. (2002). The threat to patriotism. *The New York Review of Books, XLIX*(3), *44–50.*

Eide, A. (1999). Der Prozess der Universalisierung der Menschenrechte und seine Bedrohung im Zeitalter der Globalisierung [The threat to the universalism of human rights in the age of globalisation]. In W. Krull (Ed.), *Zukunftsstreit* (pp. 32–50). Weilerswit: Velbrueck Wissenschaft.

Eide, A., & Skogly, S. (Eds.). (1988). *Human rights and the media*. Oslo: Norwegian Institute of Human Rights Publications.

Eide, A., Alfredsson, G., Melander, G., Rehof, L. A., & Rosas, A. (Eds.). (1992). *The universal declaration of human rights*: *A commentary*. Oxford: Oxford University Press.

Ellinor, L., & Gerard, G. (1998). *Dialogue*. New York: Wiley.

Evans, T. (2001). *The politics of human rights*. London: Pluto.

Falk, R. (1981). *Human rights and state sovereignty*. New York: Holms & Meier.

Falk, R. (1999). A half century of human rights: Geopolitics and values. In B. H. Weston & S.P. Marks (Eds.), *The future of international human rights (*pp. 1–24). New York: Transnational Publishers.

Fasching, D. J., & Dechant, D. (2001). *Comparative religious ethics*. Oxford: Blackwell.

Feilitzen, C. von, & Bucht, C. (2001). *Outlooks on children and media*. Goteborg: UNESCO/NORDICM.

Fisher, D. (1982). *The right to communicate. A status report* (Series Reports and Papers on Mass Communication, No. 94). Paris: UNESCO.

Fisher, D., & Harms, L. S. (Eds.). (1983). *The right to communicate: A new human right*? Dublin: Boole.

Forsythe, D. P. (1989). *Human rights and world politics*. Lincoln and London: University of Nebraska Press.

Freeman, M. (2000). Universal rights and particular cultures. In M. Jocabsen & O. Bruun (Eds.), *Human rights and Asian values* (pp. 43–58). Richmond: Curzon Press.

Gallagher, M. (2001). *Gender setting*, London: Zed Books.

Galtung, J. (1994). *Human rights in another key*. Oxford: Polity.

Garcia-Sayan, D. (1995). New path for economic, social and cultural rights. *The Review. International Commission of Jurists*, *55*, 75–80.

Gay, P. (1973). *The enlightenment: An interpretation. Part 2: The science of freedom.* London: Wildwood House.

Gewirth, A. (1982). *Human rights: Essays on justification and applications.* Chicago: University of Chicago Press.

Ghai, Y. (1999). Rights, social justice and globalization in East Asia. In J. R. Bauer & D. A. Bell (Eds.), *The East Asian challenge for human rights* (pp. 241–263). Cambridge: Cambridge University Press.

Giddens, A. (1991a). *The consequences of modernity.* Oxford: Polity.

Giddens, A. (1991b). *Modernity and self-identity. Self and society in the late modern age.* Oxford: Polity.

Ginneken, J. van (1998). *Understanding global news.* London: Sage.

Goldhagen, D. J. (1996). *Hitler's willing executioners.* New York: Vintage Books.

Goldstein, P. (1994). *Copyright's highway. The law and lore of copyright from Gutenberg to the celestial jukebox.* New York: Hill & Wang.

Gould, C. C. (1988). *Rethinking democracy.* Cambridge: Cambridge University Press.

Halliday, F. (1996). *Islam and the myth of confrontation: Religion and politics in the Middle East.* London: I.B.Tauris.

Hamelink, C. J. (1988). Communication and human rights: The international dimension. *Media Development, XXXV*(4), 6–8.

Hamelink, C. J. (1991, October). The Gulf War, the media and human rights. *Media Development* [Special Issue], pp. 2–4.

Hamelink, C. J. (1994a). *Culture.* In C. J. Hamelink (Ed.), *The politics of world communication* (pp. 186–195). London: Sage.

Hamelink, C. J. (1994b). *The politics of world communication.* London: Sage.

Hamelink, C. J. (1995a). *World communication. Disempowerment & self-empowerment.* London: Zed Books

Hamelink, C. J. (1995b). The democratic deal and its enemies. In P. Lee (Ed.), *The democratization of communication* (pp. 15–37). Cardiff: University of Wales Press.

Hamelink, C. J. (1997). Media, ethnic conflict and culpability. In J. Servaes & R. Lie (Eds.), *Media & politics on transition* (pp. 29–38). Leuven: Acco.

Hamelink, C. J. (2000a). *The ethics of cyberspace.* London: Sage.

Hamelink, C. J. (2000b). *Preserving media independence: Regulatory frameworks.* Paris: UNESCO.

Hannikainen, L. (1988). *Peremptory norms (Ius Cogens) in international law.* Helsinki: Finnish Lawyers.

Hannikainen, L., & Myntti, K. (1992). Article 19. In A. Eide, G. Alfredsson, G. Melander, L.A. Rehof, & A. Rosas. (Eds.), *The universal declaration of human rights: A commentary* (pp. 275–298). Oxford: Oxford University Press.

Hedebro, G. (1982). *Communication and social change in developing nations.* Ames: Iowa State University Press.

Henkin, L. (Ed.). (1981). *The international bill of rights.* New York: Columbia University Press.

Herman, E. S., & Chomsky, N. (1988). *Manufacturing consent.* New York: Pantheon.

Herman, E. S., & McChesney, R. W. (1997). *The global media. The new missionaries of global capitalism.* London: Cassell.

Hick, S., Halpin, E. F., & Hoskins, E. (2000). *Human rights and the internet.* London: MacMillan.

Hobbes, T. (1651). Leviathan. Harmondsworth: Penguin (1968)

Hossain, K. (1997). *Promoting human rights in the global market place*. Amsterdam: Vrije Universiteit.

Hossain, K. (1999). Globalization and human rights: Clash of universal aspirations and special interests. In B. H. Weston, & S.P. Marks (Eds.), *The future of international human rights* (pp. 187–200). New York: Transnational Publishers.

Hugenholtz, P. B. (Ed.). (1996). *The future of copyright in a digital environment*. The Hague. Kluwer Law International.

International Commission for the Study of Communication Problems. (1980). *Many voices, one world*. Paris: UNESCO.

Jacobson, M., & Bruun, O. (Eds). (2000). *Human rights and Asian values*. Richmond: Curzon.

Jacobson, Th. L., & Jang, W. J. (2001). Rights, culture and cosmopolitan democracy. *Communication Theory, 11*(4), 434–453.

Jagers, N. (1999). The legal status of the multinational corporation under international law. In M. K. Addo (Ed.), *Human rights standards and the responsibility of transnational corporations* (pp. 259–270). The Hague: Kluwer Law International.

Jansen, S. C. (1991). *Censorship*. Oxford: Oxford University Press.

Jokinen, P. (1996, August 22–25). *The promise of the information society for sustainable development*. Paper for the Telecommunications and Sustainability Workshop at the Conference on Challenges of Sustainable Development, Amsterdam.

Jones, Th. D. (1997). *Human rights: Group defamation, freedom of expression and the law of nations*. The Hague: Kluwer.

Jongman, J. J., & Schmidt, A. P. (1994). *Monitoring human rights*. Leiden: PIOOM.

Jungk, M. (1999). A practical guide to addressing human rights concerns for companies operating abroad. In M. K. Addo (Ed.), *Human rights standards and the responsibility of transnational corporations* (pp. 171–186). The Hague: Kluwer Law International.

Juusela, P. (1991). *Journalistic codes of ethics in the CSCE countries*. Tampere: University of Tampere.

Kiss, A.C. (1981). Permissible limitations on rights. In L. Henkin (Ed.), *The international bill of rights* (pp. 290–310). New York: Columbia University Press.

Kleinwächter, W. (1988). The right to participate in the cultural life of society. *Media Development, XXXV(4)*, 9–10.

Korten, D. C. (1995). *When corporations rule the world*. West Hartford: Kumarian.

Kretzmer, D., & Hazan, F. K. (Eds.). (2000). *Freedom of speech and incitement against democracy*. The Hague: Kluwer.

Kubka, J., & Nordenstreng, K. (1986). *Useful recollections. Part I*. Prague: International Organization of Journalists.

Kung, H., & Schmidt, H. (Eds.). (1998). *Global effects and global responsibilities*. London: SCM.

Leslie, J. (1996). *The end of the world*. London: Routledge.

Lessig, L. (1998, October 9). Life, liberty, copyright. *The Atlantic Monthly Unbound*.

Lessig, L. (1999). *Code and other laws of cyberspace*. New York: Basic Books.

Lukes, S. (1993). Five fables about human rights, In S. Shute & S. Hurley (Eds.), *On human rights* (pp. 19–40). New York: Basic Books.

Makridakis, S. (1995, August 27). The forthcoming information revolution: Its impact on society and firms. *Futures*, pp. 799–821.

Manji, F., Jaffer, M., & Njuguna, E. N. (2000). Using ICTs to enhance the capacity of human rights organizations in Southern Africa. In *Voices from Africa (9); information and communication technologies* (pp. 19–31). Geneva: UN Non-Governmental Liaison Service.

Marquardt, P. D. (1995). Law without borders: The constitutionality of an international criminal court. *Columbia Journal of Transnational Law*, *33*(1), 76–95.

Martenson, J. (1992). The preamble of the universal declaration of human rights and the UN human rights programme. In Eide, A., Alfredsson, G., Melander, G., Rehof, L. A., & Rosas, A. (Eds.), *The universal declaration of human rights: A commentary* (pp. 17–30). Oxford: Oxford University Press.

Mayer, A. E. (1999). *Islam and human rights: Tradition and politics*. Oxford: Westview.

McQuail, D. (1992). *Media performance. Mass communication and the public interest.* London: Sage.

McWhinney, E. (1984). *United Nations law making*. New York: Holmes & Meier.

Melander, G. (1992). Article 27. In Eide, A., Alfredsson, G., Melander, G., Rehof, L. A., & Rosas, A. (Eds.), *The universal declaration of human rights: A commentary* (pp. 429–432). Oxford: Oxford University Press.

Merrill, J. C., & Barney, R. D. (1975). *Ethics and the press. Readings in mass media morality*. New York: Hastings House.

Mertus, J. A. (1999). Human rights and the promise of transnational civil society. In B.H. Weston & S.P. Marks (Eds.), *The future of international human rights* (pp. 433–456). New York: Transnational Publishers.

Michael, J. (1994). *Privacy and human rights*. Paris: UNESCO.

Nickel, J. W. (1987). *Making sense of human rights*. Berkeley: University of California Press.

Nino, C. S. (1993). *The ethics of human rights*. Oxford, Clarendon Press

Orücü. E. (1986). The core of rights and freedoms: The limit of limits. In T. Campbell, D. Goldberg, S. McLean, & T. Mullen (Eds.), *Human rights. From rhetoric to reality* (pp. 37–59). Oxford: Basil Blackwell.

Othman, N. (1999). Grounding human rights arguments in non-Western culture: Shari'a and the citizenship rights of women in a modern Islamic state. In J. R. Bauer & D.A. Bell (Eds.), *The East Asian challenge for human rights* (pp. 169–192). Cambridge: Cambridge University Press.

Otto, D. (1997). Rethinking the universality of human rights law, 29 Colum. Hum. Rts. L.Rev. 1, 3 1997

Ovsiovitch, J. S., (1999). News coverage of human rights. In K. Nordenstreng & M. Griffin (Eds.), *International media monitoring* (pp. 243–262). Cresskill: Hampton Press.

Partsch, K. J. (1981). Freedom of conscience and expression, and political freedoms. In L. Henkin (Ed.), *The international bill of rights* (pp. 209–245). New York: Columbia University Press.

Perkins, M. (2003). International law and the search for universal principles. *Journal of Mass Media Ethics*, *17*(3), 193–208.

Phillipson, R. (Ed.). (2000). *Rights to language. Equity, power, and education*. London: Erlbaum.

Raes, K. (1995). Vrijheid van meningsuiting en de revisionistische geschiedvervalsing. In G. A. I. Schuijt & D. Voorhoof (Eds.), *Vrijheid van meningsuiting. Racisme en revisionisme* (pp. 31–77). Gent: Academia Press.

Ramcharan, B. G. (1981). Equality and non-discrimination. In L. Henkin (Ed.), *The international bill of rights* (pp. 246–269). New York: Columbia University Press.

Ramcharan, B. G. (1989). Universality of human rights in a pluralistic world. In *Proceedings of the Colloquy* organized by the Council of Europe in cooperation with the International Institute of Human Rights, Strasbourg.

Ramcharan, B. G. (1994). The universality of human rights. *The Review, 53*, 105–117.

Rehof, L. A. (1992). Article 12. In Eide, A., Alfredsson, G., Melander, G., Rehof, L. A., & Rosas, A. (Eds.), *The universal declaration of human rights: A commentary* (pp. 187–202). Oxford: Oxford University Press.

Renteln, A. D. (1990). *International human rights, universalism versus relativism*. London: Sage.

Riley, T. (Ed.). (1986). *Access to government records: International perspectives and trends*. Lund: Studentlitteratur.

Rivers, W. L., & Schramm, W. (1969). *Responsibility in mass communication*. New York: Harper & Row.

Robertson, G., & Nicol, A. G. L. (1984). *Media law. The rights of journalists, broadcasters and publishers*. London: Sage.

Roht-Arriaza, N. (Ed.). (1995). *Impunity and human rights in international law and practice*. Oxford: Oxford University Press.

Runzo, J., & Martin, N. M. (2001). *Ethics in the world religions*. Oxford: One World Publications.

Said, A.A. ((Ed.). (1998). *Human rights in world order*. New York: Praeger.

Sanders, D. (1991). Collective rights. *Human Rights Quarterly, 13*, 368–386.

Santoro, J. (1992).Unpublished dissertation about the early history of IAMCR. Paris. [In French].

Savio, R. (1994). Raising awareness. In *Human rights, the new consensus* (pp. 48–51). London: Regency Press.

Scheinin, M. (1992). Article 18. In In Eide, A., Alfredsson, G., Melander, G., Rehof, L. A., & Rosas, A. (Eds.), *The universal declaration of human rights: A commentary* (pp. 263–274). Oxford: Oxford University Press.

Sen, A. K. (1999). *Culture and human rights. Development as freedom*. Oxford: Oxford University Press.

Servaes, J. (1988). The right to communicate is a basic human right. *Media Development, XXXV*(4), 15–18.

Shannon, C., & Weaver, W. (1949). *The mathematical theory of communication*. Urbana: University of Illinois Press.

Shiva, V. (2001). *Protect or plunder. Understanding intellectual property rights*. London: ZED Books.

Sieghart, P. (1986). *The lawful rights of mankind*. Oxford: Oxford University Press.

Skogly, S. I. (1999). Economic and social human rights, private actors and international obligations. In M. K. Addo (Ed.), *Human rights standards and the responsibility of transnational corporations* (pp. 239–258). The Hague: Kluwer Law International.

Skutnabb-Kangas, T., & Phillipson, R. (1997). Linguistic human rights and development. In C. J. Hamelink (Ed.), *Ethics and development* (pp. 56–69). Kampen: Kok.

Skutnabb-Kangas, T., & Phillipson, R. (1998). Language in human rights. *Gazette, 60*(1), 27–46.

South Commission. (1990). *The challenge to the south*. Oxford: Oxford University Press.

Spaink, K. (2003). Freedom of the media in the digital age. In *From quill to cursor* (pp. 9–30). Vienna: Organization for Security and Co-operation in Europe (OSCE).

Steiner, H. J., & Alston, Ph. (2000). *International human rights in context*. Oxford: Oxford University Press.

Symonides, J. (1998). The implementation of cultural rights by the international community. *Gazette, 60*(1), 7–26.

Symonides, J., & Volodin, V. (1996). *UNESCO and human rights*. Paris: UNESCO.

Symonides, J., & Volodin, V. (1999). *Human rights of women*. Paris: UNESCO.

Szabo, I. (1974). *Cultural rights*. Leiden: Sijthoff.

Traer, R. (1991). *Faith in human rights*. Washington, DC: Georgetown University Press.

UNESCO (1970). *Cultural rights as human rights*. Paris: UNESCO.

Ventureli, S. (1998). Cultural rights and world trade agreements in the information society. *Gazette, 60*(1), 47–76.

Voorhoof, D. (1991). *Critical perspectives on the scope and interpretation of Article 10 of the European Convention on Human Rights. Council of Europe, CDMM (93) 36.* Strasbourg, France.

Wacks, R. (1995). *Privacy and press freedom*. London: Blackstone.

Waldron, J. (Ed.). (1984). *Theories of rights*. Oxford: Oxford University Press.

Weeramantry, C. G. (Ed.) (1990). *Human rights and scientific and technological development*. Tokyo: United Nations University Press.

Weeramantry, C. G. (Ed.). (1993). *The impact of technology on human rights. Global case-studies*. Tokyo: United Nations University Press.

Wells, C. (1987). *The UN, UNESCO and the politics of knowledge*. London: MacMillan.

Weston, B. H. (1999). The universality of human rights in a multicultured world: Toward respectful decision-making. In B.H. Weston & S.P. Marks (Eds.), *The future of international human rights* (pp. 65–100). New York: Transnational Publishers.

Weston, B. H., & Marks, S.P. (Eds.). (1999). *The future of international human rights*. New York: Transnational Publishers.

Whitaker, R. (1999). *The end of privacy*. New York: The New Press.

Wissema, J. G. (1997). *Rijden managers door rood licht?* [Do managers run traffic-lights?]. Assen: Van Gorcum.

World Commission on Culture and Development. (1995). *Our creative diversity*. Paris: UNESCO.

Yasuaki, O. (1999). Toward an intercivilizational approach to human rights. In J.R. Bauer & D. A. Bell (Eds.), *The East Asian challenge for human rights* (pp. 103–123). Cambridge: Cambridge University Press.

Author Index

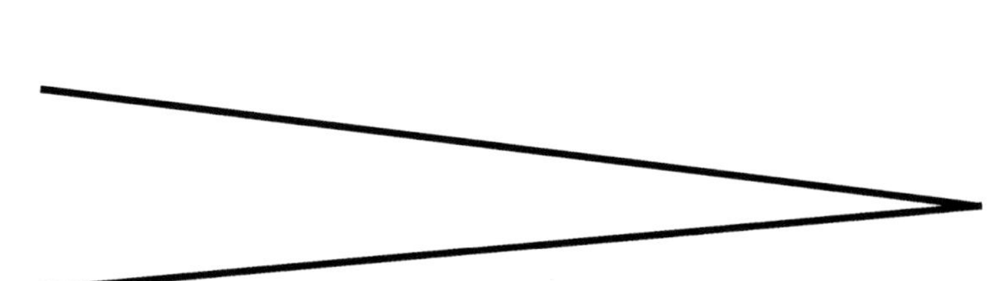

Subject Index

D

E

Printed in the United States
20609LVS00001B/229-273